Grand Rapids

RENAISSANCE ON THE GRAND

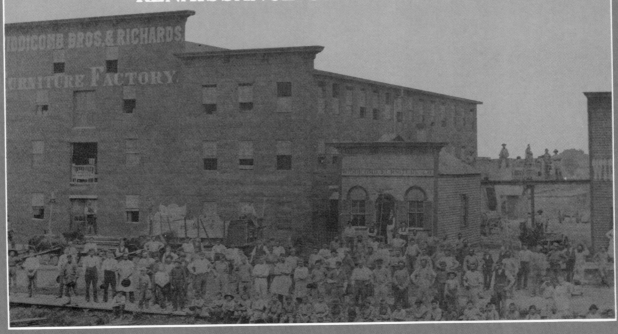

by Gerald Elliott
with Ellen Arlinsky, Marg Ed Conn Kwapil and Barbara McGuirl
photography by Phillip Radcliffe

Grand Rapids: Renaissance on the Grand

by Gerald Elliott with Ellen Arlinsky, Marg Ed Conn Kwapil and Barbara McGuirl

Publishers:
Larry P. Silvey
Douglas Drown

Managing Editor:
Kitty Gibbons Silvey
Associate Editor:
Marie Flagg

Art Director:
Rusty Johnson
Assistant Art Director:
James Michael Martin

Project Director:
Joyce Moffett
Current Photographer:
Phillip Radcliffe

During the 1880s, Reeds Lake was a favorite recreational spot. There were private clubs and public refreshment gardens along the shore, rowboats for rent at the dock, and steamboat cruises on the lake.

Library of Congress Catalogue Card Number: 81-86569
ISBN: 0-932986-22-6

Grand Rapids: Renaissance on the Grand is one of the American Portrait Series published by Continental Heritage Press. Others include:

Akron: City at the Summit
Anchorage: Star of the North
Charlotte: Spirit of the New South
Cleveland: Prodigy of the Western Reserve
Columbus: America's Crossroads
Denver: Rocky Mountain Gold
Des Moines: Capital City
Detroit: American Urban Renaissance
Fort Worth: The Civilized West
Houston: A History of a Giant
Indianapolis: Hoosiers' Circle City
Los Angeles Two Hundred

Miami: The Magic City
Milwaukee: At the Gathering of the Waters
Oakland: Hub of the West
Pensacola: Deep Water City
Philadelphia: Dream for the Keeping
Phoenix: Valley of the Sun
The Saint Louis Portrait
The San Antonio Story
San Diego: California's Cornerstone
San Jose: California's First City
Toledo: Gateway to the Great Lakes
Tulsa Spirit

I have always been proud of Grand Rapids—proud to call this city home and proud to have represented its 5th Congressional District for 25 years in the House of Representatives.

Grand Rapids has a vitality and a spirit of concern and caring that make it a very special place. Many strengths have shaped the city. Ethnic diversity contributes strong faith and cultural richness. Energetic citizens, who care deeply about their city, play a significant and active role in civic and cultural affairs. They demonstrate a remarkable ability for getting things done and they display a constant commitment to enriching the quality of city life. Grand Rapids is truly an All-America City, well deserving of that title, which it received in 1981 for the third time in three decades.

Throughout my years in Congress, I looked forward to coming home to Grand Rapids. Traveling around the countryside each fall and meeting with constituents strengthed my ties to the people and the city. The community never failed to make me welcome and I was always eager to return.

At the 1981 "Celebration On The Grand," Betty and I returned once again—to the traditionally warm Grand Rapids welcome, and to a new Grand Rapids, a city rejuvenated and revitalized through the tireless efforts of its citizens, its business community and its government.

The downtown renaissance and the publication of this book reflect the fact that Grand Rapids has always had a sense of its own history.

The city has passed through many stages since its

4

founding more than 156 years ago. Once a tiny settlement on the banks of the Grand, it grew into a lumbering town, a manufacturing hub and into the Furniture Capital of the World. It survived war and depression and urban decay to emerge stable and prosperous. Today's industrial diversity, fiscal strength, social awareness and cultural vigor promise a bright and secure future.

At the same time, Grand Rapids has carefully restored and preserved much of its past. The old Federal Building, where I once had an office, has become the new Art Musuem; the old Pantlind Hotel, a downtown landmark for most of this century, has been restored and transformed into the new Amway Grand Plaza Hotel. Neighborhoods are being refurbished and revitalized as citizens take renewed pride in their heritage and in their city.

Even the new pays tribute to the old. The Performing Arts Center is evidence of the community's abiding love of music. Ah-Nab-Awen Bicentennial Park reminds visitors of the history of this nation and of the Indian tribes who lived beside the Grand before the European settlers came. I am greatly honored that the Gerald R. Ford Presidential Museum, which overlooks the park, has been so warmly received and supported by the citizens of Grand Rapids and that it, too, is playing a role in the city's continuing renaissance.

Gerald R. Ford

Sponsors and Benefactors

The following Grand Rapids area firms, organizations and individuals have invested toward the quality production of this historic book and have thereby expressed their commitment to the future of this great city and to the support of the book's principal sponsor, Grand Rapids Area Chamber of Commerce

American Laundry & Cleaners, Inc.
*American Seating Company
*Amway Corporation
*Amway Grand Plaza Hotel
 Amway International Department
 Arthur Andersen & Co.
 Aves Advertising Inc.
*Barclay, Ayers & BERTSCH Co.
 Baxter & Associates
 Howard A. Beadner, M.D., P.C.
 J. A. Besteman Produce Co.
*Bissel Inc.
 Bixby
 Eldon M. Bliek

 H. L. Bolkema Decorating
 The Bouma Corporation
 Building Facilities Corporation
 Center Manufacturing Inc.
 Clary, Nantz, Wood, Hoffius Rankin & Cooper
 Consumers Power Company
 Mr. and Mrs. Peter C. Cook
 Corporate Color Services Inc.
 Cox & Vogel, Inc.
*Davenport College of Business
*Daverman Associates, Inc.
 Davidson Plyforms Inc.
 Deloitte Haskins & Sells
 Mr. Richard DeVos
*DeWinter and Associates
*DeWitt Barrels, Inc.
 Evans Products Co.
 Mr. Fables Systems Inc.
 Fairbrother & Gunther, Inc.
*Gerald R. Ford Museum
*Foremost Corporation of America
 Henry A. Fox Sales Co.
*Furniture Manufacturers Association

*General Motors Corporation
 J. Larry Gillie
*Grand Rapids Historical Organizations
*Grand Rapids Junior College
*Grand Rapids Press
*Grand Rapids Supply Company
 Alexander Grant & Company
 Graybar Electric Company
 Great Lakes Sales Inc.
*Groskopfs Luggage
*Guardsman Chemicals, Inc.
 Hartger & Willard Mortgage Associates, Inc.
*Haviland Enterprises, Inc.
 Hertel Plumbing & Heating Company, Inc.
 Holland American Wafer Co.
*Houseman's Clothing Company
 Industrial Fuel & Asphalt Corp.
 Interphase Office Systems, Inc.
 The Island Fan Co. of Grand Rapids
*Israels Designs for Living, Inc.
 Jackson Products
 Jobbers Warehouse Service, Inc.
 Keeler Brass Company
 Keller Transfer Line Inc.

Downtown Grand Rapids, looking north along Monroe Avenue towards the Pantlind Hotel, circa 1905.

*Kendall School of Design
 Kent Intermediate School District
 Kent Manufacturing Company
*Knape & Vogt
 Kregel, Raterink, Kingma & Co.
 Landman, Luyendyk, Latimer, Clink &
   Robb
 Law, Weathers & Richardson
*Leitelt Iron Works
 Maghielse Tool & Die Co. Inc.
 Marshall & Wells Co.
 Mattson Tool & Die Corp.
 May's of Michigan
 Mazda Distributors Great Lakes
*Meijer Inc.
 Merrill Lynch, Pierce, Fenner & Smith, Inc.
 Michigan Consolidated Gas Company
*Michigan National Bank Central
*Michigan National Corporation Banks
*Monarch Road Machinery Company
*S. A. Morman & Co.
 Murphy, Burns & McINERNEY, P.C.
 F. R. Neuman Insurance
 Newhof & Winer Inc.

Old Kent Bank & Trust Company
 Chris Panopoulos Salons, Inc.
 Cholette Perkins & Buchanan
*Phoenix Contractors, Inc.
*Pioneer Construction Company
 Preferred Bldg. Maintenance Inc.
*Preusser Jewelers
 Price Waterhouse
 Quality Trane Heating and Airconditioning
 Quimby-Walstrom Paper Company
 Rasmussen Siding & Roofing Co., Inc.
*The Roman Catholic Diocese of Grand
   Rapids
 Ronda Tire Inc.
 S & S Brokerage Co.
 Sackner
 Hon. Harold S. Sawyer
 Schiefler Tools Corporation
 Schmidt, Howlett, Van't Hof, Snell, and Vana
*Seidman & Seidman
 Lear Siegler, Inc., Instrument Division
 SmeeLink Optical Service
*Spartan Stores, Inc.
 Stiles Machinery Inc.

*Steelcase Inc.
*Stow/Davis Furniture Company
 Sysco/Frost-Pack Food Services, Inc.
*Time-Life Broadcast
 Touche Ross & Co.
 Twin Lakes Nursery, Inc.
*Union Bank & Trust Co., N.A.
*The Universal Companies, Inc.
 Mr. Jay Van Andel
 Tamsen R. Vanderwier
*Warner, Norcross & Judd
 Waterfield Mortgage Company, Inc.
*Waters Building Corporation
*Westinghouse Electric Corporation
   Architectural Systems
*John Widdicomb Co.
 Wing & Jabaay, Inc.
*Wolverine World Wide, Inc.
 Robert J. Wyma
*WZZM-TV13
 Yamaha Musical Products
*The Zondervan Corporation

*Denotes Corporate Sponsors. The histories of these organizations
 and individuals appear in a special section beginning on page 181.

From trading post to renaissance city

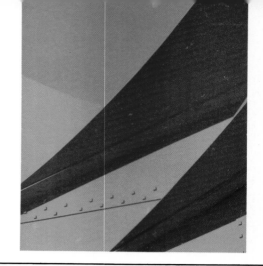

Alexander Calder's stabile, La Grande Vitesse *(right), dedicated on June 14, 1969, symbolizes Grand Rapids, a city surging ever more swiftly away from trading post days. In contrast (below), Grab Corners as it was in 1873. (Antoine Campau's store, built in 1835, and the Jefferson Morrison general store were adjacent.)*

Nationally, the 1980s have not had a propitious dawning. The country is wracked by inflation, high interest rates, a gargantuan national debt and rising unemployment. Michigan has been particularly hard hit. But while the eastern half of the state grapples with an ailing automobile industry and high unemployment, Grand Rapids has been described as "an island of stability in a sea of economic turmoil."

Settled in the 1830s, Grand Rapids grew quickly— on the one hand a brawling frontier town with its share of lumberjacks, mill hands and saloons, and on the other hand a staid and industrious community peopled by a solid, sober nucleus of citizens bent on building the good life for themselves.

Grand Rapids is the head of navigation for the Grand River, longest river in the state. People came to the valley, not by happenstance, but deliberately, to take advantage of the river as a waterway and a source of power and to farm the rich lands left centuries earlier by receding waters.

Too far from Lake Michigan to develop as a port, off the path of major roads linking trade centers or government outposts, the community was geographically isolated. Unaffected by trends, strongly moral in character, the town developed as a self-reliant, self-supporting entity.

Even though its initial flush of fame was as the furniture capital of the world, Grand Rapids had other, satellite industries which sprang up to support the furniture industry. When furniture manufacturers moved south to more readily accessible materials and cheaper labor, the satellite industries stayed on, developing new products and seeking new markets.

Grand Rapids grew according to no particular design or thought. Its greatest natural resource—the Grand River—was harnessed, channeled, dug up, filled in, redirected and eventually poisoned with the flotsam of civilization. And by the 1960s, the creeping deterioration and apathy that had overtaken many of America's cities were threatening Grand Rapids.

"Revitalization" became a byword, and the city began to move, sometimes briskly, sometimes falteringly, to reclaim the vision on which it was founded.

Civic leaders worked diligently to bring about the renewal. Capped by a glittering week of celebration the reconstruction of downtown and the cleanup of the river and its banks left the city with a soaring sense of achievement and self-confidence. And self-confidence is important to continued progress. "You can build on that," observed Stuart Cok, president of the Grand Rapids Area Chamber of Commerce.

Perhaps Grand Rapids' most remarkable resource is its ability to shake itself out of a decline and move forward. The city has always been blessed with both the foresight to see that an infusion of initiative and innovation is needed to turn onto a new track, and with the willingness and energy to take on the job.

Grand Rapids is on the upswing once more—a renaissance city where bold plans not only sprout but bear fruit. And where renewal is a portent of continuing progress.

8

A distinctive culture: Since its founding in 1826, Grand Rapids has blended its geographical location, its ethnic diversity and its natural resources into a unique and pleasing harmony; (clockwise, from right), Romanesque window in the Fountain Street Church; children at play on the John Ball statue in John Ball Park; St. Andrew's Catholic Cathedral; Campau Square; entertainment at the John Ball Park Zoo.

9

In 1928, Fulton Street (looking west toward La Grave
Avenue and beyond) was still primarily residential.

Contents

The first people

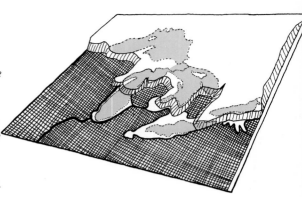

The Pleistocene Age: After the glacial blanket of the last Ice Age receded from the Great Lakes region (map), mastodons (far right) were among large game tracked into Michigan and the Grand River valley by small family bands of Paleoindians. Later tribes such as the Potawatomi and Ojibwa, were in Michigan for centuries before French explorers and missionaries arrived. The scene (below) is from a painting by Robert Thom depicting a Michigan Indian village as it might have appeared in the 1500s.

Long before the first man or beast crossed the Michigan lands to forage an existence from the earth—even longer before the dense forests of pine, hemlock, hickory and tamarack sprouted in the fertile ground—the form and quality, and thus the destiny, of the land to be called Grand Rapids was beginning to take shape.

Fifteen thousand years ago, the earth was bitter cold, buried beneath the glacial blanket of the last Ice Age. Ice sheets two miles thick crept slowly across the North American continent, giving shape to its features. The great glaciers piled rocks and debris ahead of them, forming the ridges—or moraines—of Michigan's rolling terrain. Glacial claws gouged deep valleys and depressions into the land below.

And then, almost imperceptibly at first, the earth began to warm. The heat of the sun assaulted the vulnerable ice, forcing the glaciers into a final, inevitable retreat. Great puddles of meltwater filled the basins and valleys, forming the Great Lakes and Grand River and the thousands of lakes and streams which dot the Michigan countryside. Meltwater flowed through the glacial drift, creating ancient lakes that have long since silted over into rich fertile soil, and washing away the original clay, leaving deposits of sand and gravel.

THE FIRST FOOTFALL

As the glaciers receded, groups of hunters moved from Asia into the New World, following a trail blazed by their prey. It is generally speculated that the woolly mammoth, mastodon, musk ox and their human trackers crossed the Bering Sea over a 1,000-mile-wide land bridge connecting Asia to Alaska. Hunter and hunted spread south and then east.

By the year 9,000 B.C., small family bands, who were descended from those earliest hunters, had moved into Michigan and the Grand River valley to track the big game. Called Paleoindians (*paleo,* ancient) by archaeologists, they chipped spearheads out of flint and used flint scrapers and knives to make clothing and shelter from animal hides.

Over the centuries dense forests grew as the melting glaciers continued their northerly retreat. The big-game animals moved steadily north to forage and the Paleoindian big-game hunters followed. The climate grew much warmer and the mastodon and mammoth

During the Woodland Period, maple sugar was a staple of the Ottawa Indian diet. In early spring, when the sap began to flow, the Ottawa tapped the sugar maples, caught the sap in birchbark baskets and boiled it in large kettles until it was reduced to brown sugar. What they did not use themselves, they traded.

eventually disappeared, replaced by deer, caribou and other faster-moving game. Paleoindian times gave way to what archaeologists now call the Archaic Period.

Over a span of 5,000 years, the Archaic peoples of Michigan changed their hunting tools and methods and learned to supplement the meat they caught with foodstuffs they could gather. They were less nomadic than their Paleoindian predecessors and their tools were more sophisticated—grooved axes to build wood shelters and to hollow logs into dugout canoes; pestles and grinding stones to prepare their food.

Population increased—the result of a better food supply—and the patterns of life became more complex.

In the north of Michigan, about 3,000 years ago, men who were among the first metalworkers in the world began mining copper and hammering it into knives and spear points, axes and ornaments. They traded these and bits of raw copper for shell ornaments and other exotic items from the peoples to the south. Just as once the great glaciers had spread their tentacles over a vast land area, now a trading network stretched its way across the continent from Lake Superior to the Gulf of Mexico. Around the trade goods and the objects that could be made from them arose elaborate rituals and burial ceremonies which added texture to an existence once concerned wholly with survival.

THE THREE FIRES

Michigan's principal native American tribes were the Ojibwa (the name was later corrupted to Chippewa), Potawatomi and Ottawa.

The Ojibwa, hunters and fishermen of northern Michigan, were the first native Americans the French encountered in Michigan. The Potawatomi lived further south, tending fields and growing crops. The Ottawa, traders and middlemen, lived in the forests which were a transition zone between northern and southern Michigan.

In the eighteenth century, the three tribes, who shared a similar cultural tradition and a common Algonquian dialect, formed a "Council of the Three Fires," a loosely defined confederacy to defend against European encroachment. The tribes referred to themselves as brothers—the Ojibwa were the Elder Brother, the Ottawa the Next Older Brother and the Potawatomi the Younger Brother.

THE MOUND BUILDERS

The years wore on and cultural patterns evolved into what is known as the Woodland Period, which began about 1,000 B.C. The people of the Grand River valley learned to grow plants for food and to make pottery for storing seeds and grain.

Although the practice of burying the dead beneath mounds of earth began in earlier times, mound building in the Grand River valley reached its peak during the middle of the Woodland Period.

The Mound Builders were part of a larger group whose culture and burial practices spread from Kansas to New England. They lived along the Grand River in small, scattered villages, gathering wild seeds and planting and harvesting sunflowers, squash and corn.

They also maintained a far-flung network of trade. Obsidian from the Rockies, galena from Missouri, copper from northern Michigan, flint from Ohio and conch shells from the Gulf of Mexico represented wealth and power to the Mound Builders. The trade goods, along with carved turtle-shell bowls, pottery jars and effigy pipes crafted by their own artisans, were ceremonial objects to be buried with their dead.

As part of a ritual regularly enacted on the shores of the Grand, the Mound Builders dug pits into which the deceased were placed along with tools, points, mica mirrors, bowls and ornaments that would perhaps ease their passage to the afterworld. Workers built pine ramps around the pits and then covered the site with bark and soil to form a mound. Each mound took many years to complete and required the labor of hundreds of workers.

The Mound Builders' culture flourished as the Roman Empire rose and fell. It vanished nearly 1,500 years ago, leaving its remnants behind in the burial mounds built by its people. One of the first burial mounds to be excavated was on the land of an Ohio farmer named Hopewell, and archaeologists applied the name Hopewell to the Mound Builders. (A group of Hopewell mounds remains in Grand Rapids today. Called the Norton group, the mounds are among the best preserved in the Great Lakes region).

Mound building ceased about A.D. 500 and new cultural patterns emerged among Michigan's native peoples that lasted well into the seventeenth century.

The French influence: Jesuit Father Jacques Marquette (left) founded Michigan's first French mission in 1668 at Sault Ste. Marie where he first met French explorer Louis Jolliet. Marquette, in company with Jolliet, explored St. Ignace (below) and founded a mission on the north shore of the Straits of Mackinac in 1671.

FROM A FARAWAY WORLD

Other lives and other ways, however, were eventually to intrude on the tribes living beside the river they called Owashtanong, the faraway water. The French cast the first shadow, beginning their New World explorations early in the sixteenth century and later sending missionaries, traders and soldiers to protect and expand their empire.

In exchange for annual gifts to the people called Indians, the French established their forts and missions unopposed. Jesuit Father Jacques Marquette founded Michigan's first French mission in 1668 at Sault Ste. Marie; French explorers passed through the Grand River valley in the 1680s. Fur traders and other missionaries followed.

The Ottawa Indians moved into Michigan in the early 1700s, pushed west by a series of Indian Wars. They established one of their permanent year-round villages in the Grand Rapids area and called it Paw-Qua-Ting, place at the rapids. The Ottawa served as middlemen —Ottawa, in fact, means trader—in the increasingly profitable fur trade with the French.

In the earliest years of European contact, French and Indian interests were compatible. Indian trappers supplied French traders with furs in exchange for manufactured goods that soon became essential to their way of life. Indian warriors fought beside the French and received gifts of guns and ammunition which made them more powerful than enemies armed with traditional weapons. Indians agreed to be baptized by Catholic

15

French traders and missionaries: Indian hunters and trappers exchanged beaver, mink, lynx and other pelts for such items as fabric, knives, kettles, shirts and snowshoes (below). A cross of trade silver (right) was presented to the Indians by the Jesuit fathers in 1660.

THE TRADING GAME

Fur trading in the 1820s was big business—as Dwight Goss, an early resident historian, recorded,

There was such sharp competition in the fur trade that the local traders would not wait for the Indians to bring their furs to market, but would often send messengers with goods directly to the Indian camps. Late in the fall the Indians would separate, and each family would go into camp for hunting and trapping during the winter when the traders in the Rapids would dispatch men for the furs.

Furs commanded about the following prices in trade: Beaver, $1.25 a pound, weighed by hand, which means that the trader guesses at the weight and paid the Indian accordingly. It is needless to add that the furs never fell short of weight when weighed at the warehouse. Mink commanded from fifty cents to $1. Smoke skin (buckskin), $1 each. Martin, $1 to $1.25; lynx, $1 to $1.25; muskrat, five cents each. Wolf and bear skins were not of much value. Fashions did not change and the above prices continued for years.

In the wilderness: The earliest known map (below) of the Great Lakes region was published by the French in 1703—a time when their trading with the Ottawa Indians was brisk. Chief Pontiac (left), an Ottawa Indian chief, later led an uprising, known as Pontiac's War or Conspiracy, against the British in 1763.

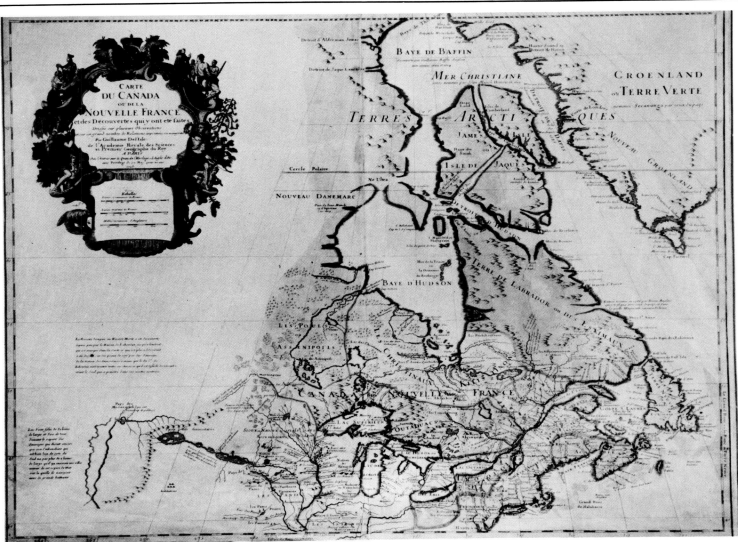

missionaries and were given rings, silver crosses and medallions in exchange.

But England had also set its sights on the New World, and the Indian tribes soon became pawns in a political and economic struggle that spanned three continents and lasted two centuries.

Michigan Indians played their own part in that struggle. In 1755, Charles Langlade, half-French, half-Ottawa, established a trading post at the mouth of the Grand River at Grand Haven. When he wasn't trading, he was leading war parties of Ottawa braves—many from the Grand River valley—against British forts and settlements in the Ohio valley. Langlade and his Indian

warriors were at the Plains of Abraham in 1759 when Quebec fell to the British, signaling the French defeat a year later and British ascendancy in the New World.

Life under British domination became increasingly difficult for the Michigan tribes, whose loyalties remained with the French. The Indians deeply resented the official British policy denying them credit at the trading posts and discontinuing the gifts of clothing and ammunition on which they had come to depend. They could foresee, moreover, the unchecked occupation of their lands by British colonists.

In 1763, the Ottawa chief, Pontiac, led a carefully plotted uprising against the British, and many of the

In October 1779, the British sloop Felicity (below, from a painting by Homer Lynn) was ordered to sail around Lake Michigan to confiscate suspected caches of grain in order to prevent them from falling into the hands of George Rogers Clark and the American revolutionaries. After anchoring at the mouth of the Muskegon River, the sloop's commander, Samuel Robertson, met with Black Piter, who ran a trading post on the Muskegon. Like other Caribbean blacks, who had accompanied the French to Canada as slaves or as servants, Black Piter probably bought or otherwise obtained his freedom and then became involved in the fur trade.

Black Piter told Robertson that a large supply of corn was stored along the Grand River. The Felicity sailed to the Grand and sent a small boat upriver to capture or destroy the grain, but the supply was never found.

warriors recruited by his agents were from the Grand River valley. Although Pontiac's rebellion was crushed by the British forces that same year, the uprising helped stave off temporarily the encroachment of European settlers into Michigan territory. The bloodshed that Pontiac visited upon the frontier forts and settlements caused the British to issue a crown proclamation prohibiting all settlement west of the Alleghenies. But Britain's loss in the Revolutionary War and later the War of 1812 opened the way for American settlement and foreshadowed an end to Indian dominion in the West.

Control over the lucrative Michigan fur trade was an issue in both wars. Michigan was rich in fur-bearing animals, and Indian trappers, who competed against each other for a share of the trade, supplied the territory's many traders with pelts. Fur trader Joseph La Framboise made annual trips to the Grand River valley beginning in the 1780s. He and his wife, Magdelaine, whom he married in 1796, established a permanent trading post on the Grand River near Lowell in 1809, acting as agents for John Jacob Astor's American Fur Company. Magdelaine, a woman "highly esteemed by both whites and Indians," ran the trading post for more

than a decade after her husband Joseph's death, and in 1821 she sold it to Rix Robinson. A lawyer by training, Robinson came west during the War of 1812 to make his fortune as a fur trader. He, too, became an agent of the American Fur Company which, by 1827, had twenty or more posts around Michigan. But overtrapping reaped scarcity, and in 1837 Rix Robinson retired to become a farmer, politician and land speculator. The Michigan fur trade was rapidly disappearing, and the Indians, once so useful as trappers, were now regarded simply as an obstacle to western settlement.

THE HUNGER FOR LAND

Epidemics of European diseases and increasing Indian dependence on European weapons and manufactured goods weakened the fabric of traditional Indian life. The American hunger for land would damage it beyond repair.

In 1809, when the La Framboises established their trading post on the Grand River, almost all of the land in Michigan belonged to the Indians. But the encourage-

Michigan territorial map, 1822.

19

Land Fever: In the 1800s, government policy displaced the native people through Indian land cession agreements (map). By the time Rix Robinson (left) purchased the La Framboise trading post in 1821, most of the Indian lands had been whittled away. During the following decade, much of Michigan was caught up in a period of land fever as represented by Robert Thom's painting of the Kalamazoo Land Office (below).

ment of white settlement was the official policy of Lewis Cass, Michigan territorial governor between 1813 and 1831. The Indians, overpowered and outnumbered, began ceding their lands. By the time Rix Robinson purchased the La Framboise trading post in 1821, most of the Indian lands in the eastern half of the state had been whittled away by treaty; the Treaty of Chicago, signed in 1821, began the same process in the western part of the state. Within 40 years, all but a few square miles of Michigan would be in American hands.

The Indians gave up their lands in exchange for reservations, individual land allotments, cash annuity payments, hunting and fishing rights, and for teachers, farmers and blacksmiths who would instruct them in the settlers' ways.

But greed, corruption and unscrupulous practices among the merchants, traders, land speculators and Indian agents served to defraud the Indians of even those modest treaty guarantees. As one early Grand Rapids historian noted:

When first visited by Europeans, [Michigan's Indians] numbered a quarter of a million [a questionable figure]; but the white man's aggressive spirit; his destructive vices; and above all, his fiery rum, have destroyed the Algonquin nation.

The floodgates had been opened to a tide of settlement that Michigan's native peoples were powerless to stem.

from trading post to village

The Reverend John Booth sketched Grand Rapids as it was in 1831 (below). The three buildings on the right are Louis Campau's cabin, trading post and blacksmith shop (site of today's Civic Auditorium); across the river is the Baptist mission; and in the foreground, at the left, Chief Noonday's camp. Territorial Governor Lewis Cass (facing page) negotiated treaties with the Indians and opened the Michigan lands to settlers at $1.25 per acre.

"**T**his has been the choicest, dearest spot to the unfortunate Indian, and now is the pride of the white man."
These words, appearing in the first editorial of the first newspaper in Grand Rapids, the *Grand River Times,* were printed on April 18, 1837, barely a handful of years after a tiny but permanent settlement built its dwellings and planted its roots beside the rapids of the Grand.

"Like other villages of the West," the editorial continued, "its transition from the savage to a civilized state has been as sudden as its prospects are now flattering."

In fact, the chain of events leading to the settlement of Michigan and Grand Rapids had been set in motion by the French fur traders and missionaries of an earlier age. Many hard-fought battles, broken treaties, shifting alliances and a revolution later, Michigan became a United States territory, administered by a government eager to annex Indian lands and to open them for white settlement.

"INCULCATE PROPER SENTIMENTS..."

In return for the cession of Indian lands south of the Grand River, the Chicago Treaty of 1821 established an annual fund to provide the displaced tribes with blacksmiths, farm and blacksmithing tools and experts to teach them farming techniques. The Reverend Leonard McCoy, a Baptist missionary, sought and was granted an appointment by Territorial Governor Lewis Cass to carry out the treaty provisions by establishing two mission stations—one for the Potawatomi on the St. Joseph River, and another for the Ottawa Indians on the Grand.

McCoy was well briefed on what his job would be:

Give the Indians, young and old, such instructions as are deemed best suited to their habits and condition; exercising discretion as to the proportion of moral and religious instructions.

Inculcate proper sentiments toward the Government and citizens of the United States, and strive to wean the Indians of their affection toward any foreign power.

Labor assiduously against the use of ardent spirits, and to prevent the free introduction of whiskey among the natives.

Watch the conduct of traders, and report infractions of the laws to the nearest agent.

Strive to induce the Indians to engage in agriculture and rearing of domestic animals.

Instruct them as to the best mode of expending their annuities, and against unlawful traffic.

Seek to promote the general good of the Indians, and to persuade them to stay at home.

McCoy, his family, pupils and assistants—32 in all— founded the Carey Station on the St. Joseph River a week before Christmas in 1822. When the bitter cold of those first months subsided, McCoy and two members of his party set out through the forests and across the

Men of devotion: Father Frederic Baraga (below left) wrote to his superiors in 1834 expressing concern that the policy of Indian removal would force "my poor Indians to wander. However, I console them with the assurance that I shall never abandon them." He spent much of his life among the Indians, established a mission in Grand Rapids and later served as Vicar Apostolic of the Upper Peninsula until his death in 1868. The hand-carved crucifix and glass rosary beads (right) are said to have been worn by an Indian in the nineteenth century. The Reverend Leonard Slater (below right) also spent most of his life among Michigan's Indians, first at the Baptist mission in Grand Rapids and later in Barry County and Kalamazoo.

Grand River to find the site earmarked for his Ottawa mission station. But nothing in the vicinity matched the government's descriptions of the designated site, and when the Ottawas expressed dissatisfaction with the treaty terms, McCoy was forced to postpone his plans.

By 1824, however, the "brave, noble and dignified" Ottawa chief, Noonday—Qua-ke-zik in his own language—agreed to the establishment of the Thomas Mission Station. McCoy chose his own site—a traditional Indian gathering place on the west bank of the Grand River at the foot of the rapids for which the city would be named. The sound of the rushing water, tumbling over limestone ledges (between present-day Leonard and Pearl streets) in its gradual, eighteen-foot drop, could be heard more than a mile away. Said McCoy of the spot, "The place we had selected for the establishment of the mission we could easily perceive would one day become a place of great importance—much more so than that which had originally been selected for it by the United States Commissioner."

Within two years, McCoy's group had constructed permanent log buildings on the mission reserve, a teacher and a blacksmith had joined the settlement, and cattle grazed within the newly fenced acreage. The wigwams of Ottawa villages clustered around the area.

OF RELIGION AND RIVALRY

The Reverend Leonard Slater arrived in 1827, with his pregnant bride of less than a year, to take charge of the Thomas Station. Slater mastered the Ottawa's language and numbered Chief Noonday himself among his earliest converts.

During Slater's tenure, the mission grew and so did his family. Sarah Emily Slater, born on August 12, 1827, was the first white child born in Grand Rapids. But in less than ten years, Sarah, her parents and the three other children born to them at the Thomas Station would be gone from the banks of the Grand and the mission itself would be disbanded.

St. Mary's, the Roman Catholic mission established by Father Frederic Baraga in 1833, half a mile downriver from Thomas Station, met the same fate.

Father Baraga, like his Baptist colleague Slater, was fluent in the Ottawa language, and the two men became intense rivals. Slater believed that indoctrination must

precede baptism. Baraga, on the other hand, baptized 46 Indians, by his own account, on the occasion of his first preaching in the valley. Slater and his followers bitterly protested the priest's arrival in Grand Rapids while Baraga countered that Slater "has been able in nine years to convert only ten Indians."

Although in the end, both men left the valley, their rivalry was not the reason. Catholic and Baptist missions alike had outlived their usefulness in the face of further Indian land cessions in 1836 and the federal government's increasingly adamant policy of Indian removal.

But even before the mission days ended, the era of permanent settlement began.

THE LYON AND THE FOX

First came Louis Campau, Detroit-born Frenchman, fur trader and town character known to one and all as Uncle Louis. Variously described by his contemporaries as irascible, amiable, childishly whimsical, benevolent, willful-minded and kind, he would one day be immortalized, somewhat inaccurately, in his epitaph as

"The founder of the original village in 1826, Now city of Grand Rapids."

Campau, after more than a dozen years as a fur trader in the Saginaw valley, came to Grand Rapids in 1826 to trade with the Ottawa. The following spring, he returned to stay.

For the price of 72 beaver pelts: In the 1820s, Louis
Campau brought his wife, Sophie (below right),
from Detroit to the new settlement when it was still
a wilderness. A shrewd trader, Louis Campau (below
left) recognized the value of the land along the
river and purchased 72 acres bounded by today's
Michigan Street on the north, Fulton on the south,
Division Avenue on the east and the river on the
west. The cost was $90, and Campau registered his
purchase in the federal land office at White Pigeon
where he received a Western District receipt for
payment in full (below).

No. 723

RECEIVER'S OFFICE, WESTERN DISTRICT, M.T.

White Pigeon, 20th Sept. 1831

RECEIVED from Louis Campau Sen. of Kalamazoo Co. M. Ty.

the sum of Ninety DOLLARS and CENTS, being in full for the

North East fraction of Section No. 25 in Township No. 7 North of range

No. Twelve West, containing Twenty two acres, at the rate of $1.25 per acre. $90.00

Wm. C. Sheldon
Receiver.

Campau built his log-cabin home, a trading post and a blacksmith shop on the east side of the river, opposite Thomas Station, and brought his French-speaking wife, Sophie, from Detroit. The fur trade was still profitable in those days, and Campau was soon on his way to becoming a man of property.

For the first few years after Campau's arrival, the settlement attracted little outside attention. Apart from missionaries and an occasional traveler, most of the newcomers came because of Louis Campau. Among them were a few helpers working at the trading post and several relatives—Campau's wife, Sophie, his mother and a brother, Toussaint. Two more brothers, George and Antoine, came later as did his wife's sister, Emily de Marsac, who later married Toussaint.

In 1831, the federal government survey of the Northwest Territory reached the Grand River. The survey fixed the boundaries of Kent County, named for prominent New York state jurist James Kent. When the government offered public lands for sale, Louis Campau purchased 72 acres. That land, which eventually became the heart of a thriving downtown, cost Campau $1.25 an acre—$90 in all.

Campau, of course, was not the only person shrewd enough to recognize the potential value of the land along the river and beyond. Lucius Lyon, the government surveyor, wasted little time in buying his own chunk to the north of Campau's tract.

Between them, Lyon and Campau owned all the prime land in the future downtown area. Lyon and his associates—calling themselves the Proprietors of Kent—formed a land-speculating combine and did a brisk business. Campau did business, too. In need of money to plat the rest of his property, Campau sold the northern portion of his original holdings to none other than Lucius Lyon.

Despite that sale, Campau and Lyon remained bitter rivals. Campau platted the streets in his tract in the French manner, angled off the old Indian trail—Monroe Avenue—which ran diagonally from the river. Lyon, however, platted his streets according to compass

directions. Feelings between the two men continued to run high, and Campau finally platted a line of lots along Pearl Street to separate his holdings from Lyon's and to prevent Lyon's streets from connecting with his own. That spite fence was eventually breached, but it created an obstacle to getting around downtown that would take years to correct.

Campau named his tract Grand Rapids; Lyon called his holdings the Village of Kent. (In 1838, Grand Rapids was officially adopted as the township and the village name.)

Federal land policies had put Grand Rapids on the map. Territorial surveys followed by land sales at bargain-basement prices opened the West to settlement; the Erie Canal, completed in 1825, offered the way. News of stately forests and rich farmland filtered east to New England and New York. Settlers began streaming west.

One New York "land-looker" and would-be settler was Samuel Dexter, who liked what he saw around west Michigan in 1832. After buying land in what is now Ionia, he returned to Herkimer County in eastern New York state to organize a colony of 63 settlers. They came by way of the Erie Canal and booked steamer passage from Buffalo across Lake Erie to Detroit. After a brief stopover to replenish their supplies, they spent sixteen days cutting through the Michigan wilderness. It wasn't an easy trip. Samuel Dexter's 2-year-old son died along the way and the saddened settlers finally reached the Grand River in May 1833, more than a month after their journey began.

On their way to the federal land office in White Pigeon, Dexter and Joel Guild, a member of Dexter's group, stopped at Campau's trading post for the night. Ever the wily trader, Campau, nicknamed "the Fox" by local Indians, sensed an opportunity to make a profit on his land. If Guild would buy one of Campau's lots for $25, Campau would help move his family there. Guild accepted the offer, purchased two lots for $45, and within two months, he, his wife, six daughters and a son were in their new home, the first frame house in the valley. It wasn't long before the Guilds had neighbors living within a few miles of the river and its rapids.

Louis Campau, interested in making a profit on the land he had purchased, divided his land into lots. Two of these he sold to Joel Guild who built the first frame home in the valley (left). A plat map, drawn in the 1830s, shows Louis Campau's Village of Grand Rapids and Lucius Lyon's Village of Kent (below). Although Lyon's streets ran according to compass directions, Louis Campau's did not. Campau did not want Lyon's streets to connect with his, and once said "If Lyon wants to come to my plat, he will have to come around by Division."

TRAGEDY ALONG THE TRAIL

For the Dexters and the Guilds—early settlers to Grand Rapids—the westward journey from New York in 1833 proved more trying than any might have predicted. Several years later, Harriet Guild—19 years old at the time of the trek—described the tragedy that befell the group.

At Pontiac Mrs. Dexter's youngest child, a boy, became sick with scarlet fever, and seemed to grow worse every day. But we could not stop, for our progress was slow and our supplies running short, so we traveled on to the Shiawassee where we procured a guide. It was raining when we reached the Looking-Glass River, and that night the little boy was so sick that his mother and Mrs. Yeomans, whose babe was but four weeks old when we started, and myself, sat up all night, holding umbrellas over the two little ones, and nursing them. It was late when we started the next day, and we went only about four miles before reaching heavily timbered land. Thus far we had been traveling through burr oak openings. That night the boy grew worse, and his mother and I sat up nearly all night with him.

Our provisions were nearly gone, and we could not stop, but about noon Mrs. Dexter called a halt, noticing a change in the boy. Dr. Lincoln gave him some medicine, but in a few minutes the little sufferer was dead. We could not tarry, but went sadly on carrying his body, and camped early; when my mother furnished a small trunk that had been used for carrying food and dishes, which served for a coffin, and by Muskrat Creek, as the sun was going down, the little one was buried. A large elm by the grave was marked, and logs were put over the mound and fastened there, to protect it from the wolves that were then plenty in that vicinity. The only service over the little grave was a prayer by Mr. Dexter. The mother seemed broken-hearted, and we were all grieved, but could not tarry there.

Most of those first families came from New York and New England, drawn by the abundance of cheap land and driven by dreams of a prosperous future. Many were farmers. Even those with other trades farmed part-time until they could support themselves. However, until the newly cultivated fields yielded crops, provisions were scarce, and supplies—often several weeks in transit—had to be shipped in from Detroit and Mackinac. The settlers, in historian Albert Baxter's words, were "forced to practice the most rigid economy and frugality, being compelled to live for weeks at a time on potatoes and salt, or codfish and potatoes, or milk and rice only." Nevertheless, the settlers weathered shortages and floods, withstood hardship and disease and even found time for merriment and dances. "They survived, sound and hardy, as a rule," said Baxter, "with the remembrance of their experience to add zest to the better times that followed."

Not all prospective settlers were pleased. Two disappointed farmers from Vermont disparaged the little settlement as being "a hundred miles from nowhere" with land that was just "middlin' good." Nevertheless, the settlers kept on coming.

In 1834, they organized the Township of Kent, later renamed Grand Rapids Township. Four years later, the Village of Grand Rapids, newly incorporated within the Township of Kent, held its first election, and Louis Campau was elected one of seven village trustees by a landslide of 141 votes.

SPECULATIVE FEVER

Land was the most sought after commodity and speculative fever was a national affliction. John Ball arrived in Grand Rapids in 1836, acting as the agent for a group of New York speculators. His original intention was to purchase in Detroit, but prices were too high. "I made up my mind," he later wrote, "that the Grand River district was the promised land, or at least the most promising one for my operations." And so it was. Land sales soared and prices skyrocketed.

The little settlement became a boomtown. Population shot from 40 to 400. In the spring of 1836, the young village boasted thirteen buildings. By August of the next year, that number had tripled. Wildcat banks and local

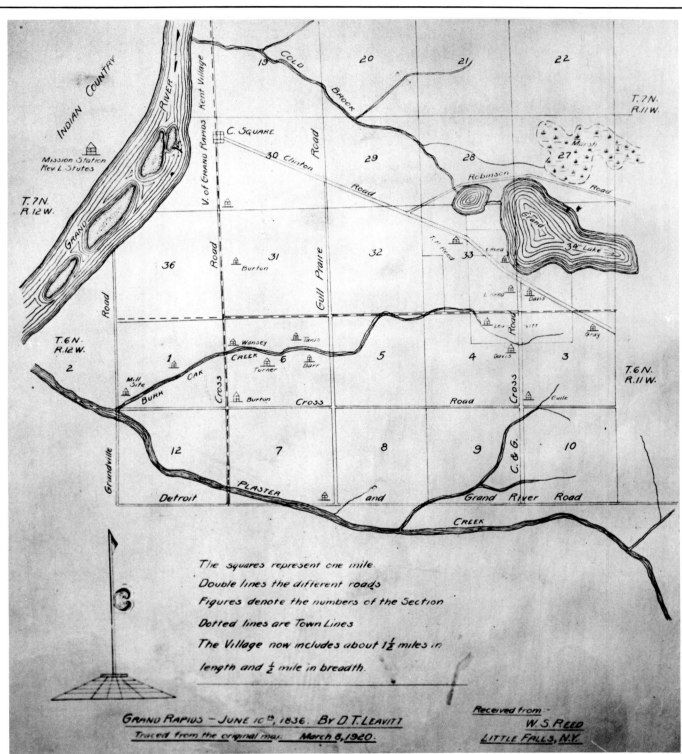

The squares represent one mile.

Double lines the different roads

Figures denote the numbers of the Section

Dotted lines are Town Lines

The Village now includes about 1½ miles in

length and ½ mile in breadth.

GRAND RAPIDS — JUNE 10th, 1836. BY D.T.LEAVITT

Traced from the original map. March 8, 1920.

Received from :-
W. S. REED
LITTLE FALLS, N.Y.

29

Many of the first families to settle in Grand Rapids were farmers from New York and New England. The farm (below), with its log cabin, covered well and woodpile, stood just outside Grand Rapids.

merchants issued their own paper currencies. There wasn't much robbery or theft at the time, John Ball later noted. When it came to land deals, however, sharp practices and even outright swindles were the order of the day.

As Grand Rapids boomed, so did business. In 1835, Jefferson Morrison had opened one of the first general stores; others, including Campau's brother George, soon followed suit. Before long, merchants, tradesmen and craftsmen of all kinds were setting up shop in a bustling downtown area. Tailors and shoemakers, coopers and saddlers, tanners and millers, blacksmiths, cabinetmakers, wainwrights, surveyors and hardware vendors all began to find markets for their services and customers for their wares.

The discriminating shopper, stopping in at establishments clustered here and there in the emerging downtown business district, could find an ample supply of merchandise—from axes and vinegar, boots and whiskey, to candles and crockery, spices and snuff boxes.

OF SKIFFS, SCOWS AND ROWBOATS

For more than 30 years, boatbuilding was an important business in Grand Rapids. The early boats were skiffs, scows and rowboats. Then came pole boats made by Richard Godfroy.

Later, several steamships were built in Grand Rapids, along with hulls for ships that sailed the Great Lakes and a number of canal boats for the Illinois Canal.

The first steamboat on the Grand was built and launched in 1837, from a shipyard at the foot of Lyon Street, and was christened the Mason, *for Stevens T. Mason, Michigan governor at the time.*

According to Charles Belknap in The Yesterdays of Grand Rapids, *"Steam whistles had not been invented and Alanson Cramton stood upon the deck in front of the pilot house with a bugle, which was really more appropriate to the occasion. Can you not imagine how the people who had settled along the river and those who were coming down in canoes and on rafts were startled by the notes?"*

In the mid-1850s, there were several steamboats on the river—the Algoma, *the* Michigan, *the* Empire *and the* Hummingbird *below the dam, the* Porter *and the* Kansas *above the dam.*

Most of the steamers were flat-bottomed, shallow-draft sidewheelers, and carried both freight and passengers. The Olive Branch, *however, was, says Belknap, a "regular Mississippi stern-wheeler staterooms with lace curtains, cabins and carpets on the top deck and a dining room that looked like a banquet hall."*

By the 1890s, river transportation was much less important, and only two steamboats ran regularly from Grand Haven to Grand Rapids. Pleasure boating, however, became very popular, with many small steamers and rowboats on the river.

THE BUBBLE BURSTS

But the nation's banking practices were in severe disarray. A torrent of paper currencies, issued by wildcat banks, inundated the states. Credit was overextended, hard coinage became increasingly scarce and the speculative bubble burst, leaving in its aftermath the panic of 1837.

In Grand Rapids, the "air was rife with rumors" of impending bank failures, and "the panic-stricken people were filled with dire forebodings and alarm."

Their apprehension became fact as the local economy virtually collapsed. John Ball wrote of those years, "There was no money, and our merchants who tried to do business had to trust the farmers on the strength of their growing crops. . . . We had enough to eat, but little to wear; and if we could get enough money to pay postage, it was all we expected."

Louis Campau, who had amassed a considerable fortune through land speculation, was one of a number of prominent citizens who suffered severe financial reverses. Although he and Sophie continued to live in their impressive and newly built mansion on Fulton Street Hill, Campau was forced into receivership in 1839 and had to deed some of his property to other family members in order to avoid total ruin.

The panic left the village bankrupt, and its board of trustees took the step of issuing several hundred dollars' worth of one- and two-dollar bills which came to be known as shinplasters—a form of poorly secured paper money. Depression hung over the valley, with even partial recovery several years away.

By 1845, as Frank Little, then a young shop clerk, later observed, "the people were beginning to take heart, to crawl out from under cover, and business was reviving." Land sales increased again, but the period of wild

speculation was over and this time purchasers came to stay. The new post-boom and post-depression stability marked the real beginnings of the city.

DIAMOND IN THE ROUGH

Slowly, the village began to acquire the veneer of civilization, though some of the rough edges remained. "In the late fall and early spring, Monroe Street, from Division to Canal Street, became literally a river of mud . . . frequently from six to eight inches deep . . . and thick like hasty pudding," reported Frank Little. There were no sidewalks, and

Regular stage-line service from Grand Rapids began in 1842 with coaches that were little more than wooden farm wagons. Stage traffic increased greatly in 1855 with the completion of the Kalamazoo plank road, and Concord-style coaches were introduced, enabling passengers to travel in comfort and style.

runaway horse teams were an almost daily occurrence. Franklin Everett, who came to Grand Rapids in 1846 as principal of the Grand Rapids Academy, wrote of a "fine musical frog pond" west of Division and north of Fountain. "As regards the appearance of the village and its surroundings," Everett said, "there was a primitive air to the whole."

Nevertheless, continued growth brought increasing urbanity and the amenities associated with urban life. By the late 1840s, a number of public and private schools replaced the early mission schools which had served Indian and settler children alike. The village boasted fine residences of frame or stone, several downtown hotels, twelve lawyers, six physicians, a fire engine with a hand pump, three breweries, a temperance society and churches in an assortment of denominations.

Catholicism had come early to the village with the Campau family and with Father Baraga, the missionary, who celebrated the village's first mass in Louis Campau's home in 1833. Soon afterwards, Baraga established St. Mary's mission and school for his newly baptized Indian converts and the Catholic families among the settlers.

Originally built as a Catholic church, but never used as such, the Old Yellow Warehouse (right) became the home of Grand Rapids' earliest theatrical entertainments. Louis Campau's Catholic church (left), built in 1837 on the corner of Division and Monroe, burned down in 1872. Its 1,000-pound bell was the first of its size in the city.

CAMPAU'S CROSS

he city's first Catholic parish church, St. Andrew's, was started on the west side of the Grand River, at Father Baraga's Indian mission. But Louis Campau believed that the church belonged on the east side where the white settlers lived. He had Barney Burton steal the building by pulling it behind a yoke of oxen across the frozen river. But Father Baraga, the village's only priest, chose to remain on the west side among the Indians, and Catholic settlers were obliged to worship there in a log structure consecrated as a chapel. The stolen building, painted yellow and put to other uses, came to be known as the Old Yellow Warehouse.

In 1837, Campau built a new church on the east side, and Catholic settlers began attending services there. But Campau, in the midst of a feud with church authorities, reneged on his promise to deed the church to the bishop. Feelings ran so high between Campau and the Reverend Andreas Viszoczky, Baraga's successor, that one Sunday, in the middle of a service, the priest led his parishioners en masse out of the new church and back across the river to the old log chapel. Campau retaliated by selling his church to the Congregationalists in 1841, all but the iron cross atop the building; that was not for sale.

It wasn't until 1846 that the cross came down. Removal was difficult, and when the first attempt failed, a workman, John Post, was sent to saw if off. Cross and worker tumbled from the roof and Post was killed instantly.

34

From these small beginnings grew St. Andrew's, the city's first Catholic parish.

Until the 1850s, St. Andrew's parish and its pastor, the Reverend Andreas Viszoczky—Father Baraga's successor—worshipped in temporary sanctuaries. So, for the most part, did the members of many other church groups—Baptists, Methodists, Episcopalians, Reformed, Christian Reformed and their various offshoots. But as congregations grew, their church spires and steeples injected a note of piety into the rough-hewn landscape.

A BLENDING OF FAITHS AND CULTURES

The churches represented not only many faiths, but many nationalities as Dutch, German and Irish came to join the French- and English-speaking settlers.

The first Dutch settlement in Michigan was the colony of Holland, founded by Albertus Van Raalte in 1847. The Dutch colonists planted settlements named Holland and Zeeland for the places they left behind. But many would have to leave these places, too, because they could not afford to buy land or replenish their dwindling supplies. Economic necessity forced some of them, and their working-age children, to seek employment in Grand Rapids.

As crop failures, famine and political unrest drove hundreds of thousands of Germans and Irish from their homelands, they also made their way to America. Encouraged by state-appointed immigration agents to settle in Michigan, large numbers of Germans, many of them skilled mechanics and tradesmen, came to Grand Rapids. A small group of Irish found work in Grand Rapids as early as 1835. Lucius Lyon, Campau's rival, had hired John Almy, a civil engineer who later served as an immigration agent, to plat his downtown property and design an east-side canal to bypass the rapids. Nehemiah Sargeant, Lyon's partner in the Kent Company, recruited laborers in Detroit to dig the canal. In July 1835, a crew of 40 workers—New Englanders and Irish—marched into the settlement to the tune of bugle fanfares played by Alanson Cramton. (Cramton played for many local dances and frolics; his bugling services later would prove handy on a Grand River steamer which had no whistle.)

Several black families also settled in the county during the 1830s, the Hardys, the Hawleys and Minisees, among

35

Recruiting for settlers: John Almy (right), a surveyor and civil engineer, who laid out the Kent plat for Kent Company proprietors Lucius Lyon and Nehemiah Sargeant during the 1830s, went to New York as a boomer to attract settlers to the newly platted Village of Kent. Maps, such as the Tourist Pocket Map of Michigan (facing page)—published in 1839 and circulated throughout the East—showed new roads and road distances. The improved roads encouraged new settlers to bring all their worldly goods. They also brought their virtues of morality and thrift and their desire for education and religion. St. Mark's Episcopal Church (below) joined the increasing number of churches. It was built in 1848 of limestone hauled to the site by oxen, but climate eventually damaged the limestone and prompted the parish to have the facade entirely covered with stucco in 1855, as shown below. Nearly a century later, the stucco shell was removed and the original limestone treated to preserve it.

them. Hardy was elected township supervisor in Gaines Township, and his son Eugene was later the first black to graduate from Grand Rapids Central High School. The Minisees, a family of substantial means, lived on the city's southwest side.

Sometime during the 1840s, two black slaves were able to purchase their freedom from their Southern masters. They came to the village because they believed that their status as free men would be recognized in Grand Rapids.

Less than two decades after Louis Campau established his trading post on the Grand, the village, according to a pamphlet designed to attract immigrants, was home to "twenty dry goods, two hardware, two clothing, four drug, two hat and cap and two book stores, twelve grocery and provision, ten boot and shoe stores, eight public houses and victualling establishments and two printing offices. There were also two tanneries, three flour mills, five saw mills, between 40 and 50 factories and mechanical shops of various kinds, three bakeries, two meat markets and about 100 carpenters and joiners. There were seven churches with eight resident ministers, twelve lawyers and six physicians."

Diversity shaped Grand Rapids from the beginning. Business and industry prospered and grew and provided a firm base for the workers, tradesmen, craftsmen and entrepreneurs who continued to find the opportunities they were seeking in the village beside the Grand.

In 1850, its population grown to almost 3,000, the village became a city. It adopted a city charter, elected a mayor, organized a council of aldermen and even had a town seal fashioned. High on the new government's list of things to do were the public improvements that would turn quagmires into streets and sidewalks, encourage private companies to build toll bridges across the river and transform a primitive frontier town into a city in fact as well as name.

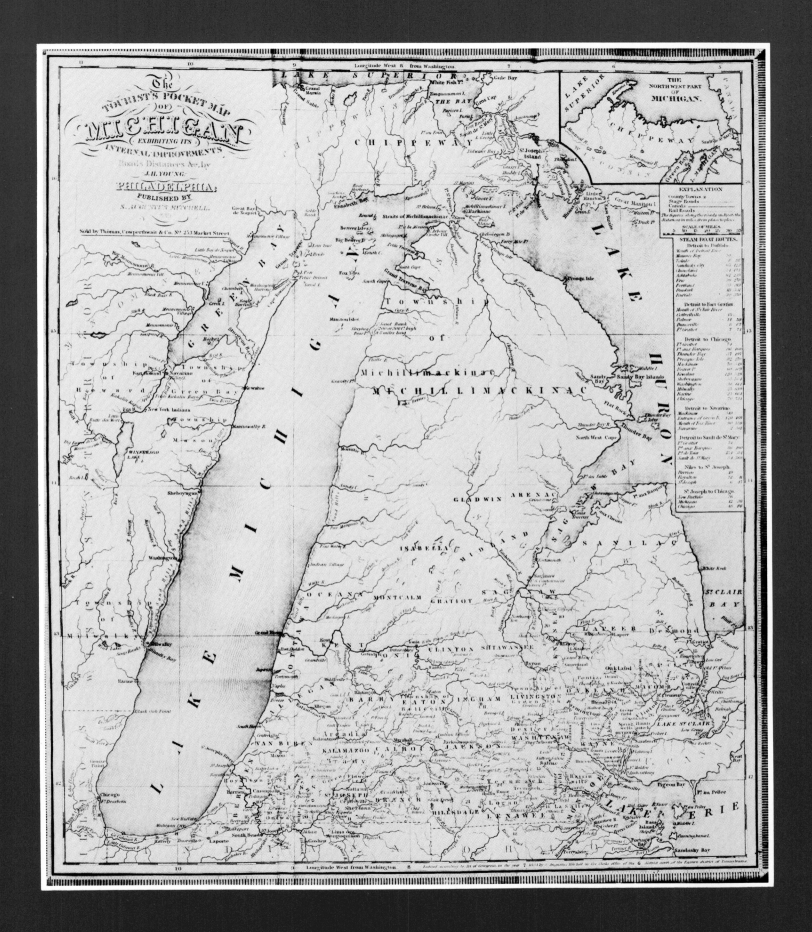

Oliver Bleak, who came to Grand Rapids in 1848, built a grocery store in 1856 at the corner of La Grave and Fulton streets and ran it for many years. The building, still standing, now houses the West Michigan Tourist Association.

Great Seal of the Territory of Michigan. The Latin motto, Tandem Fit Surculus Arbor, *inscribed beneath the two eagles, says, "A shoot at length becomes a tree."*

A RICH HARVEST OF SILVER

The shortage of hard coin remained a problem, relieved to some extent by the Indian "annuity days"—federal payments for ceded lands—that had been a yearly sign of summer for more than a decade.

With the signing of the Washington Treaty in 1836, the year Michigan became a state, the Indians relinquished all their remaining lands in the lower peninsula to the federal government in return for cash payments of $18,000 a year for twenty years. Once a year, in a downtown warehouse, federal agents handed out the payments.

Albert Baxter's early chronicle described the proceedings:

In a large room would be a long table, or counter, upon which were the receipts and little piles of coin for each Indian, and about which were seated the agents, clerks and interpreters.

The Indians would enter the front door one by one, sign their receipts or make their marks thereon, receive their money and walk out the back door, where stood a crowd of hungry traders, who quickly transferred most of the money from the hands of the Indians to their own pockets, for the payment of old debts. The traders commonly claimed all they could see, and the Indians, as a rule, gave it up without protest.

Frank Little, as a teenager, watched this annual ritual in 1838. "The leading French traders with the Indians—the Messrs. Louis, Antoine, and Toussaint Campau, and the Godfroys—garnered a rich harvest of silver half-dollars, until their measures were full to overflowing."

By the time the annuity payments ended in the late 1850s, few Indians were left in Grand Rapids. The rivers in which they once fished and the forests through which they tracked game were being put to other—and in the settlers' point of view—more compelling uses.

YEA IN MICHIGANIA

Settlers made up their minds to head west to the tune of such popular songs as this one:

Come all ye Yankee farmers who wish to change your lot,
Who've spunk enough to travel beyond your native spot,
And leave behind the village where Pa and Ma do stay,
Come follow me and settle in Michigania,
(Mi-chi-gān-ī-ā)—
Yea, yea, yea in Michigania!

A city emerges

Grand Rapids' destiny was determined by several factors—among them extensive forests and the state's longest river.

It was inevitable that Michigan, heavily timbered with both hardwoods and softwoods, would develop a logging industry. In 1850, the state ranked fifth, behind New York, Pennsylvania, Maine and Ohio. A decade later Michigan moved to third place behind Pennsylvania and New York, and within less than five years after that it surpassed all lumber-producing states—and would continue to do so through the 1880s when its total annual production almost equalled the combined output of the next three states.

Grand Rapids—and its people—were in a superb position. The city sat astride the natural dividing line between the hardwood and softwood forests—the soft white pine, jack pine, Norway pine, spruce, white cedar, hemlock and tamarack to the north; ash, hickory, beech, sugar maple and walnut to the south. Pine was the chief wood sought in the early days, the hardwoods falling to the lumberman's ax only after they became important to the furniture industry.

There were plentiful pine forests along the Rogue, Flat and other rivers flowing into the Grand, and the rivers were the only means by which to move large quantities of logs to sawmills for processing or to Grand Haven for transport across the lake to Chicago and Milwaukee.

Grand Rapids became both a logging and a sawmill center, and the huge log flotillas were an annual event for nearly 40 years.

Lumbermen cut the timber in the winter and rivermen rafted the logs in the spring when the ice melted and the rivers were still high. Theirs was a brutal and dangerous business that required stout and hardy men, impervious to hardship and capable of grueling work in primitive conditions. The lumberjacks felled the trees and by team and wagon or bobsled got them to the water's edge. The rivermen, in their high, spiked boots, rode the logs down river, day and night, to their destination.

At the end of the season the loggers got paid. Immediately they converged on the nearest town to rid themselves of the effects of long months of temperance and celibacy in the logging camps. And they were thorough in their celebrations. Long after the men returned to their camps, stories flourished of lumberjacks who embarked on sprees that left them nothing to show for their season's work but broken heads or monumental hangovers, or both.

Lumberjacks and rivermen: Logging was a major industry for western and northern Michigan. The rivermen (below), wearing spiked boots, rode the logs downriver, freed snagged and jammed logs and kept the floating logs moving. Logs were branded with the owner's name to discourage "hogging" or stealing of another lumberman's logs by "shinglewavers," small-time mill operators who established camps along the riverbanks and made shingles. A logging crew (left) dragged logs by horse team out of the forest to the river where they were floated downstream for processing at sawmills or for shipping across Lake Michigan to the Chicago and Milwaukee markets.

43

A group of rivermen posed aboard a raft carrying their cook shanty, circa 1880. Rivermen were the most skilled loggers and earned the highest wages because log driving was the most hazardous job and required sound judgment. The slightest error in positioning the logs could bring on a major logjam that would take several hours to break up.

Grand Rapids never lacked for drinking establishments. As early as 1859, the city supported 25 saloons. After the German beer makers arrived in 1847, the population acquired a great taste for lager beer. And by the 1870s, there were 58 saloons, five breweries, one beer garden and eight billiard saloons.

Although Michigan was officially dry, under the provisions of the Maine Law, enacted in 1853, there were no effective means of enforcing the law. The sale and consumption of liquor went on unabated, and the saloon proprietors happily reaped the gains of the lumbermen's months in the woods. But because liquor was illegal, no municipal liquor licenses could be sold, and the city of Grand Rapids lost its opportunity to profit from the rowdiness of the times.

FURNITURE FACTORIES AND FORTUNES

Among the many Easterners who traveled west to make, or at least to improve, their fortunes, were cabinetmakers, carpenters and joiners. They came from New England and New York towns where building and furniture-making had been well-established crafts since the 1700s.

Several such men found their way to Grand Rapids, and by 1860 nearly all the men who would soon make their names and the city's name in the furniture business were in town and in business.

A few were cabinetmakers, a few were in the sawmill business, some were in sash, door and blind manufacturing, some in logging. Some had interests in three or more such endeavors.

William (Deacon) Haldane claimed to be the first furniture maker to set up shop in Grand Rapids. He came west, first to Ohio and then to Michigan, from Delaware County, New York. In his early teens Haldane had been apprenticed to a New York carpenter and joiner, and at 20 he opened his own shop in Painesville, Ohio, employing his brothers as apprentices. Haldane came to Grand Rapids in 1837 and immediately found a need among the inhabitants for his craft.

In 1847, William T. Powers, another Easterner with cabinetmaking skills, arrived in Grand Rapids. He teamed with Haldane briefly to manufacture and sell furniture, but in 1849 set up business for himself. In November of that year he formed a partnership with Ebenezer Morris Ball, a New Hampshire schoolteacher who had some

William (Deacon) Haldane arrived in Grand Rapids in 1837 and set up a furniture making shop. Haldane has been credited with founding the city's furniture manufacturing industry.

capital but no manufacturing experience.

Powers, Ball and Company made steady headway as a commercial enterprise. Powers was the first to have a salesroom separate from his workrooms, and from the beginning he looked beyond the local market, traveling to Chicago and New York to find customers.

By 1851, Powers, Ball and Company was both prosperous and efficient enough to be able to fill an order for 10,000 chairs for a Chicago client. In 1853, the firm built the first local steam-powered sawmill—the first local sawmill equipped with a circular saw—to supply wood to its furniture manufacturing business.

Up until this time, local furniture was handmade, and style was less important than function. Haldane's brother owned a sash and blind factory and used water-powered, belt-driven machines such as a circular saw and a lathe. Haldane adapted this machinery for use in furniture-making. Powers followed suit, adding a boring machine. The two men vastly increased their production capacity, converted local furniture-making to a factory system and gave life to an industry. By the mid-1850s, furniture-making was profitable enough to be recognized by one of the local newspapers as an emerging industry.

"Beauty and good taste, costliness and durability combine in an endless variety of forms to make our Furniture Rooms attractive." Dealer/manufacturers named in the article were Winchester Brothers, Powers, Haldane and Abbot. (Haldane entered into a number of partnerships during his years in the business.) Also mentioned was furniture retailer William E. Carr.

Grand Rapids claimed many other successful and much larger industries—flour mills, boat works, sash, door and blind factories, tanneries, knitting mills, foundries and wagon works were all well established and prospering. But lumber and furniture gave the city its identity. Grand Rapids was a thriving place now, with a bright and promising future.

PROGRESS AND PROSPERITY

The Michigan state legislature approved Grand Rapids' first city charter in April 1850, fixing the city's boundaries at two miles square and dividing it into five wards.

Seven men (for city officials were all men in those days)—an alderman from each ward, a "recorder" and the mayor—constituted the Common Council.

Such obligations as building and maintaining streets, alleys, water mains and sewers; fire protection; procurement and sale of malt and "spiritous liquors"; and the establishment of a board of health, fell to these elected men. To provide the wherewithal for their mission, they were empowered to levy taxes. In recompense, each man received $1 a year.

The charter also established a mayor's court with jurisdiction over criminal and civil matters arising in violation of the city's ordinances.

Politics were fairly spirited, with the county usually voting Democratic and the city voting Whig. The first City Council officers were all Whigs (the party that was the forerunner of the Republican Party formed in 1854 at Jackson, Michigan).

The city was becoming a city not only in name but in fact. The population tripled in the decade of the '50s, from 2,686 in 1850 to 8,085 in 1860. The government was hardpressed to keep up with the growing need for services and improvements.

In 1857 the charter was revised to extend the city boundaries. The new city limits stretched three miles from east to west and three-and-a-half miles from north to south. The revision added several more elective offices, including a second alderman from each ward.

THE TRAPPINGS OF A CITY

Along with her status as a city, Grand Rapids was acquiring the trappings. In November 1857, several Monroe Street customers of the recently established Grand Rapids Gas Light Company lit their show windows with the modern lamps. Two enterprising merchants arranged little gas jets across their store fronts to spell out their store names, and the city ordered and installed twenty street lamps.

Before 1856, the city had no organized police. A town constable was responsible for necessary law enforcement. However, merchants felt some need for vigilance at night, so they pooled their resources to hire a night watchman. The 1857 charter empowered the Common Council to appoint constables and watchmen from each ward, but few were named before 1871.

Because wood was the chief building material of that era and such fiercely flammable stuffs as straw ticks were in common use, fire was a persistent hazard for any population.

Most cities and towns had volunteer fire companies. Grand Rapids' first organized companies were formed in the 1840s but were terribly inefficient. The first effective companies were organized in 1849, and the village spent $675 for a hand-pumped fire engine that could throw five gallons of water a minute over the highest buildings on Monroe. This was considered something of a feat.

After 1850, the Common Council assumed jurisdiction of the fire companies. However, they were still volunteer units, and they were not officially recognized as the city's fire department. The department was reorganized in 1859, under the revised charter, giving a board of police and fire commissioners responsibility to appoint the chief engineer, assistant engineers and a fire warden from each ward.

GETTING THERE

Providing adequate streets was one of the concerns of the early city government. Up until the mid-1850s, the streets were a haphazard assortment of dirt roads running past residences and businesses, with wagon roads and extensions of regional roads leading in and out of town. Their condition depended on the weather—quagmires in wet weather, dusty but passable in dry.

Sometimes individual merchants took the initiative in making navigable the portion of street fronting their own establishments. The county also made some improvements and many people worked out their highway taxes by working on the roads. But even at their best, the roads were merely serviceable. In 1855, street improvements, with public funds, began in earnest.

Living up to their obligations to build and maintain streets for the residents, the city fathers, in a perverse struggle against the natural terrain, carved away at Prospect Hill for the next twenty years. Grading and cutting, they strove to level the hill, or cut their way through, carting the resulting gravel and dirt to the bottom of the hill to fill the river channels and boggy lowlands and build up the level of the streets.

It was costly and time-consuming work. When they wanted to raise the grade of a lowland street, sometimes as much as fifteen feet, the builders had to jack up the buildings along the street and lift them to the new grade, one by one.

Fire brigades: The horse-drawn hook and ladder truck (left) was manufactured by the Michigan Fire Ladder and Engine Company, located in Grand Rapids, circa 1870. Its scaling ladders could be extended to 100 feet. The Kent Street Company of volunteer firemen (below) had to use a hand-pumper to put out fires, received no salary and were fined fifty cents for each fire they missed.

Looking northwest on Monroe Avenue from Ottawa in 1859. The cobblestone paving and Luce's block, on the left, dated from 1856. Daniel Ball's bank, new in 1859, was behind the Commercial block at the foot of the street.

A boost to commerce: Daniel Ball's Prospect Hill residence, built in 1850, served in 1881 as the first home of the Peninsular Club. The 1857 view of his home (below) shows the initial grading of the hill that was eventually leveled. The constant improvement of streets, roads and river transportation spurred business. By the mid-1850s, Grand Rapids was a thriving commercial center and could boast numerous well-developed industries, such as the Kusterer Brewery Co. (facing page). Local beers were produced in Grand Rapids for more than a century, until competition from better known, nationally advertised beers forced the local breweries out of business.

OF CARGOES AND COMMERCE

From the 1830s until the advent of the railroads, Grand Rapids residents relied on the river for travel and to transport their goods. The river was an avenue, and commerce—both social and commercial—moved freely by riverboat, scow and canoe. The rapids, however, were an obstacle.

Because the early settlers were so dependent on the river, demands came early for river improvements. In 1838, two years after Michigan became a state, the fledgling legislature appropriated $30,000 to improve the Grand Rapids harbor. At that time, there had been regular steamboat service between Grand Rapids and Grand Haven for a year.

In 1835, Lucius Lyon of the Proprietors of Kent, and his partner, N.O. Sargeant, began digging an east-side canal from the head of the rapids to a place near Michigan Street. When it was completed in 1842, the canal was

nearly a mile long, 80 feet wide and five feet deep. At the north end of the canal, near Sixth Street, a wing dam turned the river current into the canal.

As river traffic increased, further improvements became necessary. In 1847, the state legislature appropriated 25,000 acres for a much larger canal, locks to enable boats to travel around the rapids and a new dam across the river.

The canal was a boon to the mills situated along its banks, but money ran out and the locks were never completed.

By 1854, two competing riverboat lines served Grand Haven and Grand Rapids with arrivals and departures four times a week. Two years later, they offered daily service.

Winter shut down the boat traffic, an inconvenience to travelers and those depending on the river for shipping or receiving goods. But for residents, it meant easy access by foot or team across the ice to the other side.

Only one bridge connected the city's east and west sides—the Bridge Street bridge built by the county in 1845 with money appropriated by the state.

The "free" Bridge Street bridge lasted until 1852 and then was rebuilt as a toll bridge. A gatekeeper at the west side of the bridge collected a penny toll from pedestrians, two cents from a person on horseback, three cents for one-horse- and four cents for two-horse-vehicles. The bane of the tollkeeper was the east-side young people who would stroll from their side of the bridge to within a few feet of the west-side toll gate and then stroll east again.

Private concerns built two more bridges—the Leonard Street bridge in June 1858 and the Pearl Street bridge in November. Both of these were toll bridges. A railroad bridge for the Detroit, Grand Haven and Milwaukee Railroad also was built in 1858.

Commerce assumed an important role early in the development of Grand Rapids, and by the mid-1850s, the area was a thriving commercial center with well-developed industries and diversified products— flour; wood products such as sash and doors, cabinetry and lumber; gypsum and produce. Exports in 1855, mostly lumber and wood products shipped across the lake to the lucrative Chicago and Milwaukee markets, amounted to $1 million.

A long-awaited plank road between Kalamazoo and Grand Rapids was completed in 1855 and gave some impetus to passenger travel and freight shipping, for Kalamazoo had been served by the Central Railroad since 1847.

But even with the plank road, it was difficult to exploit markets to the south and east. Transporting freight by wagon to Kalamazoo and on by train was slow and cumbersome. Clearly, the city needed train service.

SHARING THE WEALTH

In 1858, George K. Johnson and Francis H. Cuming, businessmen who had built lovely homes at the top of a rather large hill, decided to give a parcel of their land to the city for a park. Their beneficence may have been dictated in part by a desire to guarantee a beautiful green setting for their homes, but the result, nevertheless, was Grand Rapids' first formally declared park.

The crescent-shaped hillside, stretching west from Bostwick Avenue halfway to Division Avenue, was graded and rounded that first year, under the direction of Dr. Cuming. It took many years to complete Crescent Park, but the addition of the elaborate fountain and the "56 massive stone steps, cut from the best Joliet stone, with side coping to match," made the park, with its magnificent view of the valley below, an agreeable spot to spend an idle hour or two.

53

THE EVENING'S ENTERTAINMENT

Back in the days when movies, radio and television entertainment were not available, public gatherings played an important role in Grand Rapids. Theatres and public halls were popular spots.

Grand Rapids' first large public hall was Luce Hall, built in 1856. Squier's Opera Hall was built in 1859, and until it burned in 1872, was the only properly equipped theatre in the city. It was in constant use for theatrical presentations, lectures and expositions.

The year Squier's opened, a traveling theatre company presented Uncle Tom's Cabin, a popular play in that age of abolitionist fervor. The show ran for two nights and the audience packed the theatre each night, weeping for Eliza and Little Eva, mourning Uncle Tom and hissing Simon Legree.

Lectures, a popular entertainment of the 1800s, were frequent and on a variety of such edifying and uplifting themes as the ravages of demon rum, the Second Coming, phrenology, and local, state and national politics. Such noted lecturers as Horace Greeley, Frederick Douglass, Charles Sumner and Henry Ward Beecher appeared in local theatres and halls.

During the last three decades of the 1800s, traveling companies booked theatres regularly, arriving for a week and often presenting a different play each night. The quality of the performances ranged from stellar to mundane.

In one week at the Powers Theatre, the "highly talented actress" Ida Van Cortland performed in Caught in the Web, Forget-Me-Not, The Dangerous Woman and The Creole.

Edwin Booth played in Hamlet and Othello at different times. In 1887, Dumas' The Count of Monte Cristo was performed twice—in September with Arden Benedict and in May with James O'Neill, father of the playwright Eugene O'Neill.

Julia Marlowe appeared in W.S. Gilbert's three-act play, Pygmalion and Galatea; Miss Francis Bishop, "America's greatest living soubrette," appeared in "two of the funniest plays ever written. . .produced with New and Elegant Scenery, singing and dancing." The plays were Muggs Landing and Gyp.

And in a Powers Theatre playbill of December 6, 1889, Swetland's Restaurant, 134 Monroe Street, advertised itself as "the only nice place to take a lady to get Oysters as you like them."

The Rathbun House, at Waterloo and Monroe, was built by Louis Campau as his first Grand Rapids home. Under new ownership, it was later enlarged to become a boarding house and then a hotel. The stone addition was built in 1846, and the hotel closed in 1885.

A thumb in every pie: Daniel Ball (left), who came to Grand Rapids in 1841, was a man of "unbounded faith in the future of Grand Rapids" and one of "tireless activity in many business lines." His interests and investments involved him in a broad range of ventures, from steamboat building and real estate sales to manufacturing and banking. During the height of his days in Grand Rapids, he and his fellow citizens traveled from place to place on plank roads and on wooden sidewalks (below) that were in use in the city until the 1890s.

As early as 1845, townspeople began pressuring for rail service. In that year, citizens held a meeting and agreed to petition the state legislature for a railroad charter from Battle Creek to Grand Rapids. Meetings and agitation continued for the next nine years. Finally, in July 1858, the Detroit and Milwaukee Railway Company completed tracks into Grand Rapids and regular service between the east and west sides of the state began twelve days later. By September 1, the line was complete from Detroit to Grand Haven. The city at last had rail service, at least east and west.

Another benefit that came with the railroad was

Western Union. Up until that time, important messages came to Grand Rapids from Kalamazoo by stage or special messenger.

The D&M was the only rail line to serve the city for eleven years. First the financial panic of 1857 and then the Civil War intervened, stifling new railroad development.

THE PANIC OF '57

The financial panic of 1857, precipitated by overspeculation in railroad building and securities, shook to the breaking point the nation's confidence in the entire financial system.

Grand Rapids fared no better than other localities. Businesses failed, men were ruined. For the farmer or small tradesman who could barter in goods and services, it was possible to survive; not comfortably, perhaps, but survive. Men who dealt in cash and credit, however, had little chance of coming through unscathed, and many such businesses did not survive.

Daniel Ball and William Welles were only two of those who were hard-hit. Ball, who came to the valley in 1841 with high optimism for its future and with considerable business acumen, founded an exchange bank in 1853. The business suffered such losses in '57-'58 that Ball was never able to recoup and in 1861 had to close the doors. William Welles, who had opened a banking and exchange office in 1851, was also forced to close. The two men eventually paid off their creditors, but neither regained his former prosperity.

THE HAZARDS OF EARLY DAY BANKING

Setting forth the banking history of the city, the December 8, 1883, Grand Rapids Saturday Globe stated, "It is an enjoyable feast to gain the attention of one of the 'old settlers' and listen to him, as for hours he will dilate upon the primitive conditions of the banks in an early day. Old, tumbledown frame rookeries appeared to be first choice with the bankers, and where to-day institutions are all provided with ample room, in those days, cramped, musty, dingy quarters seemed to best suit the money lenders."

Banking offered some hazards to depositors. Ravilla H. Wells had a banking business from 1857 to 1859, but according to the Globe, "His career was short and he went away suddenly, leaving many creditors with aching hearts and empty pockets."

And in 1870, David Latourette opened a private bank and "by means of promises of heavy rates of interest succeeded in securing some $75,000 from depositors. In a short time he turned up missing. Where he went to no one was ever able to say, but from all the Globe can learn, he languishes beneath some orange tree in a tropical atmosphere, while his creditors are obliged to pass their lives in a bleak Michigan climate."

For nearly 100 years, beginning in 1855, the Kent County agricultural fair was held at the 40-acre fairground in the Madison Square area. At the 1860 fair (below), fruits were displayed outdoors.

57

Proud and patriotic: Michigan sent more soldiers to the Civil War than any other state to serve under the Union flag. Troops of the Second Michigan Infantry (right) mustered in 1861. The Civil War poster (below) offered government bounty money as an additional inducement to encourage enlistment.

RALLY ROUND

THE UNION FOREVER

THE FLAG, BOYS!

100 MEN WANTED!!

For the 23d Mich. Infantry.

Enlist before April 1st, secure the Government Bounty of $300 00,

AND "KEEP OUT OF THE DRAFT!"

Government Bounty, $300; State Bounty, $100; Town Bounty, $100.

Apply to WM. SICKELS, St. Johns, or

O. L. SPAULDING,

Lieut. Col., 23d Mich. Infantry, Corunna.

March , 1864.

("REPUBLICAN" PRINT, ST. JOHNS.)

THE CALL TO ARMS

It was war—civil war—that finally brought the country's economy back to its feet again.

According to historian Albert Baxter, the onslaught of the Civil War was "to the people of this valley like a peal of thunder from a clear sky."

In April 1861, "President Lincoln, calling for 75,000 men for three months' service in behalf of the Union, roused the military ardor of our people to the highest pitch of enthusiasm. The response was prompt, and the rush to arms instantaneous."

Americans had always maintained state and local

59

Michigan troops were the first troops west of the Alleghenies to reach the nation's capital. Their arrival reassured President Lincoln that the western states would remain loyal. He is said to have exclaimed, "Thank God for Michigan."

militia, and Grand Rapids had four military companies—the Valley City Guards, the Grand Rapids Artillery, the Ringgold Light Artillery (all mustered into the Fifty-first Regiment Uniformed Michigan Militia) and the Grand Rapids Rifles (a company of mostly local German citizens).

At the call for arms, the Valley City Guards and the Grand Rapids Rifles each went as a unit, to a man, into the Union Army.

Each state had to organize and finance its own military units. Michigan was asked for only one regiment, but sent many more. The state had a sorry lack of funds, so Michigan citizens, in the grip of patriotic fervor, raised by subscription $100,000 to equip state men for war. Later, when the state was solvent, the money was reimbursed.

The Third Michigan Infantry was mustered in at Grand Rapids. The fairground south of the city was transformed into "Cantonmont Anderson," and remained an active assembly point throughout the war. Men from around the state arrived throughout May and early June to swell the ranks of the Third to more than 1,000.

Grand Rapids women responded to the call with the same resolve as the men. On April 22, they held a formal meeting and resolved, "That the ladies of the Valley City are not unmindful of the perils which threaten our country, and they appreciate the patriotism which impels their fathers, husbands, brothers and sons to take the field in defense of the Flag of our Union."

On June 4, they presented the Third with a silk banner inscribed in gold, "Presented by the Ladies of Grand Rapids to the Third Michigan Infantry."

The women also made bandages, organized aid societies to take care of the sick and diseased and to care for wives and children left widowed and orphaned.

On June 13, the regiment marched to war and five days later saw action. The departure was described by Baxter:

"There was a general suspension of business in the city, as the regiment marched in solid ranks through the streets to the railway station, receiving from the thousands as they passed benediction of mingled pride and cheers and tears, and prayers for the success of the noble cause for which they had volunteered. No such pageant had ever before been seen here, though similar scenes were destined to become familiar before the trouble ended."

In 1863, the federal government asked the states for additional funds to finance the war. Michigan's coffers were empty, but citizens again met the call. Grand Rapids

first raised $23,000, and two months later, $80,000.

Of the Michigan regiments, the Second, Third, Sixth, Seventh and the Tenth Cavalry were mustered in at Grand Rapids. Michigan sent more men per capita than any other state to serve under the Union flag, and suffered more casualties, losing nearly 15,000 men.

Kent County sent 4,214 men to the war—537 died in action.

By war's end, hardly a family had been left untouched. Nearly everyone had a relative, close or near, who had served for the Union and had been wounded, maimed or had not returned at all.

The day after Lee's surrender on April 9, 1865, the Grand Rapids *Daily Eagle* proclaimed, "Babylon Has Fallen!" The mayor's published statement began, "We now have assurance that the greatest and most unholy rebellion which the world ever saw is at an end."

The city went wild. People poured into the streets, blowing whistles, banging on drums or anything else that would make a noise. Church bells rang and steam whistles blew. An impromptu procession wound through the town, collecting participants at every step. Veterans of the "glorious 'Old Third'" clambered aboard a wagon, waving their tattered battle flags and joyously whooping for victory. The celebration lasted through the day and ended with speeches that night at the Rathbun House.

On the following day, the *Eagle's* account ended, "The news was glorious and gloriously was it received and welcomed by our people. All is well! Hail Columbia!"

Four days later, the *Eagle* sadly proclaimed, "The wine of life is spilled. . . . The times are dark again."

Abraham Lincoln was dead.

Although Michigan was intensely loyal to the Union cause, there were among state citizens a fair share of "Copperheads"—Northerners sympathetic to the Southern cause.

One such local was holding forth on the steps of the Rathbun House, lauding Lincoln's assassination. Louis Campau, a man now in his 70s, raised his walking stick and smote the fellow across the back, knocking him into the mud. Broken walking stick in hand, Campau stalked off.

THE UNION FOREVER

Furniture city

Looking north down Ransom Street from the schoolhouse tower. Union-Central High was built at Lyon Street and Ransom Avenue in 1849 and boasted an octagonal dome with a tin roof, paid for by popular-subscription funds.

To the soldiers who returned to pick up the thread of their lives that spring and summer of 1865, city life had not changed perceptibly. When Harry and John Widdicomb got back to Grand Rapids, they found that their father, George Sr., had been forced to close down the cabinetry shop he had opened in 1859 with Harry and John and his two other sons, George Jr. and William. By 1868, the brothers were back in business, running a small furniture factory with 28 employees. A number of partnership changes eventually led to formation of the Widdicomb Furniture Company in 1873.

The Widdicombs had plenty of competition. Grand Rapids' days as "The Furniture City" were in full swing.

Julius Berkey, after an unsuccessful initial start, opened a furniture-making shop in 1861. Elias Matter joined him in 1862, followed by Julius' brother William in 1863 and George W. Gay in 1866. Like the Widdicomb firm, the Berkey enterprise underwent a series of owner changes before emerging as Berkey and Gay Furniture Company in 1873.

William Berkey broke away in 1873 to reorganize the Phoenix Manufacturing Company into the Phoenix Furniture Company. Berkey had the notion, startling for the time, that a factory should present a pleasant and comfortable environment for workers. He built a new factory in 1873 and insisted on large rooms with plenty of windows and white walls. Such an arrangement also captured an extra half hour of daylight in the winter.

In 1857, Charles Comstock had acquired the Winchester furniture manufacturing firm when the Winchesters were "embarrassed," as one writer put it, by the panic of 1857. Comstock was not initially inclined to run a furniture manufacturing business, but the economic climate made it impossible to sell the business so he chose to stick with it and make it profitable.

One of his techniques was, in 1861, to produce furniture for sale outside the Grand Rapids market. He made "cheaper grades" of furniture which he sold in Grand Haven, Milwaukee and Chicago. He later opened showrooms in Peoria and St. Louis. Response to these sales techniques was so good he was soon able to upgrade the quality of his furniture.

In 1863, James and Ezra Nelson, sawmill and logging owners since the mid-1830s, purchased a half interest in the Comstock factory. When, in 1870, Elias Matter left Julius Berkey to buy out the rest of Comstock, the factory was renamed Nelson–Matter and Company.

63

The rise of industry: Charles Carter (C.C.) Comstock (left), a man of considerable energy and ability, owned at various times a sash, blind and door factory, a pail and tub factory and furniture factories. Two other furniture factories in Grand Rapids at the turn of the century were the Widdicomb Furniture Factory (facing page, top) and the Berkey and Gay Furniture Co. Employees pose in front of the Berkey and Gay building (facing page, bottom).

The furniture men were ambitious, innovative and bold. Over the next three decades they would introduce many new concepts and practices that would substantially affect the nation's furniture industry.

Such foreign markets as Canada, Cuba, Hawaii, South America, the Philippines and Puerto Rico were developed in the early 1870s, but substantial sales to the European market did not exist before the 1876 Philadelphia Exposition. One manufacturer remarked that during the 1873 recession "Canada saved us from bankruptcy. It was the only market of importance for our goods for which we were promptly paid in real money."

City directories of 1873 listed eighteen furniture manufacturing firms. The recession that year reduced the number to seven. However, by 1880, the economy had recovered and eighteen firms were doing business.

Besides furniture manufacturing, a large network of satellite industries sprang up, producing such furniture-related items as mattresses, excelsior, furniture hardware, casters, varnish and veneers.

TO THE FURNITURE FAIR

Furniture makers had been exhibiting their wares at county and regional fairs as far back as the 1840s, when Haldane and Powers won awards for their entries. But the Philadelphia Centennial Exposition of 1876 put Grand Rapids and its furniture industry on the map.

Three firms, Berkey and Gay, the Phoenix Company and Nelson-Matter, had displays. The Berkey and Gay entry was a bedroom suite fairly typical of the Victorian period—massive, ornately carved, with very high foot- and headboards on the bed.

The Nelson–Matter entry, also a bedroom suite, was truly a centennial celebration in wood. The towering headboard was graced by a large carved eagle with outspread wings. Both the bed and the dresser had numerous niches and pedestals which held carved statues of Christopher Columbus, George Washington and other eminent figures. Made of oak, it required a

COMSTOCK ROW

The many enterprises of Grand Rapids businessman and politician C.C. Comstock included the ownership and operation of a pail and tub factory from 1863 until he closed it in 1883.

Comstock built a large factory at Canal and Newberry streets (now lower Monroe and Sixth) for the venture and in 1874 imported a number of blacks as workers.

To house the laborers and their families, Comstock constructed a building on a site adjacent to the factory. The tenement was immediately dubbed Comstock Row.

Edith May, a writer for the Evening Leader, made a visit to Comstock Row in 1890—a daring thing for a white woman to do at the time. She was cordially received and she described her visit at length, including an account of the history and appearance of the area.

The site whereon the row stands was originally purchased by C.C. Comstock for railway purposes. Failing in his railroad intentions, Mr. Comstock determined to make the land pay some way and erected the long tenement building at an expense of $3,000. It was built in 1874 and the architect, it is said, immediately hanged himself upon its completion. It was built upon the plan of a large old-fashioned barn, divided into 20 different compartments, each one of which was dignified with the name of 'house.' Canal street has been graded since the building was erected and it is thus left several feet below the street. There is no sewer connection and the outhouses are few in number....The river is a godsend and in a measure serves as a depository for accumulated filth, and without a doubt prevents what might otherwise prove a breeding place for disease.

65

A spark of ingenuity: The Bissell hand carpet sweeper was invented in Grand Rapids during the 1870s. The first Bissell sweeper had corner casters and a sweeping brush that was rotated by cogwheels which contacted the floor and adjusted the brush to irregular floor surfaces. Made of attractive polished wood, it also had a hinged top that could be opened for emptying. The design was patented in 1876, but the sweeper did not take the market by storm. Finally, after a number of design revisions, Melville Bissell, the inventor, put rubber tires on the sweeper's iron wheels, thereby creating friction on the brush roller. Almost immediately, the Bissell Carpet Sweeper had a national and soon an international market. By 1893, the company was producing 1,000 sweepers per day.

FLAGS, FLOWERS AND FIREWORKS

The 1876 Centennial was an occasion for prolonged and elaborate celebration—public rallies, rousing patriotic speeches, band concerts and fireworks.

Preparations had begun a week in advance. A Centennial Arch was erected on Campau Place (in more recent times known as Campau Square). It was actually a series of three arches—the center arch was 84 feet high, the two side arches were 56 feet high. The entire memorial was wound with evergreens and cedar twigs entwined with red, white and blue strips. The state seal of Michigan with the slogan "Hallelujah for One Hundred Years" was painted on canvas and hung on one side; a statue of a female figure representing Michigan was placed on the other side.

Flags, paintings, mottos, flowers and "numerous other patriotic devices and sayings" were arranged over the entire structure. Smaller arches were erected at Canal and Bridge streets.

Twenty thousand people came out for the holiday. After the dedication of the arches, they paraded to the park for speeches and concerts by civilian and military bands.

The celebration was brought to a close with a "fine display of fireworks" in the evening.

Between 1860 and 1870, the population of Grand Rapids doubled, and Grab Corners (below) suffered from the city's growing pains. Grab Corners (now Campau Square) was first named so during the late 1860s by Robert Wilson, a reporter for the Grand Rapids Eagle, in a series of satirical articles decrying the area's run-down condition.

Made in the valley: The "Made in Grand Rapids" trademark (left) was designed back when Grand Rapids had become the furniture capital of the world. The trademark is still protected by the Grand Rapids Furniture Manufacturers Association, founded in 1881 for that specific purpose.

A WARNING IGNORED

In 1850, Michigan's plentiful forests seemed unending, the timber supply infinite. Enormous fortunes were made in the lumber business, and by the 1890s, nearly every town in the state had at least one resident who had become wealthy from lumbering.

For 40 years lumbermen ravaged the forests with little regard for the future. The woodcutters were paid by the stump, so they cut every tree in sight. However, lumber company inspectors often rejected many logs, which were left on the ground to rot. There was no thought of conserving or replanting to maintain the forests.

Still, there were those who predicted the results of excessive cutting without replenishing. Historian Albert Baxter wrote in 1890, "These forests...have furnished thousands of millions of feet of the finest of pine timber, but under the destroying hand of the lumberman, have been rapidly stripped until the supply is almost gone.

"The young man of 20 to-day will see, at 50 or 60 years, little or no wood for manufacture, for building, or even for fuel." Baxter's prediction came true within twenty years.

room with eighteen-foot ceilings and sturdy underpinnings.

Grand Rapids furniture makers had been gradually establishing themselves as manufacturers of fine quality goods, but with the exposition they achieved a position of prestige in the market. New showrooms opened in Grand Rapids, and in 1878 the manufacturers cooperated in promoting and staging the first buyers market. They invited furniture buyers from out of town to view and order Grand Rapids furniture. Only eleven buyers came to the first market, but by 1882, so many were visiting the twice-annual markets—in January and July—that the manufacturers began to establish retail outlets in other cities.

Soon, Eastern firms were coming to the markets to exhibit their lines. The local manufacturers exhibited in their factories, but the outsiders had to rent space. Dealers leased whatever vacant space they could find—stores, third-story lofts, hotel lobbies. The Morton House leased its billiard room to a St. Louis firm for $800.

In 1860, the furniture industry had ranked behind plaster, lumber, flour, meal and clothing manufacturing in the local economy. Between 1880 and 1884, the number of furniture factories jumped from 18 to 32, and the $5.5 million industry dominated the city's economy.

GROWING PAINS

As the furniture industry grew up during the post-war decades, so did the rest of Grand Rapids.

Between 1860 and 1870 the population doubled, going from 8,000 to 16,000. Many of the new faces were immigrants from the east, or from abroad, and many were returning soldiers, who with their families, chose not to go back to the farms and villages from which they had come but to settle in the city.

Grand Rapids began to suffer all the growing pains of other midwestern cities. At the same time, it enjoyed the benefits of new technology.

In 1865, the city paid $5,600 for its first steam fire engine. Some residents objected to being taxed for the machine, but most felt it would greatly improve firefighting because the engine could throw a stream of water a remarkable 80 feet into the air.

Unfortunately, the city's two privately owned water supply companies were rarely able to produce sufficient

69

Putting out the fires: The fire of 1873 (below), which left 130 families homeless, destroyed a considerable portion of downtown between Canal and Ionia and was one of the worst fires in the city's history. The Grand Rapids Fire Department began motorizing its vehicles in 1910. The gasoline engine, combination hose and pumper truck was purchased in 1915 (left).

water pressure to force the water even two stories high. A series of disastrous fires in the early '70s prompted citizens to demand that the city provide its own water service.

The city complied—adding its services to those of the two private companies—and spent the next 30 years laying mains, constructing and improving reservoirs, pumping stations, settling basins and purification cribs.

Reservoirs were built at strategic points around the city, and even though the number of fires increased, total losses fell from $353,000 in 1875 to $80,000 in 1876 to a mere $18,000 in 1877.

Many other municipal services—neglected during the war years—were reestablished during the 1860s and '70s. Although the city had begun a primitive sewer system in the early 1850s—laying pine boxes end to end without regard for the varying levels and grades of streets and whether water could flow from one to another—it did not develop a more comprehensive and efficient system until 1865. That year, a large granite boulder was placed at the corner of Monroe and Division as a grade-level point of reference and was used for many years in determining the grades of east-side sewers and streets.

A couple of streets had been cobblestoned in the late 1850s, but not much more paving was done until after the war. In 1874, paving materials were changed from stone to wood. Builders cut blocks of wood from four-inch pine planks and set them on end in gravel beds, packing sand and gravel between the blocks. When the pine blocks

Getting from here to there: The Leonard Street Bridge (left) was built in 1879 by the city. It replaced an earlier bridge built in 1858 by a private company and operated as a toll bridge until 1873 when the city bought it and abolished the toll. Fulton Street (looking east from College Avenue) was still a dirt road in the 1870s (below).

deteriorated in a few years, they were replaced with six-inch cedar blocks. Cedar proved much more durable, and cedar-paved streets were still in use well into the twentieth century. Wooden sidewalks served until 1890.

Modern, public transportation made its debut with horse-drawn railway streetcars. The streetcar line ran from the railway depot at Coldbrook and Plainfield down Canal Street and up Monroe and Fulton to Jefferson Avenue. "The streetcars are now a fixed institution in our city. . . . To the astonishment of many 'prophets,' they appear to be doing a good paying business," reported the *Daily Eagle*.

In 1865, William T. Powers purchased land on the west side of the river and built the West Side Water Power Canal. His company and the owners of the east-side canal joined forces to build a new dam across the Grand River near Fourth Street. Powers built the half of the dam west of the center chute, and the East Side Water Power Company built the eastern half. Both companies agreed to share maintenance expenses. Together the two canals provided waterpower, estimated to equal 2,400 horsepower, for manufacturing concerns along the riverbank.

Rechanneling and filling in the river was an ongoing process. When the first settlers arrived in Grand Rapids, there were four wooded islands in the river at the foot of the rapids. But the islands, like the rapids, were considered a barrier to transportation. Over the years, settlers chipped away at the limestone ledges beneath the rapids, using the stone to build houses and churches. A series of channels, canals and millraces diverted the

The age of trains: The Grand Rapids and Indiana Railroad (left) was the third rail line to reach the city. It began service in September 1870 and ran from Fort Wayne to Grand Rapids. In 1873, the line was extended to Petoskey and ten years later was opened to Mackinaw City. The road contributed to the opening of northern Michigan and linked the rural north to the big city of Grand Rapids. Union Station (below), built in 1900, replaced the original wooden station. As increased dependence on the automobile and the airplane for travel and shipping of freight diminished rail service, the need for the large station dwindled, and the structure was torn down in 1961 to make way for an interstate freeway.

river's course westward. The islands, viewed as useful downtown building sites, were attached to the mainland by filling in the shallow channels that had once separated them from the shore. Island No. 2 became the site in 1872 of the Kent County jail, the "handsomest edifice . . . owned by the county."

Railroad building—slowed to a snail's pace nationwide during the war—resumed. The Lake Shore and Michigan Southern Railroad reached Grand Rapids in 1869; the Grand River Valley Railroad from Jackson came in January 1870, and the last rail of the Grand Rapids and Indiana Railroad was laid in September of that same year.

Expanded rail service was of particular benefit to the manufacturing community, particularly the furniture industry, for it provided a fast, inexpensive means of shipping products to distant markets in every direction. And it made Grand Rapids accessible to western markets, giving local manufacturers an advantage over their eastern competitors.

AMERICAN GALOSHES

When J. Hendricks Ter Braak settled in Grand Rapids he found his new homeland to be missing one necessity—a ready source of wooden shoes. To remedy the situation, he began the Grand Rapids Wooden Shoe Factory in 1873 with a capital investment of $2,000. By 1888, the factory was turning out 12,000 pairs of shoes annually, all carved by hand with special tools.

Ter Braak's factory was Michigan's only source of the "galoshes"—practical footgear when the city's dirt streets and paths turned to muck in the rain.

MICHIGAN'S MELTING POT

During the 1870s, furniture manufacturers recruited European wood-carvers and designers, but as the demand for Grand Rapids lines increased, these highly skilled artisans came to Grand Rapids on their own to pursue their craft in the local industry. They came from Germany, Italy, the Netherlands, Scotland, Denmark,

The first federal building in Grand Rapids was built in 1879 on Ionia between Pearl and Lyon (left). It was replaced in 1909 by the Beaux Arts-style building which served as a post office and federal court and today houses the Grand Rapids Art Museum.

Sweden, England and France.

Less skilled immigrants came, too, and each of the incoming ethnic groups settled in specific areas of the city, forming their own cultural and religious pockets.

There had been German settlers on the west side, in the Bridge Street area, since the 1840s; and until the 1880s, Germans were the dominant ethnic group on the west side. The Swedes and Danes also settled in the Bridge Street area.

Many early Dutch settlers had settled on the southeast side of the city. Later arrivals—those employed in the furniture factories—settled in the Creston area, known as the "north end," or on the southwest side of town, in the Grandville and Roosevelt Park areas. A very few of them lived on the west side, near Leonard Street, west of Alpine Avenue.

Armenians established a community in the 1890s along Front Street between First and Seventh streets. Lithuanians, coming around 1875, lived in the West Grand area near Leonard and Turner.

The Polish were west siders, and the Irish settled mostly in the north end or around Bridge Street.

Italians did not come in significant numbers until the 1880s. They settled in the South Division–Franklin area. Later arrivals from Italy also clustered near John Ball Park.

MILL TOWN NO LONGER

The constantly growing population—it doubled each decade from 1860 to 1890—meant building homes, schools, factories and government buildings. Stone and brick replaced wood as building materials, diminishing the frequency of fires and changing the city's character. Architecture became grander, more ambitious, and reflected the eclectic taste of the population.

The first plate glass storefront windows appeared in 1869 and almost immediately became *de rigueur* for commercial establishments.

The growing population naturally resulted in an increased number of school children. In 1871, the state legislature decreed that the city's three school districts be consolidated, and the quality of education for the city's children improved markedly. The number of schools increased from eleven in 1871 to 23 in 1889. In 1885, Michigan granted women the right to vote in school

elections. Three years later, Harriet A. Cook, with active support from the local suffrage league, became the first woman to be elected to the Grand Rapids Board of Education.

As the task of administering a growing city became more complex, the need for suitable city and county government quarters was a subject annually renewed for discussion. Both units of government had conducted business in a variety of rented rooms for several decades.

In 1872, the city fathers voted to build a city hall and purchased land at the southeast corner of Pearl and Ottawa streets. But they then debated the matter for another twelve years and changed the site before finally laying the cornerstone at the northeast corner of Ottawa

CHAMPION OF MANY WEIGHTS

Grand Rapids has had more than its share of better-than-average boxers. But the one who became truly legendary was Stanislaus Kiecal, better known in his boxing days as Stanley Ketchel.

Although Ketchel weighed only 154 pounds, he fought against all weights. In February 1906, he fought Jack Sullivan to a twenty-round draw in Butte, Montana. Then he fought Joe Thomas, the best middleweight of his day, to a twenty-round draw. Not satisfied, Ketchel enticed Thomas into a rematch. The second fight went 32 rounds before Ketchel put Thomas away.

In February 1908, Ketchel wrested the world middleweight crown from Billy Papke. The following September, Ketchel agreed to fight Papke again—and was knocked out in the twelfth round.

The score was even, so the fighters met a third time two months later, and this time Ketchel punched Papke into unconsciousness in the eleventh round.

Ketchel's most famous fight was with the world heavyweight champion, Jack Johnson, in 1909. Although he weighed 48 pounds less than Johnson, Ketchel knocked the heavyweight down. But Johnson got up and ended the fight with a single punch.

Ketchel could not revive his career. In October 1910, he was shot and killed by a farmhand—some said because Ketchel had toyed with the wrong woman's affections.

On August 6, 1954, Stanley Ketchel's name was enrolled in Boxing's Hall of Fame.

73

and Lyon in 1885. The county laid the cornerstone for its building, on Ottawa and Crescent streets, in 1889.

The fire department in 1888 had eight fire stations throughout the city. The police force, with 71 men, had 27 call boxes located around the city from which the officer on the beat could phone headquarters.

Electric streetcars came in 1890, but several businesses, including Sweet's Hotel and Preusser Jewelry Store, had already blazed with electric lights for a decade. The Grand Rapids Electric Light and Power Company also supplied a number of factories with electricity to run their machinery, and the city installed a dozen streetlights along Monroe Avenue.

The number of beautiful mansions in the Hill District (now known as Heritage Hill) increased yearly, and three opera houses provided access to theatrical and other cultural entertainments. William T. Powers completed his Grand Opera House in 1874. T.H. Redmond opened his opera house in 1882, and William B. Smith, who had operated the Ball's Adelphia Theatre from 1875 to 1885, opened his opera house in 1885.

The Schubert Club, a male singing group, was organized in 1883. (Now the oldest male singing organization in continuous existence in the United States, it has never failed to give an annual concert.)

Grand Rapids, at the close of the '80s, had matured in 30 years from a rough mill town to a vigorous and gracious young city, enjoying her affluence and looking forward to continued prosperity.

Good old golden rule days: The Collins School (below), in Grand Rapids Township, was a typical one-room school of the late 1800s. The first Union Benevolent Association nurses' class was in training in 1882 (inset). The association, descended from the Ladies Benevolent Association established in 1847, ran an old-age home and a hospital and was the forerunner of Blodgett Hospital, oldest of the city's general hospitals.

Raising the buildings: In 1860, the Kent County Board of Supervisors constructed a building (right) at the corner of Kent and Lyon streets for the county offices, but it was large enough only for the county clerk, treasurer, register, judge of probate and superintendent of the poor. Quarters had to be rented for the courts and board of supervisors. A larger courthouse was finally built in 1889. After decades of debate about the need for a city hall, construction on the edifice finally began in 1885. Dedicated on September 26, 1888, the new building (facing page) housed city administrative offices for 80 years. It was then demolished to make way for urban renewal. Sweet's Hotel (below), which became the Pantlind in 1902 and the Amway Grand Plaza in 1981, had its grand opening in 1869—rooms to let at $2 a day. Built by Martin Sweet, on land he created by filling in the river channel between the east bank and Island No. 1, the building was raised four feet in 1874 to bring it above flood level. Operations proceeded normally during the four days it took to raise the building, and it is said not a dish was broken.

During the 1870s and 1880s, before the larger Reeds Lake steamers were put into service, two smaller steamers, the Victor *and the* Sport, *took turns towing Crook's barge out into the lake. Merrymakers on board the barge enjoyed relaxing in the parlor, drinking at the bar and trying out the latest steps on the dance floor.*

Into
the Twentieth
century

In his 1890 inaugural address, Mayor Edwin F. Uhl described Grand Rapids as a city whose substance lagged behind its image. "While we boast—and justly, too—of a city advanced, progressive and in most respects metropolitan, yet. . .it is a matter of comment by strangers who visit us that we have not outgrown the habits and peculiarities of the country village."

It was a time of change and Grand Rapids struggled to keep pace and to transform country habits into modern, urban public services. In 1891, annexations added seven square miles, 10,000 new citizens and $2 million in tax valuations to the city's assets. Electric streetcar lines and interurban railways moved residents through the city to Lake Michigan beaches and resorts. City streets were graded and paved and iron-truss bridges were built across the Grand. Police and fire departments modernized their operations.

Horsepower replaced horse power, first on police paddy wagons and then on fire engines. In dismay, many firefighters saw their dependable horses demoted to pulling garbage collection wagons.

Grand Rapids burned its refuse in open dumps, and the stench of singed and decaying garbage often pervaded the city air. Meanwhile, the smell of corruption tainted city hall.

Officials rotated through city offices in a steady stream. Patronage, political maneuvering and financial favors went hand in hand. When two city treasurers were caught with their hands in the till, neither was prosecuted; in fact, one of them—George R. Perry—went on to become the mayor in 1898.

WELL-PLACED FRIENDS

Grand Rapids closed the nineteenth century with minor scandals. It opened the twentieth century with a major one.

In 1901, Lant K. Salsbury, city attorney, proposed a project to bring Lake Michigan water to Grand Rapids. Salsbury, a sharp operator with larcenous instincts and plenty of political cronies, was not so much interested in improving the city's water supply as he was in filling his own pockets at Grand Rapids' expense. All he needed was a bond issue for more than the amount needed to finance the new water system, and the profits were his.

Protecting a nation and a city: On April 26, 1898, huge crowds turned out at Campau Square to see local troops off to the Spanish-American War. None of the men saw combat, but their return four months later was marked by the same patriotic fervor that greeted their departure (below). In 1927, the west-side police precinct station house (left), on the corner of Third and Stocking NW, provided its neighborhood with foot patrolmen and other police services. The experiment with neighborhood precinct stations ended during the Depression, after which the city maintained a single, central, downtown police station.

East side, west side—all around the town: The great flood of 1904 inundated the west side as rain and the March thaw raised the Grand River more than nineteen feet (right). Flood waters surrounded more than half the homes on the west side, stranded 10,000 residents for two days, closed factories and caused losses of nearly $2 million. Looking north along Canal Street in 1896 when both horses and electric trolley cars shared the road (facing page). Looking southwest from the east side in the 1890s, a Grand Rapids citizen could see the river, the Leonard Street Bridge and workers' houses clustered around the factories (facing page below).

Salsbury's East Coast connections were prepared to supply whatever payoffs were needed to set the plot in motion, and numerous contractors were eager to build the pipeline. If his scheme succeeded, the city would get its water, and the cash overflow would go to Salsbury and his well-placed friends.

Salsbury's biggest hurdle was getting the bonds authorized, and he bribed anyone with power to help. Payoffs financed by various slick operators totaled more than $100,000 and greased the eager palms of assorted pillars of the community, including Mayor Perry, fourteen aldermen, the city clerk, a state senator and the managers of all three Grand Rapids newspapers.

Before anything further came of the plot, the Associated Press blew the whistle on Salsbury in a report that the Grand Rapids city attorney had been indicted for theft in Chicago. According to the AP article, Salsbury had fleeced a wealthy couple and stolen their money in a scheme connected in some way with a clean-water project in Grand Rapids.

Christian Gallmeyer, future mayor, and a delegation of righteous aldermen pressed for a grand jury investigation of the Lake Michigan water contract. Salsbury, who remained city attorney throughout the grand jury hearings and subsequent trial, was convicted, sentenced to a prison term and disbarred. He eventually turned state's evidence and implicated a galaxy of local political stars—from Mayor Perry to a constellation of lesser lights.

But punishment did not necessarily fit the crime. Public excitement over the scandal gradually dissipated into apathy. Some of the men involved paid small fines; for others, charges were dropped entirely. After serving his prison term, Salsbury went on to make a fortune selling cotton in Tennessee. George Perry, whose trial ended with a hung jury, ran against George "Deacon" Ellis in the 1914 primary as the reform candidate for mayor. He lost.

QUALITY RATHER THAN QUANTITY

The water scandal did nothing to damage the city's growing reputation as the "Furniture Capital of America." Grand Rapids was not and never would be strictly a one-industry town. But, for the more than three decades that furniture predominated, the city reaped the benefits of its new-found and self-promoted fame.

By 1890, the furniture industry's heyday had begun. Grand Rapids, although never the leading producer in quantity, was calling itself a style leader and the

---

OF VAMPIRES AND VIRTUE

The following description of a Grand Rapids bordello was written by the Reverend Frank A. Ferris, superintendent of the state's Anti-Saloon League, and appeared around 1901 in a publication called the State Issue:

It is a conservative estimate to say that there are from two hundred to three hundred girls in Grand Rapids who are practically slaves in bawdy houses and dens of vice. This vice is not hidden in stairways and back rooms but is encircled around with wealth and luxury.

Approaching one of these places, your eyes fall upon the glitter of lights and the beauty of cathedral glass that would grace the finest home or adorn the richest church....

You observe in front a stairway ornamented with chains and festoons.... If you are inclined to moralize you may hesitate a moment and wonder if those chains may not prophesy of the slavery beyond. Just through the silken draperies, you enter a ballroom.... Seated at the side are musicians and you enter to the sound of delicious music. You will be invited to a seat and suddenly you are surrounded by girls dressed in the finest silken robes. Of course, the first thing is drink. What will you have, beer, wine or whiskey? Everything here goes under the inspiration of passion or wine....

A look into the faces of these girls would touch into pity the heart of anyone save the human vampire that feeds upon the virtue of misguided and unfortunate girls. The frightful burdens of their life is [sic] seen in their hollow eyes, pale cheeks and the restless anxious look. The paint and color cannot hide the marks of death that are upon nearly every face.

The description given here is not exaggerated. It is a part of Grand Rapids life today.

85

86

country's largest producer of quality furniture. The prosperity furniture brought to Grand Rapids amply justified the city's reputation in the minds of its citizens and entrepreneurs. Thirty-one furniture companies employed nearly half of all the city's industrial workers. When these companies stepped up production and increased their sales, related industries that produced woodworking tools, veneers, mirrors and trim saw rising profits as well.

Furniture manufacturers built fine new homes on the west side and in the neighborhood now known as Heritage Hill. One lot purchased in the 1890s by mill owner Carl G.A. Voigt cost $10,000. The furniture men

patronized the arts and lent their wealth and support to a variety of cultural enterprises; their wives were among those who spearheaded social reform projects.

Furniture changed the face of downtown. As many as eleven buildings—some converted from other uses, but most newly constructed between 1889 and 1916—were designed specifically for furniture exhibits. The semi-annual markets—held every January and July—attracted swarms of out-of-town buyers who descended on the city to examine new styles and place their orders.

Hotel rooms became a top priority. In 1890, the city's 40 hotels were already equipped to play host to 3,000 guests. The growth of the furniture industry ushered in a

period of expansion and renovation under the stewardship of such amiable proprietors as the Pantlinds.

A. V. Pantlind, called the "hotel king," was a hotelier of considerable experience by the time he arrived in Grand Rapids to assume charge of the Morton House in 1874. When he died in 1896, his nephew and business partner, J. Boyd Pantlind, took over the Pantlind enterprises.

In 1902, J. Boyd purchased Sweet's Hotel, built in 1868 by Martin L. Sweet, and renamed it the Pantlind. A shrewd businessman, J. Boyd set about enlarging his hotel to keep pace with the growing demand for rooms. Earlier additions led to more ambitious plans for a brand new, eleven-story, 550-room structure that would

eventually cost $2 million and cover an entire city block.

J. Boyd took his business seriously, overseeing every detail of the building project himself, down to the pictures that would hang on the walls. A natty dresser, a man who epitomized the new breed of twentieth-century businessman, J. Boyd ran his landmark hotel the way he built it—with an eye for the smallest detail. "Give them soup first and they won't want so much meat," he often said, and "what you lose on the food you make up for on the liquor."

With its official opening on January 1, 1916, the Pantlind Hotel was ready to take its place among the many new buildings put up in response to the furniture markets' growth.

The brick and stone structures built to replace the old wooden buildings of the village days were still vulnerable to the fires that occasionally raged out of control. They were also vulnerable to the changing aspirations of those who built them and who believed replacing old with new was necessary for profit and progress. And so, places like the Wonderly Building came down, replaced by other, taller structures in the neo-classical and Renaissance styles. Chicago architect Louis Sullivan likened the trend to "a virus," which "slowly spread westward contaminating everything it touched."

While their styles paid homage to the past, architects designed buildings for the future. Inexpensive structural steel, rising real estate prices and a growing population propelled turn-of-the-century commercial buildings to new and unprecedented heights. In 1892, utilities magnate Anton G. Hodenpyl and lumberman Lewis Withey built the city's first skyscraper, the ten-story Michigan Trust Building, on the southeast corner of Pearl and Ottawa.

Although the downtown was losing its provincial air, it remained what it had always been—the commercial hub of the city. It was filled with thriving and growing enterprises: banks, real estate and professional offices, clothing and specialty stores. Wurzburg's, then a leading downtown merchant, installed the city's first escalator in 1913.

Business flourished as the gaslights flickered into a new, electric-lit century. Mills and factories downtown and along the riverbanks enlarged their quarters and expanded their markets beyond the local region. An age of inventiveness and innovation produced a steady stream of goods—steam boilers, prefabricated houses, carpet sweepers, cigars, knitted apparel, bricks and cement blocks, cardboard boxes, brass hardware and bicycles.

Just before the advent of the automobile, bicycling became a national craze. Women exchanged their awkward ankle-length skirts for knickers and joined men on the bicycle paths that led to Reeds Lake and out to Lake Michigan. In 1897, six Grand Rapids bicycle companies produced a reported 30,000 bicycles a year. Two years later, the companies were gone, victims of the age of corporate monopolies and business trusts. In June 1899, the national bicycle trust bought them all out and shut them down.

88

Playing it cool: A Grand Rapids baseball team (top) was sponsored by the Leonard Refrigerator Company in the early 1900s. The early Leonard refrigerator (above) was not yet a self-contained unit. Although the refrigerator itself stood in the kitchen, the motor—connected to the refrigerator by pipes—had to be placed in the basement. In 1900, workmen at the Grand Rapids Refrigerator Company were making the Leonard Cleanable Refrigerator (right). The company began as a branch of H. Leonard and Sons—a local housewares store— and developed a unit that was far easier to clean than its competitors' models. By 1904, Leonard was turning out 150 units a day and by 1925 was the national industry leader.

The rise of unions: At the turn of the century the
Berkey and Gay Furniture Company (right) was one
of the largest, best known and most innovative of
the Grand Rapids furniture manufacturers. When
furniture workers went on strike in 1911, George
(Deacon) Ellis (below)—Grand Rapids mayor from
1906 to 1916—helped prevent enforcement of a court
injunction against striking.

DISSENSION IN THE RANKS

Grand Rapids' small but thriving industrial community, fueled by the energy of its entrepreneurs, provided the jobs that continued to draw newcomers to the city. "Another day, another dollar," was the oft-repeated workingman's refrain. The words became a battle cry for the nation's growing union movement. The year 1890 witnessed the largest number of strikes recorded in the United States in any single year of the nineteenth century. Grand Rapids, in the coming years, was not immune.

The most devastating labor dispute to hit the city was the furniture industry strike in 1911. Employers claimed they were giving a "fair day's pay for a fair day's work." Employees thought otherwise. Worker grievances centered on the ten-hour work day and low wages— averaging $1.91 a day—despite rising profits. Workers also wanted to replace the piecework system with a minimum hourly wage. The manufacturers offered few concessions. They contended that high freight rates dictated the wage and hour structures. Determined to maintain the open shop status quo, the owners rejected arbitration and refused to deal with the two unions representing the workers—the Finishers Union and the Brotherhood of Carpenters and Joiners. On April 11, more than 7,000 furniture workers walked off the job.

On May 15, when William Widdicomb attempted to drive a car crammed with strikebreakers past 300 pickets at the Widdicomb factory, someone threw a stone at the car. A full-scale riot erupted, bringing police armed with revolvers and firemen equipped with hoses to the scene. A number of people were hurt, though none seriously, before police broke up the crowd of 2,000.

The strike wore on for seventeen weeks. The manufacturers held firm in their resolve not to deal collectively with the strikers; the workers, meanwhile, began drawing union strike benefits of $4 and then $5 a week. Mayor George Ellis, whose sympathies were mainly with the strikers, created a special peace-keeping patrol whose real mission was to prevent enforcement of a court injunction against peaceful picketing. The paid force was composed largely of striking workers. On more than one occasion, Ellis' pro-union forces confronted County Sheriff William J. Hurley's anti-strike troops, deputized to break up the picket lines and protect the increasing number of strikebreakers being brought into the city.

By the end of June, the use of strikebreakers enabled four major companies to resume operations. Two weeks later, 2,500 striking workers paraded through downtown. They marched to the music of four bands and they carried banners which read: "We Stand Pat to a Man," "My dad is a striker, is yours?" and "Who Made Grand Rapids Furniture Famous?"

Despite the show of strength and the sentiments expressed by the marchers and their banners, worker solidarity was beginning to weaken. As more strike-breakers reached the city, the strikers began modifying their demands. Some went back to their jobs. Although most manufacturers refused to budge from their pre-strike position, the ranks of returning workers continued to swell. By August 17, the strike was over. The manufacturers had won.

The fires of the four-month strike, however, had ignited

flames of factionalism within the city's ethnic enclaves. In the aftermath, bitter ashes remained.

Immigrant labor had been the mainstay of the furniture industry for years. Dutch craftsmen, in particular, were sought after for their skills, industriousness and willingness to work for lower wages than their American counterparts. The Dutch made up the heart of the labor force, but they rarely advanced to the upper-echelon, supervisory positions that were generally filled by Americans and Germans.

After 1900, large numbers of Polish and Lithuanian immigrants also found work in the furniture factories as unskilled and semiskilled laborers. In the virtually unanimous decision to strike, the various nationalities had set aside their religious and cultural differences. But those very differences ultimately worked against their cause and helped bring the strike to its end.

Some of the city's most prominent clergymen adopted highly vocal positions on different sides of the strike issue. The Reverend Alfred W. Wishart, pastor of Fountain Street Baptist Church, took a pro-manufacturer stance and urged the strikers to return to work. Catholic Bishop Joseph Schrembs supported the nine-hour day and championed the workers' right to unionize. He and other Catholic leaders took immediate exception to an inflammatory statement in the *Furniture Manufacturer and Artisan,* published by the Furniture Manufacturers Association, which blamed Polish and Lithuanian strikers for the Widdicomb riot.

The Christian Reformed Church discouraged membership in non-church organizations. Individual clergymen were firm in their opposition to union membership, outspoken in their anti-strike position and persuasive in their efforts to return striking congregants to work. When the Classis, the church governing board, formally voted that church and union membership were incompatible, the union lost its opportunity to represent all of the workers and the united front crumbled.

More than a labor dispute, the furniture strike brought deep-rooted prejudices and old antagonisms to the surface and intensified existing divisions among the community's ethnic and religious groups that would take years to heal.

Workers set aside their grievances temporarily when America entered the Great War in 1917 and patriotic fervor swept the nation. In Grand Rapids, during the first eight months after America's entry, 3,500 volunteers and 144 conscripts went off to serve. Civilians contributed millions of dollars to the federal government's Liberty Loan drives; a neighboring town had its name changed from Berlin to Marne, and the teaching of German was dropped at all the local schools.

The Grand Rapids furniture industry did its part to assist the war effort. In those days, most aircraft components were made of wood. Grand Rapids already had the tools and the skilled work force, and local furniture makers plunged enthusiastically into the production of planes. They organized the Grand Rapids Airplane Company—a consortium of fifteen furniture plants—and entered into a contract with the United States Army to supply parts for the Handley-Page bomber. Devoting a third of their production capacities to the war effort, the companies turned out propellers, wing tips, struts and pilot and observer seats—for 356 complete aircraft—with the same care and precision that went into their more famous product.

FOOD FOR THOUGHT

With a large Dutch population whose religion has traditionally placed great emphasis on reading theological works, it is not surprising that Grand Rapids developed into a religious publishing center. Four Christian book publishing houses—Baker, Eerdmans, Kregel and Zondervan—are headquartered in Grand Rapids.

Kregel, the smallest and oldest of the four, had its beginnings in 1909 when Louis Kregel began selling used theological books from his home. The following year, William B. Eerdmans launched a similar home-sales enterprise, which grew to become Eerdmans Publishing Company. Two more companies emerged in the 1930s—Zondervan, today the world's largest publisher of religious books, in 1931, and Baker in 1939.

Today, each of the companies is still family owned. Publications range from biblical commentaries, encyclopedias, concordances and other scholarly reference works to textbooks, Bibles, religious classics, inspirational books and a host of titles aimed at the mass-market trade. Together, the four companies publish about 280 titles a year, and combined sales run into the millions of volumes, making Grand Rapids the Christian book publishing center of the nation—and the world.

93

94

On land and in the air: The Austin motor car, made in Grand Rapids from the early 1900s to 1918, was an aristocrat of the automobile world and came in several models which sold from $950 to $1,500 (left). Some Grand Rapids motorists in 1911 preferred to tour in a Reo (facing page), and West Fulton Street at John Ball Park was a popular place to go. One of the earliest airlines was the Furniture Capital Air Service (below right). In 1919, regular air service came to Grand Rapids, and seven years later the Kent County Airport was officially opened. There were no runway lights, however, until 1928.

THE WHEELS OF PROGRESS

Grand Rapids never developed into the national aircraft production center that some of its businessmen envisioned, but it did make a contribution to the twentieth century's other newfangled mechanical marvel—the motor car.

Walter S. Austin set up shop in Grand Rapids around the turn of the century and produced his first successful gasoline-powered auto in 1903. Austin held a number of important patents and until 1918, his company turned out elegant, hand-built models that rivaled the Detroit-built Cadillac in style and price.

Trucks and automobiles began rolling out of other local factories to be displayed at the city's annual auto shows and to be sold to a public increasingly enchanted by the prospects of owning a horseless carriage. In 1900, there were just four privately owned automobiles in Grand Rapids; by 1915 there were 3,000. The corner gas station became a regular fixture of the urban scene, and automobile agencies did their best to put more cars on the road. Traffic jams proliferated, and downtown parking limits were set. The electric trolley cars that clanged across the city were doomed to extinction.

The machinery of city government was also destined for change. The water scandal of 1901, Mayor George Ellis' support of the furniture strikers ten years later, and a tax title scandal in 1915 all helped set the stage for municipal reform.

On August 29, 1916, Grand Rapids voters approved by a narrow margin a new city charter, and the city became

95

96

In the 1900s, Ramona Park was a vast amusement area. Visitors to the park could take a cruise on the steamer Ramona, ride the roller coaster, stop at a refreshment garden, take a trip through the Laughing Gallery (left), row across the water or watch a baseball game—and if there was still any time left, enjoy the many other attractions.

THE ALL BUT FORGOTTEN FIRST

T he first night baseball game between professional teams was played at Ramona Park in East Grand Rapids, on the night of July 7, 1909. Grand Rapids Mayor George Ellis umpired the seven-inning contest between two Central League teams, Grand Rapids and Zanesville, Ohio.

The home team won, 11-10, in a game beset with pop flies and grounders dropped in the glare of incandescence.

Local skeptics predicted night baseball was a novelty that would never catch on.

For 25 years, it seemed as though they were right. But in 1935, the first major league night game was played and was hailed as an innovation.

By then, the first nighttime professional game— played in Grand Rapids—was all but forgotten.

one of the first in the nation to adopt a modified commission-city manager form of government.

The new charter consolidated the city's twelve wards into three. The First Ward encompassed the entire west side; the Second Ward represented east-side constituents North of Wealthy Street, and the Third Ward represented those east-siders south of Wealthy. The aldermen of the earlier system were replaced by seven commissioners, two from each ward and one at large, all nominated and elected by the city at large. As the city's legislative and administrative body, the commission chose the mayor from its own membership and named the city manager, who functioned as chief executive.

The charter eliminated some of the abuses and excesses of the past but created other areas of controversy. Almost from the beginning, power struggles between the mayor and the city manager were commonplace. The political boundaries of the three new wards reinforced existing divisions between the largely Catholic west side and the predominantly Dutch east side. Religious and cultural differences had often placed these factions—who lived on opposite sides of the river—on opposing sides of a variety of issues: Sunday theatre closings, liquor control regulations and the furniture industry strike of 1911. Now, with control of two wards out of three, the east-side elements formed a voting bloc of considerable political strength. (The three-ward system has not been altered since its inception, but charter amendments have brought such

changes as the return to a popularly elected mayor.
Additional revisions over the years reflect continuing
efforts at reform.)

At the time Grand Rapids adopted its new charter, the
quest for governmental reform was a national mood.
Progressivism, the outgrowth of that mood, was an
impassioned movement calling for new standards of
honesty in government, demanding ethical business
practices and expressing a growing humanitarian
concern for the poor and underprivileged.

For all its self-described conservatism, Grand
Rapids—city of many churches and strong religious
affiliations—did not lack a social conscience. Nor did its
citizens and their government neglect educational
improvements and social and cultural advances.
"Progressive" may not have been what the city called
itself, but many of its attitudes and accomplishments
were progressive nevertheless.

City taxes supported a public school system under a
politically independent board of education established
in 1906. Women, by a charter amendment of 1885, were
permitted to vote in school elections. The new charter of
1916 retained the city library commission and created
an art and museum commission, giving the city
responsibility for financing and operating the Kent
Scientific Museum, today's Grand Rapids Public Museum.
In 1914, Grand Rapids Junior College, the first junior
college in Michigan and one of only a handful in the
nation, began offering classes at Grand Rapids Central
High School. Seven years later, the church-affiliated
Calvin College became the first school in Grand Rapids
to offer a four-year, bachelor of arts degree.

Parks bloomed throughout the city. Four hospitals,
including Sunshine Hospital, the first municipally owned
tuberculosis sanatorium in the country, ministered to
the sick.

98

WOMEN AT WORK

More and more, women were becoming
involved in social issues. The Industrial
Revolution urbanized America and altered
many of women's traditional roles. Poor
women found work in factories; affluent women found
they had time on their hands. Barred from most
professions and denied the educational opportunities
available to men, women sought other avenues for

Social issues and suffrage: The Grand Rapids Equal Franchise Club, the city's major women's voting rights organization, staged suffrage parades (facing page top) and distributed handbills arguing that "the average woman is as fit to vote as the average man" and that women "will not neglect any duty for politics any more than men do." By the turn of the century, women were entering the work force in ever-increasing numbers. In Grand Rapids, cigar-making was an important local industry, and women were employed to roll the cigars (below). By 1920, more than three-quarters of the cigar-industry labor force was female. Wages averaged about $8 a week. Affluent women, who had less need of wages, became involved in volunteer service. During World War I, American Red Cross volunteers ran a canteen at Union Station (left).

Flour mills, looking west on Bridge Street, during the time of World War I.

intellectual and artistic stimulation. Clubs attracted them in ever-increasing numbers, and by the turn of the century, the women's club movement was in full swing nationwide.

At first, such local groups as the Ladies Literary Club concentrated on self-improvement. But it wasn't long before Grand Rapids clubwomen were spending considerable time and energy on a host of worthy projects to advance the fine arts, protect the welfare of children and stamp out tuberculosis, one of the scourges of the age.

Women organized the St. Cecilia Music Society in 1883 and financed the building of St. Cecilia Auditorium, the first structure of its kind in the country to be built, financed and operated entirely through the efforts of women. (Ever since its completion in 1894, the auditorium has presented to the city's music lovers a full yearly schedule of events. The society has brought to the city many young performing artists who later became stars, and since its establishment it has sought—with great success—to stimulate an interest in music among the young.)

Women were equally instrumental in forming the Grand Rapids Art Association, forerunner of today's Art Museum. Fire gutted the association's first gallery in a rented downtown building. In 1924, the association hung its works of art in the Pike House on East Fulton Street where the museum was housed until its move to new quarters in 1981.

Bringing their influence to bear on the larger issues of the progressive era, Grand Rapids clubwomen also set about solving the problems of prostitution, poverty and child neglect. Women's groups lobbied for child labor laws and civil service regulations. They provided charitable services to indigent women, organized maternity and child-care clinics and campaigned tirelessly in the battle for women's suffrage and the crusade against alcohol.

The anti-saloon interests had staunch allies in city prosecutor John S. McDonald (later a state supreme court justice) and police chief Harvey Carr. Both men were scrupulous in their efforts to enforce municipal liquor laws and close saloons found in violation. Michigan went dry in 1918, two years before the nation did. A majority of Grand Rapids voters cast their ballots in favor of both the state and national ban on liquor.

Michigan was also two years ahead of the nation in granting women the right to vote. Grand Rapids voters firmly resisted women's suffrage when the question appeared on their ballots in 1912 and 1913. But the suffragist forces pressed on, arguing in 1918 that "women have earned the right to vote through their war work." By December 3, 1918, women's suffrage in Michigan had become a fact and Grand Rapids women were registering in such numbers that there was talk of creating new voting precincts or rearranging old ones to accommodate the new voters.

For the first three decades of the twentieth century, Grand Rapids basked in prosperity, forsaking its village ways for big-city airs and amenities. Its citizens were smug in their achievements, claiming a city that was "cultural, happy, hospitable, reverent," and boasting of the national fame reaped by a furniture industry that "fixes the standard for the American home."

100

A GOOD PLACE TO START

One day in the mid-1920s, two young Milwaukee actors, dusty and sleepy from a long ride, stepped off a train in Grand Rapids. Both were intending to answer an advertisement for a job as young leading man with the Wright Players, a stock company playing in Powers Theatre.

They were friends, young men who had known each other for years and had often acted in the same companies.

They freshened up as best they could, went to the theatre and auditioned for William Wright, the pro-ducer, and John Ellis, the director.

Wright and Ellis hired only one of the young men. The other, an actor named Pat O'Brien, went on to New York, continued in the theatre, and eventually became a popular movie actor.

The man Wright and Ellis hired appeared with the Wright Company in Grand Rapids off and on for several years before he decided to make a bid for the big time. He, too, found a career on stage and screen as one of the country's leading actors—his name, Spencer Tracy.

scrip labor & city stores

The year 1926 marked prosperity across the nation and the 100th birthday of Grand Rapids. For three days in September 1926, pageants and parades heralded Grand Rapids' anniversary and the city reveled in its past. Celebrating citizens witnessed Louis Campau's grandnephew and namesake reenact Campau's arrival at the rapids. They watched thousands of costumed schoolchildren perform the folk dances of the city's ethnic groups. They applauded the costumes made and modeled by the city's clubwomen for their historical style show. And they lined the streets for the old-fashioned torchlight parade that capped the gala event.

In its centennial year, the city had much to celebrate. According to a municipal history commissioned especially for the occasion, "Grand Rapids is one of the best-governed cities in the Union. . . . The citizenship is contented, as is eloquently proved by the percentage of residents who own their homes. There is a minimum of poor and indigent persons requiring public aid, but a generous public, exceptionally well organized, provides for the support of those in need. . . . The city has no semblance to the so-called 'slum districts' of some large cities. It has no poor sections, no neglected districts."

The author may have indulged in a bit of exaggeration, but there is no doubt that the city prided itself on its low tax rate, its educational system, its charitable instincts, diverse industries and fiscal stability.

Greenhouse men and gardeners, pageants and parades: The City Market, a wholesale market built on Grand River Island No. 3 in 1896, bustled with activity in the early morning hours (facing page top). Other places of greengrocer trade included the west-side market (below)—one of several markets to which area farmers brought their produce during the early years of the twentieth century. During the 1920s, Monroe Avenue, looking toward the Pantlind Hotel, was often decorated with flags and banners for the city's many civic celebrations (facing page below).

By the 1920s, Major Amasa B. Watson's mansion—built in 1882 on the corner of Fulton and Sheldon streets in the heart of a fine residential area—was surrounded by downtown development.

TROUBLE ON THE HORIZON

But signs of impending trouble were apparent as the furniture industry began slipping from its pedestal. Although the city's reputation as the nation's furniture capital was still intact at the time of its centennial, the furniture industry was being victimized by rising competition, sagging sales and a new rival for potential buyers' dollars—the automobile. Despite the postwar sales boom, Nelson–Matter, one of the city's largest and best known furniture manufacturers, and the Macey Company had already failed.

A serious threat to Grand Rapids' preeminence was North Carolina's emergence as a furniture producer. Ready access to native hardwoods, lower labor costs and taxes, state building subsidies and cheap power sparked a rapid growth in the southern furniture industry.

Closer to home, Chicago-made furniture competed in price and quality, and Chicago had a single, huge exhibition hall to house all its furniture displays. Grand Rapids would not build a modern display facility despite manufacturers' complaints that the city did not appreciate the importance of the semiannual furniture markets. The local industry lost laborers to the Chicago factories where the pay was better, and the greater convenience of the Chicago market began luring buyers away. Sales showed a slight but discernible decline.

A shortage of skilled labor, meanwhile, drove wages up. Reluctant to increase costs at the expense of profits, the manufacturers in 1923 came up with a plan to import 200 cabinetmakers from Europe. But the U.S. Bureau of Immigration blocked the attempt. If the industry wanted artisans, it would have to pay the price.

Manufacturers had to find a way to increase the demand for Grand Rapids furniture. Many of them began to cut corners, introducing cheaper, mass-production techniques while continuing to emphasize the quality that had moved their product to the top. Berkey and Gay even held sessions to teach dealers and salesmen how to sell a luxury-priced product to a public far more inclined to spend its money on the automobile.

SWEN NELOTS IS DEAD

Grand Rapids had three daily newspapers in the '20s, the morning Herald, and the Press and the News, both afternoon papers.

Of the three, the Press was by far the richest and largest paper. Its immediate competitor was the News, but the News had neither the staff nor the money to cover every story. Nevertheless, the News seemed to come up with most of the important local events.

Lee M. Woodruff, then a Press writer, began to suspect that the News had someone planted in the Press' composing room. If his suspicions were correct, then this spy was smuggling proofs of the Press' early edition to the News offices about six blocks away.

One afternoon the Press ran a front-page headline announcing:

SWEN NELOTS
IS DEAD

Below the headline was an article giving details on Swen's life. Later that afternoon the News printed the same story, somewhat revised.

The next day the Press disclosed its secret: Swen Nelots was not dead. Swen Nelots was Stolen News, spelled backwards.

The Grand Rapids News never completely recovered from the disclosure of its purloining.

THE GOOD TIMES ROLL

Not all Grand Rapids manufacturers were suffering. The automotive manufacturers and suppliers saw only prosperity ahead. In 1928, the Hayes Body Corporation landed a $10 million contract to make Marmon auto bodies. With 3,000 workers on its payroll, Hayes was also turning out bodies for Chrysler, Reo, Willys-Overland and the local DeVaux-Hall Motor Corporation. DeVaux, a late entrant in the automobile production sweepstakes, was also optimistic about its prospects.

Even on the eve of the Great Depression, the auto industry and the city anticipated a rosy future. Grand Rapids, despite its furniture industry woes, was still on the crest of a national wave of prosperity. Housing construction boomed, wages rose and living standards were higher than ever before.

President Harding's "return to normalcy" had ushered in the new decade. There was money to spend and plenty to spend it on. The city improved its roads, built the East Beltline (the north-south road that bypassed the city), developed an airport south of town and dedicated a memorial to its World War I dead. There was even talk of

Crating

implementing a new, downtown development plan.

Commuters and shoppers traveled on a fleet of sleek, modern trolley cars bought to replace the older models burned in the car-barn fire of 1924. In 1927, merchants E.M. and William Wurzburg placed the city's first transatlantic telephone call. Plans were finally under way for the long-awaited sewage treatment plant to alleviate pollution of the Grand River. And the city boasted a steadily improving symphony orchestra.

The orchestra—established in 1921 as the Grand Rapids Civic Orchestra—was under the sponsorship of the St. Cecilia Society and under the baton of a pianist of national repute, Ottokar Malek, who had come to Grand Rapids to establish a music conservatory. Malek directed the unpaid, 60-member orchestra until his death in 1923.

That same year, Karl Wecker, a young teacher at Grand Rapids Junior College and a recent graduate of the Cincinnati Conservatory of Music, took over the baton. The orchestra itself was reorganized and named the Grand Rapids Symphony. Wecker's indefatigable efforts kept the new orchestra playing through financially difficult times. He gave recitals, lectured at service clubs and otherwise talked up the orchestra wherever he went. By 1929, its place in the community assured, the Grand Rapids Symphony Orchestra officially incorporated and began operating under a board of directors.

Prosperity seemed permanent to Grand Rapids citizens. It was a reckless age, an era of wild stock market speculation, relaxed moral standards, marathon dances (a regular occurrence in Grand Rapids until the city called a halt), bobbed hair and bared knees and a stepped-up pace of living that gained momentum from the increasingly ubiquitous automobile.

Perhaps slightly more conservative in behavior and outlook than their counterparts in other American cities, Grand Rapids citizens were nevertheless caught up in the spirit of the Roaring '20s. They danced to the music of jukeboxes, many made in Grand Rapids by American Musical Industries (AMI), Inc. They marveled at the talking pictures beginning to play the local movie theatres. They flocked to Ramona Amusement Park to ride the carousel and the roller coaster and listen to the Furniture City Band. The more affluent among them began taking to the fairways at the city's private golf clubs. So popular did golf become, that in 1927 the city commission appropriated funds for the development of Indian Trails, the city's first municipal golf course.

Like Americans everywhere, Grand Rapids citizens

clustered around their radios to hear comedy shows and campaign rhetoric. At first, the programs they listened to originated from Chicago stations. The first Grand Rapids station began broadcasting in November 1924. The original call-letters, WEBK, were changed to WOOD in recognition of the financial support supplied by the Furniture Manufacturers Association. In 1925, the Baxter dry cleaning and laundry company started another local station, first calling it WBDC for "worldwide Baxter dry cleaning," then changing the name to WASH for a catchier identification.

Those citizens in search of more cultural pursuits often went to the Powers Theatre to see many—if not most—of the era's great performers. George Arliss, Otis Skinner, Nance O'Neill and Katherine Cornell all played the Powers. Howard Thurston, the most famous magician of his day, appeared annually on the Powers stage. A less frequent but even more sensational visitor was Harry Houdini, the great escape artist.

During the 1920s, several stock companies took up residence in the city. At one time, four of them operated simultaneously, one at the Powers Theatre, one at the new Regent Theatre, one at the Kent—a one-time burlesque house—and one at the Temple, which became the Savoy and later closed after a long reign as a movie house.

William Wright's group at the Powers Theatre was the finest of the stock companies. Spencer Tracy, Porter Hall, Selena Royle and Dean Jagger were among many famous stage and screen stars who got their start in Grand Rapids on the Powers stage. The era of stock companies ended with the Great Depression.

VIEW OF
FUTURE GRAND RAPIDS
SHOWING EFFECT OF
IMPROVEMENTS PROPOSED IN CITY PLAN

BOOZE BY THE BARREL

One of the more popular recreational activities of the '20s was breaking the law—one law—prohibition.

Over the years Grand Rapids had witnessed many conflicts between the Wets and the Drys. In 1887, the Wets won when the city voted heavily against statewide prohibition. But in 1916, the Drys

A WOMAN TO BE RECKONED WITH

One of the most powerful women in American politics in the late 1930s and early 1940s was Dorothy Smith McAllister, daughter of a prominent and pioneering Grand Rapids surgeon, Dr. Richard R. Smith, and wife of Thomas McAllister, who left the Michigan Supreme Court to become a member of the Federal Sixth Circuit Court of Appeals at Cincinnati.

A Democrat, Mrs. McAllister was appointed by Governor William A. Comstock to the State Liquor Control Commission in 1933. The next year she was named national committeewoman for Michigan for Young Democrats of America. Two years later she became a delegate-at-large to the Democratic National Convention.

By 1940, she was director of the Women's Division of the Democratic National Committee. She addressed the Democratic National Convention that year—the first woman ever to address an American national political convention on a major policy issue.

McAllister had organized the Democratic women at the convention and twisted the arms of some recalcitrant male party members in positions of power. She was successful in persuading the convention to adopt as policy equal representation for women on all of the convention's major committees.

At the same time, she had the temerity to suggest in her speech that it was high time her party nominate a woman for vice president.

In later years she made her influence felt in state circles, fighting for a better life for migrant workers, fair employment practices, civil rights, better libraries, effective prepaid hospital and medical care. Six different governors, representing both major parties, named her to ten different state commissions. One of her finest achievements was to lay the groundwork, with her friend Helen Claytor, for Grand Rapids' first Human Relations Commission.

mustered enough support for a victory. In 1920, shortly after national prohibition went into effect, *Survey* magazine, a national publication, reported that "to all intents and purposes John Barleycorn is dead in Grand Rapids."

Actually, John Barleycorn had just gone under cover.

As arrests for drunkenness increased beyond preprohibition levels, regular sheriff's department raids netted illegal booze by the barrelful. And while they skillfully evaded the clutches of the law, many of the wiliest moonshiners illegally tapped gas from the city utility's pipelines to heat their stills. Many prominent citizens paid as much as $8 and $10 for a quart of whiskey. When one large bootlegging operation was nailed in 1931, the newspapers had a field day pointing out that the good stuff bought at great cost was nothing more than watered-down, artificially colored and flavored grain alcohol.

Public Safety Director John Sinke complained that prohibition "places wealth in the hands of a law-violating class and money in the hands of the underworld." The law, he said, "has created a great number of hypocrites."

Prohibition made lawbreakers out of otherwise respectable citizens and fostered cynicism and disillusionment among Americans. The ease and enthusiasm with which the law was broken exemplified a growing rejection of traditional values and represented the dark side of an era bewitched by the glitter of neon lights.

CROSSING THE COLOR LINE

Speakeasies, stills and bootleg whiskey lurked beneath the surface of Grand Rapids' respectability. Other social ills were more readily observable.

The city's black community, 1,000 in all in 1920, faced the same problems that confronted blacks everywhere; many had no employment other than menial labor; many local restaurants, bars, theatres and nightspots drew a color line; and most residential neighborhoods were strictly off-limits and would remain so for decades.

Blacks began protesting this state of affairs as early as 1904 with the formation of one of the city's first civil rights organizations—the Grand Rapids League of Independent Colored Citizens. In 1906, C.L. Stevenson

1896 - 1906
5th
CONVENTION
National
ASSOCIATION
of
COLORED
WOMEN
DETROIT, MICH.
JULY 9 - 14
1906

Moving toward equal opportunity: The nineteenth-century National Association of Colored Women was organized in 1896 to provide cultural opportunities for black citizens. Its Grand Rapids representative Myrtle Lasher, wore a special delegate's badge when she attended the 1906 convention in Detroit (left). Local attorney Floyd Skinner, at the microphone, and detective Walter Coe spoke at a March of Dimes rally in the 1940s (below). Skinner and Coe were active in the black community with fund-raising efforts on behalf of many charities. In 1927, the congregation of St. Luke African Methodist Episcopal Church posed in front of the church which originally was a mission used as a haven for runa-way slaves. The church was organized around 1863 and is the oldest African-American church in the city (facing page above). George M. Smith (front row, fourth from the left) posed in Lansing, Michigan, where he went with the group to demonstrate support for unionism and to discuss with legislators the problems of black labor (facing page below). Smith was one of the founders of the Grand Rapids Chapter of the NAACP and was publisher of Michigan's first black-owned newspaper, The Michigan State News.

became the city's first black letter carrier.

There were other milestones. In 1913, Hattie Beverley, the city's first black schoolteacher, was hired to teach at the Henry School in the heart of a black neighborhood. In 1917, George M. Smith published the first black-owned newspaper, *The Michigan State News*. In 1922, a former baseball player, Walter Coe, joined the Grand Rapids Police Department and later became its first black captain. In 1930, Daniel Lampkin became the first black document clerk at the Statehouse, and in the same year, City Hall hired its first black clerical worker.

As the Progressive Voters League was busy getting out the black vote in the election of 1928, millions of other Americans were also casting ballots—for Herbert Hoover. Hoover, the candidate whose election seemed to promise four more years of prosperity, carried 40 states, including Michigan, and was swept into office by a margin of six million votes. But even as the new president delivered his inaugural address, fevered and unchecked stock market speculation was speeding the nation toward economic disaster. On October 29, 1929, Grand Rapids newspaper headlines announced, "Stocks Hit Bottom—Stay Down."

These were small steps forward, and there would be others, set in motion by determined black leaders and by a growing number of organizations dedicated to black rights—the local chapter of the NAACP, founded in 1915; the Citizens Voters' League; and the Progressive Voters League, established in 1928.

Milo Brown, owner of the Brown Funeral home and one of the city's first black businessmen, and attorney Floyd H. Skinner, the first black member of the Grand Rapids Bar Association, were the moving forces behind the Progressive Voters League. Their aim was to get out the black vote. "There were 1,800 eligible black voters and we had 1,400 of them voting," Brown later recalled. "But we worked, we knew every person that was able to vote. We telephoned them. We organized block by block. In the afternoon of an election day we knew everyone in a block that hadn't voted. We called them. We went in cars to get them and take them to the polls."

112

113

Keeping the bread lines open: As the Great Depression deepened, aid to destitute families increased. The city distributed free milk, bread and potatoes. In the early 1930s, the bread lines outside "Michigan Bakeries" were long and the bus-stop sign ironic (below). A Depression-era milk delivery wagon, decorated as a parade float, urged increased consumption of milk to increase employment—at least in the dairy industry (facing page above).

CHAOS AND COLLAPSE

The Depression brought the Grand Rapids furniture industry to a state of virtual collapse. Buyers stopped coming. Customers stopped buying. Sales plummeted to an all-time low. Unemployment soared, and those workers lucky enough to be kept on the payroll had their wages cut in half. Within four years, financial reverses claimed many victims. Simmons bought Berkey and Gay, perhaps the best known of all Grand Rapids furniture manufacturers. Kroehler bought the Luce Furniture Company. The new owners imposed production shortcuts and inferior materials; neither Berkey and Gay nor Luce survived. By the time the Depression ended, the lower-priced, mass-produced furniture of the South had permanently eclipsed the Grand Rapids product.

Hardships multiplied. Like Americans everywhere, Grand Rapids citizens faced bankruptcy and financial ruin, mounting debts, mortgage foreclosures, huge cuts

WINNER BUT NEVER CHAMPION

Sometimes the best are never granted the plaudits due them. Sometimes they see lesser men receive the recognition instead.

Wesley Ramey of Grand Rapids was such a man.

In the early 1930s, Wesley Ramey should have been the lightweight boxing champion of the world. He never received the crown and had only his fans' acknowledgement that he was indeed the uncrowned lightweight champion of the world.

He defeated six world champions in his division, more than enough, but he never held the title.

Ramey's greatest ambition was to meet Tony Canzoneri, world lightweight champion. On April 20, 1933, he got his chance, in Grand Rapids' Civic Auditorium.

Ramey won, and according to the unanimous decision of the sportswriters, won handily, but it was a non-title bout, with nothing but a momentary glory for Ramey.

Canzoneri avoided Ramey after that. He was smart enough not to repeat the experience.

Wes Ramey fought 194 professional bouts and was ranked among the world's top ten lightweights. But the big prize, the champion's belt, was always beyond his grasp.

115

in wages and massive and widespread unemployment. The prosperity promised by President Hoover did not lie just around the corner, and the city's established welfare machinery was unable to meet the needs of the growing ranks of poor, homeless and unemployed.

A JOB FOR EVERY MAN

George W. Welsh, by trade a printer and by instinct a master politician, was named Grand Rapids city manager in May 1929, by a 4 to 3 vote of the city commission. He brought considerable government experience to the position, having earlier served as a city alderman, a four-term representative in the Michigan House of Representatives, speaker of the Michigan House, and lieutenant governor.

Refusing his own salary and taking drastic measures to turn a million-dollar deficit into a $174,000 surplus, Welsh set about developing a radical plan to aid the needy—a citywide, city-financed relief project that pre-dated Roosevelt's New Deal by a full three years.

Welsh's plan was revolutionary in a city that traditionally voted Republican and consistently described itself as conservative. And it gained for Grand Rapids a measure of national fame as "the city where every man has a job."

Welsh believed that men had the right to preserve their honor by working for their keep. He decreed that the city would supply the jobs if the men would provide the labor. Applicants had to be heads of households and had to take an oath swearing that neither they nor their families had any available funds. Property owners, however, were ineligible, and some men, who wanted to sell their homes but couldn't, fell through the cracks in Welsh's system.

Each worker was given a complete physical examination before being assigned a job. Financial need and family size determined the number of working hours permitted, up to a maximum of 24 hours per week.

Wages were 40 cents an hour, payable in city scrip. The gas, water and electric companies accepted the scrip as payment for utility bills and were later reimbursed by the city. Workers could exchange scrip for haircuts at the city barbershop and for the food, clothing, fuel, shoes, fruit and cigarettes stocked at the city-operated, scrip grocery store where milk sold for four cents a quart.

Welsh put 3,000 unemployed men to work. Men from all walks of life worked at any job available. Bookkeepers mowed lawns and shoveled snow; businessmen cleared vacant lots and cut firewood; factory workers graded streets, laid pipelines, improved parks and playgrounds and built the Richmond Park swimming pool and the Civic Auditorium.

In 1930, Welsh pushed for the auditorium. He argued

ACCLAIMED AWAY FROM HOME

Constance Rourke, who achieved national standing as a social and literary historian, was the most scholarly of writers to be claimed as Grand Rapids' own. But, like other widely acclaimed Grand Rapids artists and literary figures, she was honored more away from home than by her own birthplace.

To her contemporaries in Grand Rapids, she was the author of Davy Crockett, *a book for children, and* Audubon, *a straightforward biography of the great naturalist. In fact, these were the least of her works.*

Constance Rourke's scholarly reputation rested on a series of impressive literary works—American Humor, *a book that has rarely been out of print in the last 50 years;* Troupers of the Gold Coast, *a chronicle of the lives of Lotta Crabtree and other entertainers; and* Trumpets of Jubilee, *lively writing about such fascinating people as Henry Ward Beecher.*

A Vassar College graduate and professor before returning to Grand Rapids in 1915 to pursue a writing career, Constance Rourke was also a recognized authority on the subject of folk art. Her interest in art extended to supporting many young Grand Rapids artists, and the walls of the home she shared with her mother were virtually covered with their works.

In 1941, Constance Rourke slipped from an icy porch and died, with what was to have been her major work incomplete. Roots of American Culture *was to be a three-volume examination of the culture of many ethnic and religious groups, including their folk art and indigenous music.*

Another literary figure, Van Wyck Brooks, completed the final chapters for the first volume, published posthumously. The remaining profuse notes—the fruit of countless hours of research—lie forgotten in some dusty file drawer.

Constance Rourke, too, has been largely forgotten by the city in which she did most of her writing. Historians and literary authorities still quote from her books, but her hometown has paid her little heed.

The Eagle Hotel on Market Street (looking north) in 1933, shortly before it fell victim to the Depression and permanently closed its doors. Built in 1883, it replaced the original Eagle, the city's first hotel.

that the project would put men to work and that the city would benefit through increased convention business. Despite the hard times, Welsh succeeded. Grand Rapids passed a $1.5 million bond issue, and the auditorium was completed in 1933. Later it was named for Welsh, whose persistence brought it into being.

By 1931, the city was spending more than one million dollars—fully one-third of its total budget—to provide relief.

Welsh's program was not without its critics. The Reverend Alfred Wishart of the Fountain Street Baptist Church, so vocal twenty years earlier in his opposition to the furniture strike, objected loudly and publicly to Welsh's purchase, with public funds, of 30,000 bushels of potatoes to feed the needy. Wishart argued, with some justification, that Welsh had violated the law by not having the city purchasing agent handle the transaction. Welsh responded that the hungry had to be fed. It took

considerable pressure on his part to have the city release the long-overdue payment to the impatient potato farmers.

Welsh's City Social Shelter—a home for jobless and single men—came under even heavier fire. Many leading citizens regarded the shelter as an "invitation to the shiftless, local and transient" and objected to the city operating such a facility.

Persistent criticism forced Welsh to appoint the so-called Committee of One Hundred to investigate his relief methods. Made up of some of the city's most prominent citizens and some of Welsh's severest critics, the committee scrutinized the entire relief operation and registered its objections in a detailed report. Among other things, the report suggested that single men be housed by the Salvation Army, that non-negotiable scrip payments and the city store were unfair competition for the local merchants and that the city was playing favorites with some of its suppliers. The use of scrip was subsequently abandoned, but city hall's commitment to the welfare program remained. Grand Rapids would care for its needy, said Mayor John D. Karel in 1932, "even at the cost of book juggling or illegality."

The flow of federal money that accompanied Franklin Roosevelt's New Deal temporarily silenced Welsh's critics and removed much of the burden of relief from the local treasury.

A LIMBER LAD OF 67

Hardly a person is left who remembers the name Ollie Praetorious.

Born on the west side of Grand Rapids shortly after the Civil War, Ollie got into baseball's record books while still a young man. For many years, the professional baseball team with which Ollie played was pictured inside the front cover of the annual Spalding's Baseball Guide. There in the front row, center, was Ollie. Ollie was there because he had set a record for strikeouts—29 batters—in a regulation game.

Normally there are 27 outs in a regulation, nine-inning, baseball game. In that game, however, two of the men who struck out reached first base because the catcher dropped the third strike and the batter beat the throw to first.

But Ollie gave up baseball for the life of a contortionist. Newspapers in such distant places as Sydney, Australia; London, England; and Vienna, Austria, ran front-page stories about the seemingly impossible things Ollie did with his body.

In 1935, when he was 67 and living in his modest Grand Rapids home off Eastern Avenue, Ollie's savings ran out and he had to apply for relief. He regaled the caseworker with stories of past exploits. Then, to prove he was still the Ollie of old, he sat on the floor, tucked his feet behind his neck and rolled through the living room, dining room, kitchen and back.

118

Jess Elster's All-Stars was a Grand Rapids black baseball team in the 1940s. Black teams were matched only against other black teams in those days, and the locally scheduled games were held at Bigelow and Valley fields.

THE BEST OF THE BEST

Juan Padron, who conceivably may have been the greatest left-handed baseball pitcher of all time, moved to Grand Rapids in 1931 and regularly pitched for local all-star teams in exhibition games against the Philadelphia Athletics, St. Louis Cardinals, Cincinnati Reds and Detroit Tigers—and just as regularly beat them. Any time Padron was scheduled to pitch, the stands were packed.

Padron was a black baseball player in the days when major league teams were all white. But he had such light-colored skin that John J. McGraw, manager of the New York Giants, tried to sneak Padron into the Southern Association as a Cuban. Padron mowed down opposing batters for several months, until someone discovered McGraw's deception, and Padron was banished.

Padron was actually a native of Cuba who had come to this country at age 16 to pitch for a Tampa, Florida, cigar factory team. He ultimately caught on with an all-black team, the Augustine Molina's Cuban Stars, and on one memorable occasion hooked up in a pitching duel with George Mullin, a one-time great Detroit Tigers pitcher. Padron struck out 22 in that nine-inning game and won the duel, 2-1.

Later he pitched for the New York Cuban Stars, Lincoln Giants and Chicago American Giants. In his years pitching in the Negro leagues, Padron said that he had faced Satchel Paige about ten times and defeated him at least seven times. In his best season, he won 62 games and lost 12.

In the 1930s, while playing with the Chicky Bar Giants of Grand Rapids, Padron pitched and won three games in one week in the state semiprofessional championship in Battle Creek. He was 47.

On a Fourth of July afternoon, when he was 52 or 53, he pitched a semipro team to victory in a 2-0 ballgame, despite the fact that his fingers were bent from injuries and arthritis.

When Juan Padron had to give up pitching, he went to work in a foundry. He wasn't sour on the world for not having had a chance to show his stuff in the big leagues. He loved baseball, loved to pitch, and he knew that he was as good as anyone around. As man and pitcher he was, as one sportswriter described him, "the best of the very best."

Grand Rapids' Civic Auditorium was built during the heart of the Depression, at the urging of City Manager George Welsh, in order to put the unemployed to work and to boost the city's sagging convention business.

CIVIC AUDITORIUM
Erected By The Citizens of Grand Rapids
OWEN-AMES-KIMBALL CO. CONSTRUCTION MANAGERS
SUB-CONTRACTORS

ACOUSTICAL CEILING
CUT STONE
ELECTRIC WIRING
GLASS & GLAZING
GLAZED TILE
MARBLE
MILLWORK
ORNAMENTAL METAL &
MISCELLANEOUS STEEL & IRON
TEMPERATURE

In 1931, the unemployed found work constructing the Civic Auditorium. In 1975, the building was renamed for George Welsh, whose persistence in providing jobs during the Depression brought the auditorium into being.

Brother, can you spare a dime: When cash was short during the Depression, the city's school teachers were paid in scrip (facing page above). The Lake Michigan freshwater pipeline project, conceived by George Welsh (by then mayor), was designed to provide jobs and was built in 1939-40 with a combination of city and federal Public Works Administration funds (below).

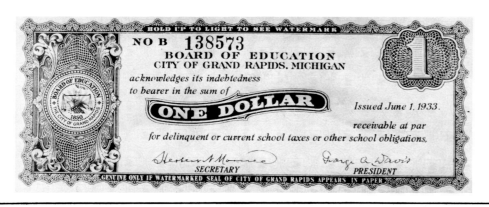

Hard times, hard work: Street-widening projects on Division Avenue in 1928 signaled the approaching demise of streetcar lines (below). The last of those lines were taken up in 1935 as part of a WPA street-widening project (left).

A time of transition: The '40s brought about a cultural shift, and women began to do things they had never done before, such as playing baseball. The Grand Rapids Chicks, a professional team in the All-American Girls Baseball League, were immensely popular and consistently drew local crowds of over 5,000 people. But reminders of a quieter past could still be found in Grand Rapids—for example, the grocery store at 752 South Division (below). Opened in 1908 by Giovanni B. Russo and his wife, Giovannina, the store was in the heart of what was then an Italian neighborhood, but it served the Lebanese and Greek ethnic communities also and was still in business in 1935.

THE CITY SURVIVES

Between 1933 and 1938, federal government welfare payments in Kent County totaled more than $57 million. All sorts of public works projects were instituted under the auspices first of the Civil Works Administration (CWA) and later the Works Progress Administration (WPA). Thousands were kept working and the city benefited with new sewers and refurbished and repaired bridges. In 1935, streets were widened and repaired and the last of the old trolley tracks were removed, paving the way for an all-bus mass-transit system. Over the next few years, the Kent County Airport was enlarged, a new Grand Rapids Public Museum was constructed and a Grand River flood control project carried out, all with the help of WPA funds.

The Great Depression rocked the nation and catapulted its citizens into an era of hard times. Few Americans escaped the heavy toll in human misery and financial ruin.

But Grand Rapids' schools never stopped running. When cash was short, teachers were paid in tax anticipation warrants. State and federal bank holidays elicited public boasts that Grand Rapids banks were sound, and they brought forth in the *Grand Rapids Press* the following bank-holiday etiquette rules:

1. Keep your head.
2. Keep your sense of humor.
3. Ignore advice of folly."

Throughout the Depression, concerned furniture manufacturers continued to promote Grand Rapids furniture. They staged a centennial celebration in 1936 and opened a furniture museum, first of its kind in the world. Some Grand Rapids businesses closed their doors permanently, but far more of them diversified, regrouped and maintained limited operations as they awaited better times.

Recovery was slow, but the city managed to survive, bolstered by an imaginative relief program which kept thousands working and supported by an economy that faltered but never entirely failed.

The home front

Meeting the '40s head on: During the war years, Grand Rapids citizens rallied to the cause. War-fund drives and generous volunteer efforts garnered the additional cash needed to supply troops and materials (facing page). U.S. Senator Arthur H. Vandenberg addressed fellow Republicans at the Grand Rapids Civic Auditorium in 1946 (inset). Although an ardent isolationist during his early years in the Senate, Vandenberg reversed his philosophy during the war, became one of the founders of the United Nations and a strong supporter of the postwar NATO alliance.

December 7, 1941, was a typically quiet Grand Rapids Sunday. The shops and bars were closed, churchgoers attended services and the city—along with the rest of the Midwest—was digging itself out from under the snowy remains of a major winter storm.

The war in Europe was still a long way from Michigan. Hawaii was a distant island—a vacation paradise—not even a state. Few had heard of a base called Pearl Harbor, and America was one of the few countries at peace.

Then, later on that quiet Sunday afternoon, Grand Rapids' two radio stations broke the news—the nation was at war.

GEARING UP

During the '30s, Americans had watched as totalitarian armies swept across Europe and Asia. Japan's invasion of China pierced the shell of American isolationism. Hitler's blitzkrieg shook the foundations of America's carefully cultivated neutrality. Over the objections of leading Senate isolationists, including Republican Arthur H. Vandenberg of Grand Rapids, Washington edged closer to the conflict.

By 1939, factories were gearing up for rearmament, and citizens—however reluctantly—began facing the eventuality of war.

More than a year before Pearl Harbor, Grand Rapids citizens were already concerned with civil and national defense. An August 1940 meeting of the Association of Commerce (the Chamber of Commerce's predecessor) featured a speech on the "importance of private enterprise in national defense." Michigan Bell, in cooperation with the Army Signal Corps, trained men in telephone communications techniques. The Grand Rapids Homing Pigeon Club offered the Corps all of its birds and roosts. Men from all over the state gathered at the Pantlind Hotel to discuss protecting water supplies; the Kent County Airport was declared off-limits to the public at night.

A group of local attorneys formed a national defense committee to protect the business and clients of drafted lawyers and the "civil welfare" of all draftees. But that Sunday morning in December, the precautionary efforts ended. In a day, the hometown became the Home Front.

Gearing up for war: Just a few days after Pearl Harbor, the Haskelite Company in Grand Rapids, makers of laminated plywood veneer used in aircraft construction, placed armed guards around its plant to prevent sabotage (left). In 1942, many servicemen said goodbye to their families at Union Station before departing for active duty (below). During the war, more than 6,000 women—many of them soldiers' wives—went to work in Grand Rapids war plants. Some women workers strung parachutes (facing page left), and some went to work in a local aircraft plant (facing page right).

ARSENAL OF DEMOCRACY

As their young men—and women—went off to war, Grand Rapids residents volunteered their services to civil defense activities and threw themselves wholeheartedly into scrap metal and wastepaper drives, practice alerts and evacuation drills.

Herpolsheimer's Department Store was the first of ten local businesses to adapt some of its trucks for easy conversion to ambulances. Sandbags protected the city pumping station and City Hall, and blackouts were scrupulously observed. Civilian concern mounted over the Japanese incendiary devices that were attached to helium balloons and floated across the Pacific for the purpose of igniting West Coast forest fires. The devices occasionally went astray, and early in the war, Grand Rapids civil defense officials held anti-incendiary training sessions at the Kent County Airport. It wasn't until V-J Day, however, that Donald S. Leonard, head of the Michigan Office of Civil Defense, revealed that one of the devices had landed in a field "near Grand Rapids" in May 1944; it was a dud.

All over the country, war production took precedence and consumer products were in increasingly short supply. Meat, gasoline and liquor were strictly rationed, so were shoes. Children's clothing was scarce, nylon stockings, introduced less than five years before, were virtually unobtainable except on the black market, and five pounds of sugar had to last each household for four months. (Just a few days before the atomic bombs fell on Hiroshima and Nagasaki, Michigan petitioned the Office of Price Administration for a greater sugar allotment; home canners needed extra sugar for the large peach crop being harvested.)

Michigan, the "arsenal of democracy," supplied the nation with war matériel and products vital to the war effort. Heavy war goods rolled off Detroit assembly lines, and farm workers from all over the state, including the Grand Rapids area, went to work in Detroit factories.

Grand Rapids industries also landed defense contracts. The Globe Knitting Works produced gas-resistant underwear for the armed forces. Owen-Ames-Kimball built prefabricated buildings for the army installation at Fort Custer, near Battle Creek, and McInerney Spring and Wire—in peacetime an automobile-spring manufacturer—turned out fragmentation

bombs, parachutes, tank armor plating, shell
containers and flare pistols. Wolverine Brass made
fuses; Michigan Wheel produced propellers and
propeller parts, and Corduroy Rubber made shell-casing
gaskets and rubber parts for tanks.

The furniture industry, damaged by the Depression
and hurt by wartime regulations requiring wooden
substitutes for metal springs in upholstered furniture,
nevertheless rallied to the national cause. Following the
precedent established during World War I when a
consortium of furniture manufacturers produced
Handley-Page bomber parts, sixteen companies banded
together in 1941 to form Grand Rapids Industries,
producing parts for gliders and observation planes.
American Seating had a contract from Beechcraft to
make airplane wings; other local furniture companies
made the furniture, ship's steering wheels, ammunition
boxes and other wood items needed by the armed forces.

Accurate weather predictions were essential for pilots
sent off on long-range bombing runs. The Pantlind Hotel,
which had once played host to thousands of out-of-town
furniture buyers each year, now hosted the Army Airforce Weather School. On January 4, 1943, the Airforce
took over the Pantlind, the Civic Auditorium, the Rowe
Hotel and other downtown buildings to hold classes
designed to teach navigators and other personnel how to
analyze worldwide weather patterns and forecast
weather conditions. Thousands of trainees attended
classes. The school operated for nine months but then
closed three months ahead of schedule when the Army
decided to move it to Illinois. The Pantlind management
sued for breach of contract and won.

RESURGENCE ON THE GRAND

134

The hardships of the Depression and the rigors
of war were all but forgotten in the
tumultuous celebration which greeted
victory. Fifty thousand people crowded into
downtown to cheer the Japanese surrender and to hail
what seemed to be the beginning of a new and
untroubled era.

All over America, the conversion from wartime to
peacetime production was accompanied by an insatiable
demand for consumer products. The economic
prosperity of the war years continued undisturbed into
the postwar years, and the Grand Rapids economy
boomed.

The furniture industry, which had virtually collapsed under the weight of the Great Depression and increasing competition from the South, never stopped promoting Grand Rapids as a quality furniture center. Two decades of financial difficulties had caused plant closures, mergers and consolidations and drove some companies to set up southern branch operations, but the industry

ATHENS OF THE WEST

On the surface, Grand Rapids seems an unlikely literary setting, but a number of authors have used the city as a backdrop for their works.

Glendon Swarthout, who achieved fame and fortune with the motion picture adaptation of his novel, They Came to Cordura, spent his boyhood years in Lowell—the small town twenty miles east of Grand Rapids. For Swarthout, as for many west Michigan residents, Grand Rapids was a citadel of the arts. In Swarthout's novel, Welcome to Thebes, published in 1962, Thebes was a thinly disguised Lowell, and Grand Rapids was labeled the "Athens of the West."

In 1935, Arnold Gingrich, a Grand Rapids native and graduate of Central High School, published Cast Down the Laurel. The novel, which satirized the ladies of a local music society and some of the more flamboyant members of the musical community, attracted a fair amount of local notoriety for its author because the characters were obviously based on real Grand Rapids socialites. Gingrich later established a nationwide reputation as the editor of Esquire magazine.

Among the more famous figures in the city's recent literary annals are several writers who attended Calvin College. Peter DeVries, author of more than twenty novels characterized by their incisive wit, irreverence and merciless examination of suburbia, has set many of his works in Grand Rapids. Feike Feikema, now known as Frederick Manfred, created a stir in his alma mater and in Grand Rapids (his hometown) with a caustic study of both in The Primitive, a novel published in 1949.

Paul Schrader, another Calvin College alumnus, was the screen writer for some of the past decade's toughest films, including Taxi Driver and Hard Core. Local audiences flocked to see Hard Core because some of the scenes were filmed in Grand Rapids, many residents had parts as extras, and because pre-release publicity labeled the film an indictment of conservative Grand Rapids values and moral standards.

itself survived. Although it never regained its earlier position of national preeminence, wartime military contracts, mutual cooperation and the determination of manufacturers to emphasize excellence saved the furniture industry from the fate suffered by local cigar-making and brewing industries. Once highly prosperous, these businesses disappeared entirely from the local postwar scene.

Buoyed by the vastly increased postwar demand for home furnishings, the industry enjoyed a resurgence between 1946 and 1950. But once that demand was met, the surge of growth receded. The industry's focus shifted from fine residential furniture to institutional seating for schools, theatres and churches, metal office furniture and quality reproductions.

Furniture was not the only item Americans had done without during the Depression and war years. As factories converted to peacetime production, wages and employment stayed high and many families put the automobile on the top of their shopping lists. Local automobile suppliers entered a boom period. So did the local construction industry.

The need to absorb thousands of veterans back into civilian life combined with wartime building slowdowns to create a serious postwar housing shortage in Grand Rapids. Some returning veterans and their families found housing in an old downtown furniture exhibition building divided into apartments. Others later took apartments in veterans' housing projects built with federal money in Coit Hills and on an unused part of Woodlawn Cemetery. Within sixteen months after the war ended, $8 million worth of construction projects were underway.

School construction had also declined sharply during the Depression and war years. After the war, with the birthrate on the upswing, cities throughout the nation faced the prospect of having to educate a rising school population in outmoded, run-down and poorly maintained buildings. Grand Rapids was no exception. School operating funds had been drastically reduced; teachers' starting salaries hovered at $900 a year; and no new schools had been built for more than a decade.

In 1948, the Grand Rapids Board of Education commissioned a citywide survey of school needs. The report, using the terms "impoverishment and decay" to describe the general deterioration of the city's schools, spurred the public in 1950 to approve a special 20-year building tax. Revised state property tax assessments

137

made additional funds available. Over the next decade, new-school construction projects in Grand Rapids totaled $12 million.

Other long-overlooked institutions also received renewed attention. John Ball Park, once the city's most popular recreation spot, had succumbed to two decades of neglect. The swimming pool was condemned and closed and the tennis courts abandoned. Only a handful of animals were left in the zoo; the others had been shot or sold during the Depression because the city could not afford to feed them. In 1948, the city commission cited lack of funds when it turned down a neighborhood petition to improve the park. However, the commission provided money the next year, and the process of modernizing park and zoo began.

At the end of the war the city began a period of hospital improvements and expansions. In 1949 and 1952 community fund drives raised a total of more than $6 million for new facilities and equipment to offer the

highest possible standard of care to Grand Rapids residents. With four acute-care hospitals and a variety of specialty hospitals, Grand Rapids was well on its way to becoming the major medical center for western Michigan. It was also the first city in the country to fluoridate its drinking water, as part of a 1945 federally funded pilot project.

Postwar prosperity throughout the nation was accompanied by an unprecedented wave of labor unrest and major-industry strikes. During the war years most unions held off striking, although there were a few wartime strikes in Grand Rapids by city garbage collectors, school custodians and the truck drivers at the Grand Rapids Gravel Company.

After the war, labor protested that wages had not kept pace with profits and that workers had made more wartime sacrifices than the manufacturers. Now that peace had returned, labor wanted its share of the new prosperity. During 1946 alone, more than four million workers were involved in almost 5,000 labor disputes nationwide.

Grand Rapids workers had never been deeply involved in unions, but during the postwar period they took part in a number of strikes. The longest was the General Motors strike which began in November 1945 and was not settled until March 1946. GM employees in 20 states stayed off the job—3,000 workers in Grand Rapids alone. Other strikes in other industries followed, as workers sought higher wages and improved benefit packages. Some of the city's leading industries—Lear, Consumers Power, R.C. Allen, Michigan Bell, Wolverine Brass and American Seating—were involved.

BELLY FULLA STRAW

David Cornel and Meindert DeJong, both Calvin College graduates, were both notable figures in literary circles between 1940 and 1970. Like other immigrants to Grand Rapids in the early twentieth century, the two young brothers from the Netherlands endured the taunts of other small boys because of their old-country ways. David was particularly bitter over such treatment. "Belly fulla straw," a jibe aimed at Dutch youngsters, became the title of his first novel. Published in 1934, it was a beautifully written story about what it meant to be a youthful immigrant in Grand Rapids in the first decade after the turn of the century.

David went on to write several other novels, all well-received by the critics, but largely ignored by the reading public. He was also a poet, and many of the country's most prestigious literary journals published his works.

Meindert DeJong, married twice but childless, became one of the country's finest authors of children's books. Among his works are The Wheel on the School, Dirk's Dog Bellow, Far Out the Long Canal and many other best-sellers for children. In 1962, he became the first American ever to win the Hans Christian Andersen award for children's literature, and he was also the winner of the Newbery Medal.

THE HOME FRONT FACTION

Citizens were also demanding change and reform on the state and municipal political scenes. Michigan was solidly Republican, and Frank McKay, the Republican state treasurer, wielded considerable influence in both state and city. But McKay's influence came under heavy attack. In 1944, a group of reform-minded local citizens, calling themselves the Home Front, wrested control of the Kent County Republican organization from McKay.

Four years later, in a Republican primary election for the U.S. House of Representatives, the Home Fronters successfully supported political newcomer Gerald R.

The political arts: George W. Welsh, Grand Rapids city manager from 1929 to 1932 and mayor from 1938 to 1949, generated considerable controversy during his years on the local political scene (left). According to his detractors, he was a political opportunist. To his admirers, however, he was a "rugged individualist" who did "what he thought would be better for the common man." In 1949, some of the citizens who were opposed to Welsh collected signatures for his recall (facing page below). Gerald R. Ford, his foot on a tractor wheel, talked with farmers during his 1948 campaign for election to the U.S. House of Representatives (facing page above).

Ford against Bartel J. Jonkman, McKay's candidate and a confirmed isolationist. Ford represented the Grand Rapids 5th Congressional District in the House of Representatives for the next 25 years and went on to become the vice president and then 38th president of the United States.

Once they had broken McKay's power, many Home Front supporters took aim at Grand Rapids municipal government. Mayor George W. Welsh, considered by many Home Fronters a cog in the McKay machine, was a prime target. Welsh, who had come under fire for his actions as city manager from 1929 to 1932, had been elected Grand Rapids mayor in 1938. Welsh's many successes kept him in office for the next decade.

As city manager, Welsh had created a city-wide relief program and at his urging the city built its Civic Auditorium. As mayor, Welsh obtained WPA funds for the freshwater pipeline to Lake Michigan, completed in 1940. He successfully engineered passage of the 1946 state constitutional sales tax diversion amendment which gave Michigan cities a greater share of state sales tax revenues. He also revitalized the city planning department, bringing in planning director Floyd Jennings

in 1944. Elected president of the United States Conference of Mayors in 1947, he was chosen two years later by "Town Hall of the Air," a popular radio show of the time, to join other prominent figures in an around-the-world, goodwill tour.

In 1949, Welsh's eleventh year in the mayor's seat, Grand Rapids was named an All-America City, the first year this national award was ever given. The mayor of the All-America City, however, was under siege by a citizens' group determined to remove him from office.

City politics had long been marked by friction and dissension, primarily between the west-side First Ward and the east-side Second and Third wards. But in 1949, voters in all three wards united behind the issue that drove Welsh from the local political scene.

The issue hinged on the question of city tax assessments. Since the adoption of the 1916 city charter, each of the city's three wards had its own assessor. Once appointed, the tax assessors were answerable to no one, and the obvious inequities bred by the system had long been a target for reformers. At the same time, city and school budgets were becoming increasingly inadequate. Welsh himself organized town meetings, and appointed a

FIRST LADY OF POLITICS

No one has ever bestowed the title on Dorothy Leonard Judd, but she, probably more than any other woman who has lived in Grand Rapids, is entitled to be called its First Lady.

The daughter of Harry Carr Leonard, Mrs. Siegel Judd, wife of a prominent local attorney, took naturally to politics, especially the nonpartisan variety.

She became a force in the Grand Rapids League of Women Voters when she joined it in 1924. In 1928 she was elected president of the Michigan League. And a couple of years later she was named to the board of directors of the National League of Women Voters.

In 1932 she was appointed to the Committee of 100 on Relief Administration and promptly crossed swords with George W. Welsh, then Grand Rapids' city manager. The two were at odds the rest of Welsh's life and, more often than not, Mrs. Judd came out the victor.

She served successively on the Citizens Tax Study Committee, the City Planning Commission, the Metropolitan Water Study Committee and the Committee of 100 on Capital Improvements.

At the state level she served on the Commission for

Revision of Election Laws, the Civil Service Study Commission, the Commission on Reform and Modernization of Government and the Commission on Election Laws. Nominally a Republican, she was honored by Republican and Democratic governors.

She, perhaps more than any other person, was responsible for Michigan's adopting civil service. And in 1961 she was elected to the Constitutional Convention that drafted a revised state constitution later adopted by the people.

The author of numerous papers, books and pamphlets on government, she has been called both gentle and feisty. Her foes have respected her and her friends have adored her. Now in her 80s, she continues to speak out whenever anything in Grand Rapids doesn't accord with her beliefs.

Citizen action: In 1949, a citizen action group, nicknamed the "Angry Order of Broom," was intent on sweeping Welsh out of office. Students carried signs supporting the ouster (below). Joseph Haraburda was one of three commissioners also under fire, but in his case, the recall effort failed. Commissioner Carl H. Richards was recalled and Lester A. Wagemaker resigned. During the winter of 1949, under new government, there was a week-long celebration of the city and of its businesses and industry. City government held open house, and the new City Manager, Frank Goebel, set up a ballot box. He then invited Grand Rapids residents to drop in their complaints and suggestions (left).

citizens' tax committee to study the problems and suggest ways to increase city tax revenues.

The citizens' committee called for a charter amendment to abolish the existing 15-mill limit on school, city and county millage elections. The voters rejected the proposal, and the committee suggested another plan to widen and equalize the tax base. This second proposal was a charter amendment calling for one assessor responsible to an independent board of review. Many members of the original Home Front were part of the newly formed Citizen Action group working to draft the amendment. Welsh's critics in the group also wanted to make sure that the mayor would not be the one to name the new assessor. Spearheaded by the Citizen Action/Home Front faction, the effort to get the amendment on the ballot succeeded. Voters approved the measure. From then on, there would be one tax assessor for the city, appointed by the city manager with the approval of the city commissioner.

THE ANGRY ORDER OF BROOM

However, City Manager Frank Goebel and the city commission, interpreted the newly passed amendment in two different lights. Goebel wanted to submit a single name for the commission's approval; the commission wanted to make its own selection from a list of candidates supplied by the city manager. Goebel stood firm and appointed an assessor; the commission rejected his appointment. In the battle of wills that followed, Goebel refused to give in and name another assessor. The commission decided to reconsider his recent reappointment to the city manager position and voted 4 to 3 for dismissal. Welsh sided with the majority, according to his critics, because he had his own candidate—a McKay functionary—for the assessor post, but Welsh steadfastly denied the allegation.

Outraged citizens jumped into the fray. The assessor question was not the major point of the protest, however. In the minds of Citizen Action members, the real issue, was the mayor. The strong-willed Welsh had clashed with community leaders before, and Citizen Action used Welsh's vote against Goebel as the wedge to remove him from office.

On May 12, 1949, a Citizen Action rally at Fulton Street Park attracted 4,000 people. Speakers Dorothy Judd, Dr. Duncan Littlefair of Fountain Street Church, and

others demanded the recall of Welsh and the three commissioners who had voted for Goebel's dismissal. Julius Amberg was named to chair a Citizen's Action recall committee. Nearly 27,000 Grand Rapids residents signed recall petitions and many of those in favor of reform nailed brooms to their front porches, symbolizing their desire to sweep the city clean.

The "Angry Order of Broom" had its way—one commissioner resigned, one was recalled, and Mayor George Welsh, in Rome, sent a telegram ordering that his letter of resignation, written before he left the city, be released. Stanley J. Davis, First Ward commissioner, became interim mayor, and in 1950, reform candidate Paul Goebel, the brother of former manager Frank Goebel, was swept into office for the first of two consecutive terms.

Welsh reappeared for a curtain call in 1954 when he managed George Veldman's successful mayoral campaign and then served for a year as city manager. But the reform faction once more gained the upper hand and Welsh left office. His disappearance from the local political scene marked the end of an era.

The fabric of city life

The affluent '50s: In 1951, too few downtown parking places prompted the city to build its first parking ramp. The site selected was on the corner of Lyon and Ionia (below). The '50s also saw the burgeoning of the suburbs as people fled the central cities for green lawns and pastoral scenes, such as found near the Lowell-Fallasburg covered bridge (right).

The peace expected after World War II was interrupted just five years after the Japanese surrendered. The Communist takeover of mainland China and invasion of Korea heated up the Cold War, and the United States was once again fighting on Asian soil, this time in Korea. A storm of anti-communist sentiment was about to explode into McCarthyism. Grand Rapids had its bomb shelters, evacuation routes and McCarthy supporters. But, for the most part, matters closer to home claimed the city's attention.

SUBURBAN BOUND

Federal spending patterns, established during the Depression and the war, continued pumping vast sums of money into the domestic economy, while a welter of federal policies gave rise to a new and nationwide phenomenon—the burgeoning of the suburbs. The Federal Housing Administration (FHA), set up during the Depression, and the GI Bill of Rights, enacted to ease the transition from military service to civilian life, made low-interest home loans available to millions of Americans. Suburban housing developments mushroomed. Tax incentives and plentiful land drew businesses, industries and shopping centers away from the city core. In turn, improved services attracted even more residents to the suburbs. All over the country, people fled the central cities. Grand Rapids saw its share of outward movement. Suburban development outstripped urban growth, businesses relocated in the suburbs and the city's population declined.

To some Grand Rapids officials, annexation was the answer to maintaining the tax base and keeping a shifting, suburban-bound population on the municipal tax rolls. However, suburbs such as Wyoming, East Grand Rapids, Paris Township (now Kentwood) and Walker were determined to maintain their own identities and preserve their own autonomy. East Grand Rapids, which had been resisting annexation attempts since 1914, again rejected annexation in 1959 and 1963. The city of Wyoming incorporated as a separate municipality in 1959; Walker and Kentwood followed suit a few years later. Grand Rapids was able to annex a few small suburbs during the 1950s, but the total land area brought under the city's jurisdiction was less than one square mile.

Finally, in 1959, the city commission and Mayor Stanley Davis adopted a get-tough stance in the form of a "no-extension" policy: Grand Rapids would no longer provide services to the unannexed communities outside its borders. The new policy had some effect. Over the next several years, annexations placed eighteen square miles and 20,000 people under Grand Rapids' jurisdiction.

City and suburban interests clashed over the years. With the completion of a new water filtration plant near the Lake Michigan pumping station in 1963, Grand Rapids officials began considering the possibility of constructing a second Lake Michigan pipeline. Negotiations with neighboring Wyoming over a joint pipeline failed, and Wyoming built its own system, picking up customers along the line who might otherwise have been future Grand Rapids pipeline customers.

In 1963, the city lost to Wyoming again, this time as the result of a Supreme Court annexation decision. The Court ruled that the area which would lose property through annexation should have as much of a voice in the decision as the core city and the area being annexed. As the area losing property, Wyoming was given a voice, and Grand Rapids had to return a sizable chunk of land, including the industrially developed area that surrounded the old Kent County Airport property south of 32nd Street.

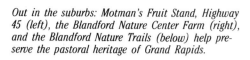
Out in the suburbs: Motman's Fruit Stand, Highway 45 (left), the Blandford Nature Center Farm (right), and the Blandford Nature Trails (below) help preserve the pastoral heritage of Grand Rapids.

Suburban growth: The city's freeway system was designed to bring motorists into its center (below). The system altered traffic patterns and was a major factor in suburban growth. The El Sombrero restaurant (right), a colorful part of the city, is representative of the growth of small businesses in Grand Rapids.

ONTO THE FAST LANE

Although federal money during the Depression and a postwar millage increase had helped modernize the airport and usher it into the jet age in the early 1950s, the facility itself was rapidly becoming inadequate. The newly extended north-south runway crossed 44th Street and had to be protected by gates. The airport was hemmed in on all sides by industrial development, and further expansion was impossible. At airport manager Tom Walsh's urging, the county board of supervisors created a new airport governing body—the Kent County Aeronautics Board. The board drew up plans for a new airport. In 1963, the same year the old airport property was returned to Wyoming, the present Kent County airport facility was opened for freight and passenger service.

The city's new freeway system afforded easy access to the new airport. Subsidized in large measure by state and federal highway funds, the network of freeways was deliberately designed, at the insistence of city officials, not to bypass Grand Rapids but to bring motorists into its center. The north-south freeway (U.S. 131), dedicated December 1962, and the east-west freeway (I-96), completed two years later, significantly altered city traffic patterns and gave additional impetus to suburban growth.

The automobile, symbol of America's postwar prosperity, changed the way Americans lived. So did television. Grand Rapids' first television station, WLAV (later purchased by WOOD-TV), began broadcasting on August 15, 1949. The fascination with this new form of entertainment never wore off, and local movie houses suffered. With the increasing popularity of television and the advent of drive-ins and suburban theatres, downtown audiences began to dwindle. Ticket prices rose and many screens went dark forever.

By 1961, the area's first truly suburban shopping mall—Rogers Plaza—opened its doors on 28th Street, just a few miles west of the first Meijer Thrifty Acres supermarket in Grand Rapids. Within a few years, other indoor malls, offering protection from the weather and an abundance of free parking, were luring more and more shoppers away from the downtown business district. Small businesses and fast-food establishments multiplied along major streets—miles from the center city, and 28th Street was well on its way to becoming the second busiest thoroughfare in the state.

146

The struggle for equality: George Smith, who published and printed the Michigan State News *helped give civil rights a voice (left). Judge John T. Letts, grandson of an escaped slave, was Michigan's first black jurist. He served for seven years in Grand Rapids Municipal Court and fourteen years as a circuit court judge (right). Black athletics owed much to the leadership of Ted Rasberry (below left), owner of the Harlem Satellites and the Kansas City Monarchs. Jackie Robinson (below right) played on the Monarchs before signing with the Brooklyn Dodgers and was the first black player in the major leagues.*

WHITE FLIGHT, BLACK RIGHTS

The flight to the suburbs was an all-white migration. The shiny new suburbs, with their private homes, new schools, property taxes and keep-out attitudes, were beyond the reach of the city's blacks. Grand Rapids' black population had increased from nearly 3,000 in 1940 to more than 11,000 in 1950. Many had come from the South in search of employment during World War II. Those who came to Grand Rapids, often at the urging of friends and relatives, found the same pattern of racial discrimination that characterized other American cities.

Inadequate housing was one problem. In 1954, a city-wide survey revealed some 7,000 substandard dwellings. But it took two years before groups—such as the Grand Rapids Urban League—achieved passage of a new Grand Rapids housing ordinance. Paul Phillips, the League's executive director for thirty years (1947–77) was a prominent figure in the city's civil rights movement, a man described as a "voice of temperance in a time of turmoil," a "great community leader" whose "style and patience led the community toward increased social justice."

In 1955, the city established a Human Relations Commission and adopted an ordinance prohibiting religious and racial job discrimination by the city or its contractors. Grand Rapids law and the 1955 Michigan civil rights law predated the federal law by nine years. Nevertheless, discrimination was a fact of life for the city's black population. And as the nationwide civil rights movement caught fire in the late '50s and '60s, such local leaders as Paul Phillips and the Reverend Albert Keith, pastor of the Messiah Baptist Church, were in the forefront of battles for equal opportunity and affirmative action programs.

Other blacks were also rising to prominence: John T. Letts became the city's first black judge. Helen Claytor was elected the first black YWCA president anywhere in the country and the first black president of the Community Health Board. But for the most part, the city's black community labored under the weight of job discrimination, real estate redlining (which made mortgage money and insurance protection unavailable), and social discrimination of all kinds. The city commission had no black members and the black population was sorely under-represented on the

employment rosters of the city's businesses, schools and other institutions.

The federal government's answer to racial tensions was a vast outpouring of money. Although such early programs as Model Cities proved less than successful, Lyndon Johnson's "war on poverty" did result in the establishment in 1964 of the Kent Community Action Program (Kent-CAP), which continues to offer a broad range of social, educational, health and employment services to city and county residents.

To many blacks, however, including Lyman Parks (who would later become the city's first black mayor), the multimillion-dollar local share of the Great Society inner city rebuilding program turned out to be "more for appeasement than helping."

As the nation's blacks struggled for equality on all fronts, tensions escalated and frustrations erupted into burnings and street violence in cities as widely different as Los Angeles and Detroit. In 1967, Grand Rapids was the

The many faces of Grand Rapids: The Reverend Lyman S. Parks (left) was mayor of Grand Rapids from 1971 to 1975, and plans for riverfront development gathered momentum during his administration. The ethnic and racial diversity of Grand Rapids has become a positive factor and can be seen reflected in the faces of its many citizens (below and facing page).

HUMAN RIGHTS ADVOCATE

Helen Jackson Wilkins was a specialist in interracial relations for the national YWCA when she made her first trip to Grand Rapids in 1942 as a speaker at a state YW meeting.

The young woman, a native of Minneapolis, was the widow of Earl Wilkins, a black journalist, and the mother of a small son, Roger, who was destined to serve not only with the U.S. Department of Justice, but later on the editorial boards of such distinguished newspapers as the Washington Post, New York Times and Washington Star.

Helen Wilkins had joined the staff of the national YWCA in 1940, a job she retained until 1944 when she came to Grand Rapids as the wife of Dr. Robert Claytor, a local physician.

Mrs. Claytor was elected to the national YW's board of directors in 1945, where she served until her retirement in 1976. She was president of the board from 1967 to 1973.

Claytor also volunteered her time to various other local committees and organizations, including the Grand Rapids Urban League and the Grand Rapids chapter of the Michigan Committee on Civil Rights. Because of her expertise in interracial relations, she was often assigned to race relations committees within those organizations. One of her particular commitments was to get black teachers hired by the Grand Rapids Board of Education.

Her work attracted local attention and she was appointed to a study committee considering the formation of a Human Relations Commission in Grand Rapids. When the commission was established in 1955, she became one of its first members.

Dr. Claytor, a graduate of Meharry Medical College in Nashville, Tennessee, came to the city in 1936. He was on the staffs of St. Mary's and Butterworth hospitals, the city's first black physician to serve on a local hospital staff.

As active as his wife in community affairs, Dr. Claytor was a charter board member of the Grand Rapids Urban League and became its first black president in 1947.

scene of similar outbreaks. The incidents, confined to inner-city neighborhoods, ultimately served to rouse the city to action. In 1968, Lyman Parks of the Third Ward was elected the city's first black commissioner. The ensuing years saw Grand Rapids and its citizens make continued efforts to move blacks and other minority groups into the city's mainstream.

149

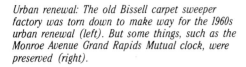

Urban renewal: The old Bissell carpet sweeper factory was torn down to make way for the 1960s urban renewal (left). But some things, such as the Monroe Avenue Grand Rapids Mutual clock, were preserved (right).

DOWN WITH THE OLD

As social and economic changes tugged at the fabric of city life, bulldozers clawed away huge portions of the city itself. By the mid-1950s, downtown Grand Rapids was sliding into a state of severe decline. Not one downtown office building had been constructed for 40 years; while the suburbs bloomed, the central business district decayed. Urban renewal became the watchword of the day.

A new downtown was not a new concept. Downtown had already undergone a number of major facelifts, and several small, successful renewal projects had been completed on the west side. What made the downtown project of the '60s so dramatically different was the presence of the federal government. Washington entered the urban renewal business and federal funds buttressed what became the prevailing philosophy—massive destruction as the solution to urban ills. The old must come down to make way for the new. The federal government would pay its portion of the costs if cities financed a local share.

In 1960, city and county voters approved a millage increase for a project to revitalize the central business district and develop a joint city-county administrative center. Federal urban renewal money came at once.

The selected site encompassed 40 acres around Lower Monroe, the part of Lucius Lyon's old Kent plat that he had purchased from Louis Campau 128 years before.

Despite some scattered opposition, the city proceeded with wholesale condemnations; bulldozers moved into the area, razing the historic along with the ramshackle to make way for $50 million of new construction. By 1966, a total of 128 buildings—many more than a century old—were leveled, ground into rubble and dumped into Riverside Park as fill for the marshy lowlands.

UP WITH THE NEW

A new post office was completed in 1962, the same year the city unveiled architects' plans for the new civic center. City and county voters, with the exception of those in Wyoming, approved another millage increase to pay for the city/county building. The Grand Rapids Area

A ONE-NEWSPAPER TOWN

Like many other major American cities, Grand Rapids has become a one-newspaper town. It has been that way since the Grand Rapids Herald discontinued publication in April 1959, leaving the field to the afternoon paper, the Grand Rapids Press.

Journalism in Grand Rapids goes back to April 18, 1837, when the Grand River Times, west Michigan's first newspaper, published its first edition. Four years after that, the Grand Rapids Enquirer, a weekly, entered the field. And three years after that, another weekly, the Eagle, appeared.

The Herald, the city's first daily newspaper, began publishing on March 19, 1855, six months before the Enquirer became a daily. Two years later, the papers were consolidated.

The Daily Morning Democrat, one of the most influential of the early newspapers, began publishing in August 1865. Then, in rapid succession, came the Daily Times, Evening Leader, Morning Telegram and Telegram-Herald.

In addition, there were at least 50 other publications—newspapers, foreign-language papers, magazines, political sheets and several religious journals—that were produced regularly toward the end of the nineteenth century.

Among the latecomers was the Morning Press, founded in 1890, a four-page daily which sold for one cent. Three months after buying the Morning Press, George G. Booth purchased the Evening Press. The winnowing process had begun in earnest, and in the ensuing years, Booth's competitors began falling by the wayside.

In 1913, Booth changed the name of his newspaper to the Grand Rapids Press, which eventually became the most prosperous in the Booth chain of eight Michigan dailies.

As the Booth newspapers prospered, the Grand Rapids Herald began sustaining losses, and in 1958 the Herald became a Booth newspaper. A year later, the Herald was still losing $1,000 a week. Booth Newspapers decided to cut its losses by closing down the Herald. The Press remained the city's sole surviving newspaper.

Late in 1976, the Booth newspapers were purchased by Samuel I. Newhouse in what was described as the largest transaction of its kind in the history of American journalism.

Making way for the new: In 1958, the old county jail was torn down (below left). The jail was built in 1872 on land that originally was Island No. 2. Health authorities had condemned the jail as early as the 1920s and its demolition was long overdue. When downtown movie audiences declined, so did the theatres, and the Regent Theatre was torn down (below right). Before the wrecking ball was finished, many landmark buildings came down (bottom).

The new complementing the old: Seventh-day Adventist Church (left); St. George's Antiochian Orthodox Church (right); City/County Building (below left); Vandenberg Plaza (below right). On the opposite page (clockwise) St. Andrew's Catholic Cathedral; St. Mark's Episcopal Church; Fountain Street Church; LaGrave Avenue Christian Reformed Church; Westminster Presbyterian Church; and the United Methodist Church.

Chamber of Commerce sponsored a county-wide contest to name the new civic center complex. The winning entry was Vandenberg Center, named for Arthur H. Vandenberg, former Grand Rapids newspaperman and United States senator. An isolationist early in his career, Vandenberg became an ardent internationalist and was the architect of America's bipartisan foreign policy.

In 1966, the Grand Rapids Press, the city's only surviving daily newspaper, moved into its new building on Michigan and Monroe. The Old Kent Bank and Trust Building rose on the site where Keith's Theatre once stood. The new police headquarters and Hall of Justice facility was dedicated. A year later, Union Bank occupied its new, ten-story headquarters, and in 1969, the City Hall/County Administration Building opened. The county also had its own new complex on Grand Rapids' northeast side. Construction began in 1960 with the building of the county jail. (The old downtown jail, on land that was originally Grand River Island No. 2, dated

ROCKET MEN

Two of the nation's astronauts have been natives of Grand Rapids. The first was Roger B. Chaffee, selected for the Apollo moon-shot program in the 1960s. In February 1967, Chaffee and two crewmates, Gus Grissom and Ed White, were taking part in a test atop the launching pad. Fire broke out in the capsule cockpit and the three astronauts were killed. Three months later, the Grand Rapids Public Museum named its planetarium after Roger B. Chaffee, the city's first space hero.

Another Grand Rapids native, Jack Lousma, was aboard the space shuttle Columbia for its third voyage. Lousma, who had spent several weeks orbiting the earth in Skylab, was at the Columbia's controls when the shuttle came in for a perfect landing on March 30, 1982.

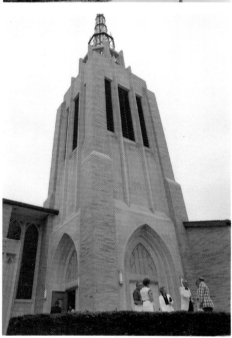

153

Urban renewal in full swing: The old Kent County building came down in the 1960s (right). In the winter of 1969, Mary Stiles chained herself to a wrecking ball in an effort to save the old City Hall clock tower (below). Members of the Joffrey Ballet (facing page left) at rehearsal in the Civic Theatre (facing page right), which was once the old Majestic. The refurbished structure became a permanent home for live theatre in 1979.

back to 1872.) By 1970, the complex included a new Juvenile Court center, a new Child Haven shelter for neglected children and a 56-bed mental hospital, Kent Oaks, the first such community-supported facility in the country. Later, the county converted Sunshine Hospital, the former tuberculosis sanatorium on the Kent Oaks grounds, into Kent Community Hospital, a chronic-disease facility.

The construction of the new county facilities preceded a major change in county government. Until 1968, Grand Rapids, with more than half of the county's population, held fewer than a third of the posts on the board of supervisors, the county's governing body. After the 1968 Supreme Court's "one-man, one-vote" decision, the county adopted a commission form of government, and rural domination of county affairs ended. The city had a voice to equal its share of the county population. The dedication of the new city/county building on Vandenberg Plaza in 1969 became the tangible symbol of a new era of cooperation between Grand Rapids and Kent County government.

THE BELL'S FINAL TOLL

At 11:30 on the night of November 3, 1969, a most unearthly sound rent the air of downtown Grand Rapids. The bell that had been silent for many years in the tower of old City Hall tolled mournfully, as if protesting the impending removal of the old structure to make room for an urban renewal project.

The clanging brought numerous complaints and a contingent of policemen, but no one could find a stairway leading to the clock tower. The only recourse was to climb to the bell tower level in the main building of the by-now nearly demolished City Hall.

From that vantage point, the policemen could see two men, taking turns with sledge hammers, as they swung at the the bell. But it wasn't until a fire truck was summoned that the police could find a way to get at the night tollers, William Bouwsema Jr., 29, and Donald D. Fassen, 30.

The men were relieved of their sledge hammers, arrested and lodged in a cell at police headquarters for the night.

The next morning the men pleaded guilty to creating a disturbance and cheerfully paid a fine of $50 each, avowing that it was worth the pleasure of having warned the citizenry of the bell tower's hour of doom.

154

A FINAL LANDMARK...A LAST PROTEST

By 1969, the urban renewal area was close to assuming its final shape. The state and federal governments announced plans for buildings of their own, and one of the last remaining landmarks of another age—the old city hall—was about to be torn down.

The site of the historic building, whose clock tower had watched over the city since 1888, was earmarked for the Union Bank parking lot. Despite the efforts of such concerned citizens as Mary Stiles, who had herself chained to the wrecking ball in a final, futile attempt to save it, the old stone structure was demolished.

MOVING THE MONUMENT

In 1864, the Kent County Soldiers' Monument Association launched a drive to raise funds for a Civil War monument. But the drive fell short of its goal, and another twenty years passed before the idea of a monument was revived.

The impetus was the Seventeenth Annual Reunion of the Society of the Army of the Cumberland, scheduled to be held in Grand Rapids on September 16 and 17, 1885. Thomas D. Gilbert, treasurer of the original monument association, saw the reunion as the perfect occasion for the dedication of a monument. Using the funds from the original subscription drive, which he had carefully invested, along with additional contributions and a generous personal donation, he commissioned the monument that would honor the men and women who had played a role in the Union victory.

On dedication day, September 17, 1885, more than 35,000 visitors crowded into the city. Flags and buntings flew, and shops, schools, banks and factories were closed in honor of the occasion.

Nearly 95 years later, the monument and the park surrounding it were moved slightly north of their original location as one of the first steps in the construction of Monroe Center mall. Along with a new location, the monument was given a new coat of paint. Its original white bronze color had oxidized to a Confederate gray and so was replaced by a more appropriate Union blue.

155

Though urban renewal made way for much that is new in Grand Rapids, much of the past was preserved. Wrought iron lamps, stone-carved columns, arched windows and doorways, stained glass windows and fire escapes with graceful curves can still be found in various places around the city—sometimes right alongside the new. In the early 1970s, La Grande Vitesse, by renowned artist Alexander Calder, was installed on the plaza in front of the city and county building (facing page). Today, the Calder, as it is popularly called, has become the city's logo. It appears on city stationery, maintenance and refuse trucks and street signs.

ART IN PUBLIC PLACES

Just a few months earlier, a new downtown landmark—the bright red Calder stabile—was installed and dedicated on nearby Vandenberg Plaza. The original plans called for a reflecting pool on the plaza outside the city/county building, but in April 1967, a new idea took root. Henry Geldzahler, associate curator of American painting and sculpture at New York's Metropolitan Museum and director of visual arts for the National Endowment for the Arts (NEA), arrived in Grand Rapids to present a lecture at the Art Museum. After seeing the plaza, he urged the city to consider placing a large piece of sculpture there. Funds were available, he said, through the NEA's newly created Arts in Public Places program.

Within weeks, Mayor Christian Sonneveldt appointed Peter Wege and Nancy Mulnix to approach the NEA for funding; the NEA, in turn, appointed an artist selection jury made up of four out-of-town experts and two local representatives. By the end of May, Alexander Calder had been selected as the sculptor and the NEA authorized a $45,000 matching-funds grant. Calder accepted the commission and the city and county accepted the grant with the proviso that no public funds be used to finance the project.

On May 12, 1969, *La Grande Vitesse*—which means great swiftness or grand rapids—arrived in the city for which it was named. It was shipped from Antwerp in pieces and assembled on the plaza exactly as Calder had specified. The stabile was dedicated, with the artist present, on June 14, 1969. The 42-ton sculpture, first in America to be financed entirely with a combination of federal and private funds, cost approximately $126,700, less than a third of which was supplied by the NEA. Grand Rapids owed its new art work to the support of local foundations, to the continuing interest and encouragement of 5th District Congressman Gerald R. Ford and to the efforts of a great many individuals such as Nancy Mulnix, Jack Busch, Miner (Mike) Keeler and Mary Ann Keeler, who gave lavishly of their time and money.

Controversial then, less so now, Calder's abstraction has come to symbolize Grand Rapids. Its dedication appeared to be one of the final steps in the city's downtown renewal. In fact, it was the harbinger of a renaissance still to come.

Festival Fever

Celebration of the arts: A young Festival-goer paints his mother's face at the popular Festival paint-in (right). The paint-in is an annual Festival event sponsored by the Arts Council of Greater Grand Rapids (facing page left). The Bethel Pentecostal Choir—Festival's traditional closing act—on the Calder stage (inset). The annual Festival continues to draw huge crowds (below). The painting by Alexander Calder on the roof of the County Building is the world's largest Calder painting. Its design was the artist's gift to the city.

At noon on the first Friday of every June, enthusiastic crowds, massed bands and a host of dignitaries assemble on Vandenberg Plaza to await the drum rolls and trumpet fanfares that signal the opening of Festival —Grand Rapids' gala, three-day celebration of the arts. As the weekend progresses, the crowds increase, swelling to nearly half a million by the time the last note has been played, the last ethnic delicacy served and the last chorus sung by the Bethel Pentecostal Choir. Festival has become an event of great magnitude, an opportunity for area residents to savor the richness of the city's artistic and musical talents and an occasion for civic pride. Yet this was not always the case. Although Festival finally captured the city's imagination in the 1970s, its slow and by no means certain genesis was the product of an earlier decade.

The first arts festival, held in 1962, was a small, virtually unnoticed affair staged in the parking lot behind the old Art Museum on Fulton Street. Its sponsors, the Friends of Art, wanted to attract attention to the city's art and cultural institutions. Their original plan was to hold the festival in the heart of the downtown business district. The Chamber of Commerce lent $1,000 to underwrite expenses, but downtown merchants rejected a proposal to block off Monroe Avenue for the festival site. The Friends of Art held the festival at the Art Museum for three years, then moved it to John Ball Park, where it languished and eventually fell victim to community apathy.

But the idea persisted. When the Arts Council of Greater Grand Rapids was formed in 1967 to coordinate many of the city's cultural activities, the idea of an arts festival was revived.

Three years later, Festival made its Vandenberg Center debut. Contributions from the Junior League and the Grand Rapids Foundation, plus the invaluable volunteer support of area businesses and individuals, made Festival a success. Each year since then has brought new innovations, larger crowds and a tremendous spirit of cooperation among all those whose efforts are so vital in making the city's enormous block party possible.

Festival is more than a showcase for the arts. The sale of ethnic foods is a moneymaker, and the Arts Council receives a percentage of the profits. Along with the contributions raised through the council's annual Combined Arts Campaign, launched in 1972, the funds help support the city's major arts and cultural institutions.

163

The seven participating members of the Arts Council—the Art Museum, Civic Ballet, Civic Theatre, Council of Performing Arts for Children, Grand Rapids Symphony Orchestra, Opera Grand Rapids and St. Cecilia Music Society—all receive Combined Arts Campaign funding.

About 32 nonprofit associate member organizations (the number varies from year to year) also benefit from council support. Associate members include all the local colleges and universities, the Grand Rapids Public Library, the Gerald R. Ford Presidential Museum, the Grand Rapids Public Museum and a number of local acting groups and semiprofessional music groups.

This roster of talent and resources has made Grand Rapids the undisputed cultural center of West Michigan. And Festival, which focuses community attention on the arts, has done much to awaken widespread appreciation of their importance to Grand Rapids.

A NEW PHILOSOPHY

The close feeling of community engendered by Festival characterized a host of other civic endeavors during the '70s. In Grand Rapids and elsewhere, concern was mounting that urban renewal's wholesale demolition was destroying the fabric of the nation and the heritage of its cities and leaving a new kind of wasteland in its wake.

In 1974, critic Robert Sherrill wrote in the *New York Times Magazine,* "Urban renewal went through Grand Rapids like a $50 million glacier, leaving behind some imposingly cold, square, glassy buildings. . . . There is absolutely no mixture of architecture, old and new, no mixture of purpose. . . . After the government workers go home, the downtown area of Grand Rapids is as lifeless as the inside of the corner mailbox after the last pickup."

Others felt as Sherrill did, and in the 1970s, a new

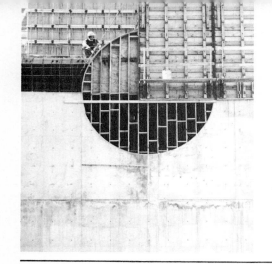

Built for the people, by the people: While Vandenburg Center (left) was still under construction, the Federal Building was dedicated and opened in 1972. It was later renamed for Gerald R. Ford, the city's favorite son. Less than ten years later, the people of Grand Rapids built and dedicated the Gerald R. Ford Presidential Museum. Gerald R. Ford and his wife Betty stand with the Reagans on the steps of the Ford Museum on dedication day, September 14. 1981 (facing page). Within the Ford Museum is a replica of former President Ford's Oval Office at the White House (inset).

philosophy of reclamation and preservation emerged. With the nation's bicentennial just a few years away, Grand Rapids focused much of its attention on the past and on the many elements of its heritage worth preserving.

Federal funding policies changed, too. The Community Development program, run by the federal department of Housing and Urban Development, replaced the ineffective Model Cities program, which was marred by widespread instances of corruption. Community Development regulations now required active citizen involvement in fund allocations and program implementation through the establishment of neighborhood councils.

The Heritage Hill Association was one neighborhood group in the vanguard of citizen reaction against the mass clearance of urban renewal. The city's first neighborhood association, it was established in 1969 to rehabilitate and preserve the fine old homes once occupied by the city's foremost citizens and now being torn down, neglected or abandoned to the process of irreversible decay. The organization, whose efforts gained national historic district status for Heritage Hill, came into being partly as a response to the College Park project, a planned expansion of the junior college which would encroach on Heritage Hill's boundaries. Neighborhood opposition to the plan yielded a compromise acceptable to residents, the junior college officials and to the city itself.

READY FOR THE TRICENTENNIAL

Grand Rapids' own time capsule—an authentic Apollo space capsule—sealed on July 4, 1976, stands waiting to be opened on July 4, 2076.

The capsule, on Lyon Street on the old City Hall site, is filled with hundreds of items considered representative of city life at the time of the nation's bicentennial. Chosen and gathered by members of Steketee's Department Store's Teen Board, the items include a skateboard, blue jeans, a chair made by American Seating (a Grand Rapids manufacturer of school and office furniture), sketches by local artist Paul Collins and the birth certificates of the city's 23 bicentennial babies. Those still living, and their descendants, will be honored guests when the capsule is opened on the 300th anniversary of the nation's founding.

City planners came to recognize the importance of community involvement, and what started out as a new philosophy soon became a city planning department mandate. Neighborhood associations formed throughout the city (in areas such as Eastown, downtown Heartside and on the west side in the vicinity of John Ball Park), and gradually became a political force, supporting and electing city commission candidates who would represent their interests. Citizen action and involvement were also key factors in the renaissance that revitalized downtown and reclaimed the Grand River from more than a century of pollution and neglect.

FAVORITE SON

While plans for the new 1970's approach to urban rebirth were taking shape, Vandenberg Center, the product of an earlier planning solution, was still under construction. The Federal Building, dedicated and opened in 1972, was later renamed for the city's favorite son and most famous citizen, Gerald R. Ford. Immensely popular in his hometown, Ford was returned to the House of Representatives in thirteen consecutive congressional elections, beginning in 1948. For 25 years, Ford's local, mobile-home office—the first ever used by a U.S. congressman—made its district rounds, maintaining personal contact with the voters. He sought their opinions, handled their problems and acknowledged the events in their lives—births, deaths, weddings and honors. None of a succession of Democratic challengers could match Ford's personal touch, and he won every election with at least 60 percent of the vote.

Equally popular with his congressional colleagues and highly skilled in the art of congressional politics, Ford rose through the ranks to become House Minority Leader. The Watergate scandal and Spiro Agnew's resignation moved him into the vice presidency in 1973. Less than a year later, Richard Nixon left office and on August 9, 1974, Gerald R. Ford became president of the United States.

At the time Ford was sworn in as vice president, Joseph Grassie was Grand Rapids' city manager and Lyman Parks was mayor. Parks, the former pastor of the First Community African Methodist Episcopal Church and the city's first black commissioner, had been named acting mayor in May 1971. Elected to a full term in

Never very far from the water: The citizens of Grand Rapids have always had an affinity for the water. The Grand River flows through their lives as much today as it did when their ancestors depended on it for transportation and to float their logs downstream. The Sixth Street Bridge, built in 1886, has been in continuous use ever since (below). In the 1970s, concerned citizens set about cleaning up The Grand River—a task brought to successful completion with the 1975 dedication of a fish ladder for salmon (right). Once again, the Grand River could support a salmon population and fishermen were quick to take the bait (left).

A diversified district: the Ryerson Building (left), the Anchor Bar (right), Central High School (below left), and the Castle (below right) are all part of the variety that makes Grand Rapids an interesting city.

November 1971, Parks prided himself on his "objectivity" and his ability to "soothe the mood of city hall and create a climate which permitted change." During his administration, he later recalled, the city added 23 minority firemen and sixteen minority policemen to the payroll, formulated downtown redevelopment plans and acquired land along the riverfront for a park.

LET THE RIVER LIVE

Grand Rapids had its beginnings on the river, and the river played a major role in the evolution of the city. Long a barrier—geographically, politically, philosophically—between the city's east and west sides, the river's early value as a source of power and as a transportation artery diminished over the years. As early as 1848, contamination was evident, and successive decades of industrial development and uncontrolled sewage and wastewater disposal turned the Grand into a sewer in which little but algae survived.

All along, there were some voices raised in dismay at the river's deterioration. Then, in the 1970s, growing concern over the environment and the establishment of organizations such as the West Michigan Environmental Action Council spurred a change in public policy and ushered in a decade of enormous environmental progress. In a massive cooperative effort, local industries, the government and concerned citizens began the clean-up of the Grand River. Clear water, the annual Coho salmon run and the 1975 dedication of Joseph Kinnebrew's Grand River Sculpture and Fish Ladder testify to its success.

Cultural connections to the past: Abe Drasin (left), a successful businessman, became a high school teacher at the age of 59. In 1971, he entered politics through a vacancy on the Grand Rapids City Commission. Since 1975, he has been the city's mayor and is the second Jewish mayor in Grand Rapids. Native Americans danced at a festival held in Ah-Nab-Awen Park—former site of a Potawatomi Indian village in the early days of Grand Rapids (below). Newcomers have always been a part of the city's history. Infant Richard Van Tran (right), born July 1975, was the first American citizen born in the city's Vietnamese community. His family (from left), Tuyet Mai, Li Ly and Tran Van Dung.

SPOKESMAN FOR THE HISPANICS

Daniel Vargas, a Grand Rapids resident since 1943 and a longtime spokesman for the city's Hispanic community, was the first Hispanic to serve on the Grand Rapids Human Relations Commission (1956-65). A champion of the rights of migrant workers, he was appointed to the Governor's Commission on Migrant Labor in 1964. He spent countless weekends traveling to migrant worker camps in Michigan, volunteering his time to translate contracts for the workers and help them negotiate for housing facilities.

Vargas was one of the founders of Our Lady of Guadeloupe Chapel in Grand Rapids and one of the originators of the annual Hispanic Festival. In recognition of his many services to the city's Hispanic community, Vargas received a special award in 1974, presented to him by then Mayor Lyman Parks.

Three years later, on the west bank of the river, Ah-Nab-Awen Park was completed. Built to commemorate the nation's bicentennial and the city's sesquicentennial anniversaries and to pay tribute to the Indians who originally inhabited the region, the park, too, was a product of citizen action. Working closely with the architects and the city planning department, a broad-based citizens' committee helped create a park design representative of the city's ecology and its history.

Resurgence of ethnic pride accompanied the renaissance of civic pride. Grand Rapids is home to many ethnic groups—from the Dutch, who began emigrating here in significant numbers more than a century ago, to the Hispanics, whose numbers have been steadily increasing since the 1950s. The Hispanic community is the fastest-growing minority group in Grand Rapids, and the success of the Hispanic business community is looked upon as something of a city phenomenon.

Although Grand Rapids did not experience the major riots and demonstrations of the Vietnam era, the war did have a lasting impact on the city's population. Many Vietnamese, who had left their homeland on the so-called Freedom Flights, were welcomed into the city. They have stayed in numbers significant enough to prompt the Grand Rapids Public Schools to extend its bilingual education program to Vietnamese as well as Hispanic students.

City schools also provide special services to the city's

Native American community, estimated at 2,500 to 3,500 in the metropolitan area. In 1970, a Grand Rapids Inter-Tribal Council was organized, and over the decade became an effective force for its constituency. And as the '70s drew to a close, Wag Wheeler, the council's executive director, remarked in an interview, "I don't know of a city this size that has a small ethnic community like the Indian community that can meet with the superintendent of schools, with the mayor, with city commissioners. . . . I know there are people that are going to disagree with me—Grand Rapids has a long way to go, but things are happening here."

CELEBRATION ON THE GRAND

The decade of the '70s saw the city's many scattered visions of urban rebirth coalesce into reality. After years of neglect, the core of Grand Rapids—the downtown—was once again being transformed into the city's heart. Historic buildings, like the Old Riverfront Building, once a telephone office, and 7 Ionia, an old Heartside warehouse, were completely and expensively refurbished. Israels, Forslund's and Rood's demonstrated their faith in downtown by moving closer to its center when many businesses were moving to the suburbs. Other long-established downtown businesses persevered in the face of parking problems and shopper

Paving stones in the form of a Tree of Dates were placed in the patio area of Ah-Nab-Awen Bicentennial Park to represent America's heritage and its future. Funds and sponsorships for each of the dates came from area businesses, churches, organizations, families and individuals. The block dated July 4, 1776, was contributed by the schoolchildren of Grand Rapids (left). Activities on the mall (below) continue to spark the downtown area. Forslund's, a furniture enterprise, moved its showroom closer to downtown at a time when other businesses were moving to the suburbs (bottom left). Today, Forslund's enjoys the rewards of having remained downtown.

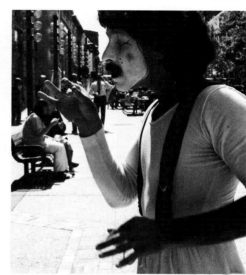

171

Kids and coneys, parks and park benches: Mustard's Last Stand (left); a park bench in Monroe Square (right); Westminster Child Development Center (facing page above); sitting on the dock at Riverside Park (facing page below).

preference for what they saw as the greater convenience of the suburban malls. The downtown believers were pinning their hopes on a changing citizen perception of the importance of downtown and on the success of the Monroe Center mall project.

The idea for a downtown pedestrian mall had surfaced during the 1950s, but it wasn't until 1976 that city officials agreed to proceed. Citizen action—this time in the form of the Downtown Improvement and Development Committee—was once again a key factor in planning the mall and generating support for the $9.4 million project. The new mall formally opened on September 12, 1980, with a ribbon-cutting ceremony at noon, a parade led by Mayor Abe Drasin and three days of festivities collectively titled the Grand Event.

Exactly one month later, the city enjoyed another grand event—a week-long Celebration on the Grand to mark the opening of a new downtown convention center and performing arts auditorium. The celebration was the culmination of years of effort by business, cultural and civic leaders who had refused to let the dream of a downtown cultural center die.

With the first phase of downtown urban renewal under way in the 1960s, tentative plans began to emerge for other development projects. Expansion of the Civic Auditorium figured prominently in assorted recommendations and feasibility studies. The aging facility was causing Grand Rapids to lose valuable convention business. At the same time, the multipurpose auditorium's deficiencies as a concert hall continually frustrated players and audiences alike.

But in 1972, voters rejected a plan to expand the convention facilities and build a music hall.

Discouraged but undeterred, concerned citizens,

GOING ON A SCULPTURE BINGE

Ever since Alexander Calder's La Grande Vitesse was placed on Vandenberg Plaza in 1969, Grand Rapids has been on an outdoor sculpture binge. Pieces by distinguished contemporary artists grace the central business district, the shopping malls and the lawns and courtyards of many public buildings.

Few cities of similar size can boast such extensive sculpture collections. Much of the credit for that goes to the Women's Committee of the Grand Rapids Art Museum. Inspired by the Calder, the committee in 1973 sponsored an outdoor sculpture exhibit which allowed

artists to create works for sites of their own selection in and around Vandenberg Center. Called "Sculpture Off the Pedestal," the exhibit was funded by the National Endowment for the Arts and many local businesses. Its purpose was twofold—to awaken interest in new forms of sculpture and to purchase as many of the works as possible for the city. Two of the works were purchased, and other acquisitions have followed.

Like the Calder, many of the sculptures installed have been highly abstract and have generated spirited controversy over their artistic merits. Such structural works as Nate Horowitz's Vesta, set in an outdoor stairwell leading to City Hall, and Mark di Suvero's Motu, a rubber tire suspended 35 feet from three iron beams just outside the Federal Building, have been the objects of heated debate. But along with other striking examples of the sculptor's craft—Joseph Kinnebrew's Fragmented Pyramid outside the Hall of Justice (left), and his unique bus shelters throughout the city; Ron Watson's Solar Painting: The Terminator, behind the Hall of Justice; Hy Zelkowitz's Lorrie's Button, in Ah-Nab-Awen Bicentennial Park; John Parker's Night Flight, outside the Art Museum; and Clement Meadmore's Split Ring, in Woodland Mall—these works have become city landmarks.

This wealth of public sculpture and its astonishing variety have captured the attention of the art world and have gained national stature for Grand Rapids.

173

The fine arts: The Civic Auditorium was designed by the Grand Rapids firm of Robinson and Campau. The classically oriented sculptured reliefs include allegorical figures representing music and other sides of life (left). Some of the volunteers, who were involved in the creation of Grand Center, pose on the pedestrian bridge over Monroe Avenue (right). Summerfest, launched in 1981, brings Grand Rapids a summertime potpourri of Broadway musicals, concerts and ballet programs (below).

municipal officials and a number of downtown development committees continued actively lobbying for a combined convention-entertainment complex to be added to the Civic Auditorium.

In 1977, five years after voters first rejected the plan, the Grand Center was under way. Funding came from bond issues, city parking fees, county hotel/motel tax revenues, state and federal grants earmarked for the Convention Center and more than $5 million in private donations to build the performing arts auditorium.

Grand Rapids citizens are generous in their support of worthy causes. Gifts to United Way, for example, doubled during the decade of the '70s. But the Performing Arts Center fund drive was something special—"the greatest success of the decade," according to one experienced fund raiser. From the $4.1 million contributed by 82 individuals, corporations and foundations, to the

The Jewish community

Julius Houseman was the city's first Jewish resident. Born in Bavaria in 1832, he first came to America when he was 18, one of many German Jews fleeing the aftereffects of the 1848 revolution. He settled first in Ohio and then went to Battle Creek, where he joined Isaac Amberg in a clothing and tailoring business. At 22, Houseman came to Grand Rapids to open a second store. Three years later, he dissolved his partnership with Amberg and retained the Grand Rapids store.

For twenty years Houseman was a clothing merchant in the city and then went into lumbering. He was not only a successful businessman, but an active member of the community. He served as alderman from 1864 to 1870, was mayor for a two-year term, served in the Michigan state legislature for one term, and then became mayor again. He also was Fifth District representative in the U.S. House of Representatives from 1883 to 1885. Houseman was on the board of directors of many local companies and built or owned considerable commercial property.

Julius Houseman's cousin, Joseph, came to Grand Rapids in 1855 and became a permanent resident in 1857. The two Housemans were partners in the clothing business for many years, offering both ready-made garments and custom tailoring.

Joseph never became active in politics as did his cousin, but nevertheless was a prominent member of

the business community. Like Julius, he served as an officer of or as a member of the board for several companies and helped to found others. He had an affection for the Ottawa Indians living on the west riverbank and often served as conciliator in disputes between whites and Indians.

Though the number of Jewish residents was never large, several more arrived shortly after Julius Houseman. In 1857, the male members of the group organized as the Benevolent and Burial Society. They purchased the southwest corner of Oakhill Cemetery for Jewish burials, and the first interment was a young French Jew who had come to the city as a trader and died of tuberculosis.

By 1872, the Benevolent and Burial Society had enough members to organize a temple, and ten years later built Temple Emanuel at the corner of Ransom and Fountain streets, which the congregation occupied until 1952, when a new temple was built at 1715 East Fulton.

In the 1880s, fifteen Temple Emanuel families left their congregation to form the conservative Ahavas Israel Congregation, which today has its synogogue at 2727 Michigan Street.

In the 1890s, there were about 300 Jewish families in Grand Rapids. Today there are 500. And once again, Grand Rapids has a Jewish mayor, the present Abe Drasin, first elected in 1975.

174

Maintaining a clean and bright city is as important aesthetically as a well-chosen frame is to a painting. Ever-present window washers (right) make sure that Grand Rapids properly reflects its beauty. The McKay Tower reflects in the Mutual Home Building (following page).

$785,000 given by smaller businesses and foundations, to the $113,000 sent in as gifts of a dollar or more by private citizens, DeVos Hall—named for its principal benefactors Richard and Helen DeVos—was a true community undertaking, an outpouring of civic determination and support unequaled in the city's history. And symbolic of the spirit in which the Performing Arts Center was built, its first public event was a Festival of Praise and Thanksgiving, an hour-long ecumenical ceremony to dedicate the hall to the "glory of God and to the use of the community."

LET THERE BE MUSIC

The 2,450-seat DeVos Hall has become home for the city's largest and most prestigious performing arts organizations—the Grand Rapids Symphony Orchestra (GRSO), Opera Grand Rapids and the Grand Rapids Civic Ballet.

The symphony is the oldest institution of the three, dating back to the 1920s. Although the GRSO has had many eminent conductors over the years, it remained a community orchestra until 1974. That year, thanks to a generous grant from the Richard and Helen DeVos Foundation, the symphony hired its first six artists-in-residence and engaged Theo Alcantara as conductor and music director.

With the board's consent, Alcantara took important steps to professionalize the orchestra, to broaden its appeal and to increase its audience. A musical explosion took place—with two annual concert series (the Grand and the Renaissance) and the formation of the DeVos String Quartet, a brass quintet, a woodwind quintet and three string quartets.

Notable, too, for its achievements is the Grand Rapids Symphonic Choir, tucked under the wing of the symphony. The choir performs at least twice each season with the orchestra and occasionally gives concerts on its own.

A salon orchestra was another offshoot of the symphony, as was the Grand Rapids Symphony Chamber Ensemble. By 1981, the GRSO had 35 full-time artists-in-residence as its core of players. In addition, duos, trios and soloists of all kinds carry the message of good music to increasing numbers of Grand Rapids citizens.

In 1980, Russian-born emigré Semyon Bychkov

succeeded Alcantara. Audiences had only to hear him once to know that the GRSO was in highly capable hands.

Opera Grand Rapids, formerly the West Michigan Opera Association, has mustered a large and loyal following since its debut in 1967. As its audience increased, so did the quality of its performances. Originally an amateur organization, the company began using talented young singers from all over the country for the lead roles in lavish productions of Mozart's *The Marriage of Figaro,* Puccini's *La Boheme, Madame Butterfly* and *Tosca,* and Donizetti's *Daughter of the Regiment.*

The opera chorus, made up of many local singers, received a two-year sustaining grant in 1980 from the *Grand Rapids Press.* The opera's alliance with the Grand Rapids Symphony Orchestra guaranteed a polished performance in the pit to match the performance onstage. The move to DeVos Hall—with its superb facilities and unlimited possibilities for scenic designers—has moved the company into first rank.

The Grand Rapids Civic Ballet, organized in 1971, often had to resort to makeshift measures to get its productions on the boards. There was never enough money in the early years to employ an orchestra on a regular basis, and the company performed in the Godwin High School auditorium.

But in the arts renaissance of the '70s, ballet gradually caught on. With grants from the Michigan Council for the Arts and other organizations, the company used guest choreographers to produce new and often original productions and, on occasion, brought in famous guest soloists.

Like its sister organizations—the orchestra and the opera—the Civic Ballet came into its own with the move to DeVos Hall in the 1980–81 season. In December 1981, more than 9,800 fans enjoyed four sell-out performances of Tchaikovsky's *The Nutcracker,* a perennial holiday favorite.

The Civic Ballet presents three ambitious programs each season, and under the leadership of Sally Seven, the company's artistic director from the beginning, it continues to expand both its repertoire and its audience.

The completion of Grand Center was the capstone of a decade of great accomplishment, a decade which had seen the flowering of urban rebirth and a renaissance of the arts. The Celebration on the Grand, which opened Grand Center, struck the opening chords in a continuing celebration of the city whose coda has not been reached.

175

176

Celebration on the Grand

CONCLUSION

A balloon race (left) was one of the many events held during Celebration Week 1981, which culminated in a glorious fireworks display (below).

 "They say you can't go home again...but they are wrong," Gerald Ford told a celebrity-studded audience on a sunny Friday in September 1981 as hometown admirers and well-wishers from around the world gathered to dedicate the Gerald R. Ford Presidential Museum.

The museum, a gleaming triangle of concrete and reflecting glass on the west bank of the Grand River, is a monument to the city's most illustrious son, the 38th president of the United States. But it is also the latest symbol of a new vision the city has of itself.

The museum dedication brought that vision into sharp focus for one brief week as the city turned itself inside out to celebrate three jubilant dedications—the Grand Rapids Art Museum, the Amway Grand Plaza Hotel and the Ford Museum.

The week of the "Celebration on the Grand" was one of great exhilaration and virtually nonstop festivities—parades, appearances by visiting celebrities, balloon races, trout and salmon fishing contests, concerts, luncheons, lectures, a bicycle tour of the city and fireworks.

The hotel was dedicated on Tuesday, September 15, the Art Museum on Wednesday and the Ford Museum on Friday.

There were so many formal dinners and dances that the city's dress shops and department stores were caught with their inventories down, and local dressmakers acquired a raft of instant customers. The local limousine livery had to borrow limos from neighboring cities.

The Ford Museum dedication brought to town such dignitaries as President and Mrs. Ronald Reagan, Canada's Prime Minister Pierre Trudeau, President Lopez Portillo of Mexico, members of Ford's Cabinet and former congressional colleagues.

Bob Hope, popular comedian and Ford's good personal friend, taped an hour-long television special featuring big names from the entertainment world.

Nine hundred newspeople arrived to record the events for print and television.

It was a gala week and it served to proclaim that the Ford Museum is more than just a museum honoring a hometown boy who made good. It is a symbol of what the city expects of its future and what it has accomplished to make those expectations realistic.

The three dedications were the culmination of great striving for several years by local groups, working separately, to build important, influential new elements into the fabric of city life.

As urban renewal became the national fever of the 1960s, an entire section of downtown was demolished and rebuilt with federal funds.

The city's two largest banks and the state, county and city governments all constructed handsome new buildings on what came to be known as Vandenberg

178

On the evening before the Ford Museum dedication, visiting dignitaries attended a gala banquet (left); seated from left, Nancy Reagan, President Ronald Reagan, Gerald and Betty Ford; standing from left, Bob Hope, Foreign Minister Sunao Sonoda of Japan, President José Lopez Portillo of Mexico, Barbara Bush, Vice President George Bush, Canadian Prime Minister Pierre Trudeau, former President Valery Giscard d'Estaing of France and Lady Bird Johnson, widow of former President Lyndon Johnson. President Ronald Reagan and former President Gerald R. Ford in discussion (below).

Plaza, named for Grand Rapids' second most illustrious son, Arthur H. Vandenberg.

The city converted Monroe Avenue, its main street, into a pedestrian mall. Two major motel chains built large motel complexes. Local corporations embarked upon expansion programs at home rather than build new plants in other parts of the country.

A massive fund-raising drive was launched to build a concert hall and update the existing convention center. Amway Corporation bought the old Pantlind Hotel (long past its prime), restored it as a fine traditional hotel and began the construction of a magnificent modern addition that would increase its capacity from 390 rooms to 700.

The private sector, too, responded to the challenge of renewing the city. Whereas before, businesses had moved away from the decaying center city, now they elected to stay, rehabilitating old buildings into stunning, efficient structures housing offices, stores and restaurants.

The New Grand Rapids Committee, made up of business people concerned with the success of the course the city had charted for itself, mounted a successful nationwide effort to promote Grand Rapids as a convention city.

All these projects took money, of course—large amounts of it. And such costly and ambitious plans didn't always have the unreserved endorsement of the entire populace. Nevertheless, it is a measure of the confidence of the city and its citizens that such bold plans succeeded.

CITY IN THE SPOTLIGHT

Taking stock, Grand Rapids finds itself not only Michigan's second city and the commercial hub of the western half of the state, but a city with many attributes.

Although General Motors is the area's largest employer with more than 8,000 workers in four plants, the automotive industry accounts for a small percent of the area's jobs (compared with the rest of state). And the products manufactured in GM's Grand Rapids plant are not subject to the radical style changes which have led to layoffs and plant closings in other parts of the state.

The region has one of the largest concentrations of electroplaters in the country, serving the auto industry with chrome-plated auto parts. Most of the firms, however, are diversified enough to survive cutbacks in the automotive industry.

The city's second largest industry is office furniture systems. Steelcase, Inc., is the world leader in this field and has demonstrated its confidence in its hometown by embarking on a $50 million headquarters building. Several other manufacturers contribute substantially to the area's reputation as an office furniture manufacturing center.

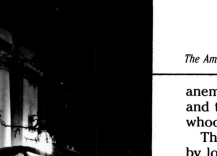

The Amway Grand Plaza Hotel at night.

Amway Corporation, the billion-dollar direct sales company, is one of the top employers and is still growing.

Grand Rapids has played host to small conventions since Civil War days. In renewing the downtown, the city pursued a role as one of the country's best medium-sized convention cities, competing with Milwaukee, Cincinnati, Indianapolis and Columbus. As more conventioneers discover the attractions of Grand Rapids and West Michigan, support services to that industry continue to expand. A host of inviting restaurants, entertainment spots and motels have sprung up, with more on the drawing boards.

The majority (53 percent) of Grand Rapids' work force is engaged in retailing and service jobs. And the city, as a regional center, is attracting business and professional service-related specialists. Law, insurance, banking and accounting firms draw West Michigan clients from the Indiana state line to the straits. The more than 40 advertising agencies and film production companies quartered in the city represent not only West Michigan firms, but national accounts as well.

The medical community is one of the most advanced and respected in the Midwest. Four acute-care hospitals, all teaching institutions, serve the area, as do such specialized medical facilities as the Mary Free Bed Hospital and Rehabilitation Center and the Ferguson Hospital. Grand Rapids physicians pioneered the design and use of artificial joints for arthritis victims, and much of the original research on prosthetic devices was done in the city. Sickle cell anemia was first diagnosed by a Grand Rapids doctor, and the pioneering work on developing an effective whooping cough vaccine took place in Grand Rapids.

The Emergency Medical Services system developed by local physicians and the Grand Rapids Police Department has been hailed as a prototype and studied by municipalities around the country.

With eight colleges in the area, education has become an industry in its own right. The city's cultural life, too, has undergone a renaissance, attracting an ever-increasing audience for the arts. Three resident arts institutions—the symphony, the opera and the ballet—perform regularly at DeVos Hall. Grand Rapids Civic Theatre, which made do for years in a series of makeshift and sometimes decrepit quarters, is now housed in the completely restored Majestic Theatre, which opened as a legitimate theatre in 1903. The current fare is remarkably diverse and sophisticated for a town that only two decades ago was known as a wasteland in which artists of all persuasions foundered and languished for want of appreciation.

The Grand Rapids Public Museum has outgrown its present quarters and is proposing to build a new facility next door to the Ford Museum. Such a museum complex will enhance the education and entertainment capacities of each. Grand Valley State Colleges is considering building a downtown campus in the same vicinity.

John Ball Zoo, always one of the city's favorite recreation spots, has embarked on a long-range expansion plan that will make it one of the most modern zoos in the country.

A little more than 150 years ago, Louis Campau first stood on the banks of the Grand River and envisioned a settlement. That settlement has evolved from a tiny trader's outpost to a metropolitan area of 500,000.

In recent years, renewal has brought new promise. With the same optimism and determination that moved the early settlers to carve a home out of the wilderness, Grand Rapids has chosen to overcome the ills of an aging city.

Renewal has brought new promise. Grand Rapids' citizens—young and old, official and ordinary—see their hometown not as a hopelessly middlebrow, slightly dowdy member of a chorus line of Midwestern cities, but as a sprightly star stepping forward with verve and confidence to claim a place in the spotlight.

Partners in Grand Rapids' Progress

The corporate community has made dynamic contributions to the growth, development and quality of life in Grand Rapids. The city's leading businesses have lent their support and financial commitment to the publishing of *Grand Rapids: Renaissance on the Grand*. Their corporate histories follow.

181

Fostering the economic vitality of Grand Rapids

In 1887, Grand Rapids was entering its heyday as a furniture manufacturing center. At the same time, the lumbering industry, which for 40 years or more had been the economic mainstay of the area, was declining. The region's forests had been depleted and the logging and sawmill industries had moved to the rich timberlands of the north.

Because Grand Rapids was not a rail center, the railroads charged higher rail rates for transporting goods in and out of the city, and the rates were hurting the city's manufacturers.

Businessmen, fearing that the combination of the disappearing lumber industry and discriminatory freight rates would spell doom for the city's economy, formed the Board of Trade to protect the interests of the business community.

Lowering the freight rates was a three-year battle, but in the end, the Board of Trade was successful, saving hundreds of thousands of dollars for the furniture manufacturers.

One of the very first projects of the new Board of Trade was the compilation of a booklet extolling the commercial and social attributes of the city—the beginning of the organization's continuing efforts over nearly a century to bring new industry to the area.

The board took an early lead in promoting the city as a convention center, and by 1898 had a convention committee charged with soliciting "organized state bodies to hold conventions in this city, offering free rent of hall, prizes for competitive drills, competitive art exhibitions, etc." The board's ways and means committee supported the project by raising funds to pay for the halls, the prizes and the etcetera.

In 1911, the board changed its name to the Association of Commerce, and a year later the association became a member of the newly founded United States Chamber of Commerce. Over the years, a series of name changes occurred—Chamber of Commerce in 1942, Greater Grand Rapids Chamber of Commerce in 1958, and the present name, Grand Rapids Area Chamber of Commerce in 1975.

The organization concerned itself with the vital issues of each age, and has often been in the forefront in promoting such progressive doctrines as clean water legislation (1904) and conservation and reforestation (1905).

Renumbering city streets on the block system, establishing an airport, formation of the Grand Rapids Foundation in 1922 to give financial aid and support to various civic organizations and endeavors, and establishing United Community Services (today's United Way) are just a few of the countless community service programs which first sprouted seed in a Chamber committee.

Economic development is the focus of Chamber activities, and several permanent Chamber committees work on such diverse issues as making local manufacturers aware of export trade opportunities, increasing participation by local area governments in regional economic development issues, developing a metro energy conservation program and seeking improved ground and air transport systems for the area.

More than 90 percent of the Chamber's members are businesses employing fewer than 50 persons. In 1980, the Chamber saw a need to emphasize services directed toward the concerns of small businesses and established the Small Business Council.

Over the last two decades, the Chamber has played a leading role in the renewal and revitalization of Grand Rapids' downtown. The Chamber coordinated the 1981 campaign by city businessmen and government officials to capture the All America City designation awarded by the National Municipal League—the third time Grand Rapids has won the title.

Grand Rapids is regarded as one of the 25 fastest growing areas in the United States. The city's growth and prosperity can be traced to the concern and determination of its citizens to keep their city a pleasant and satisfying place in which to live.

The Grand Rapids Area Chamber of Commerce is proud to be a part of that tradition. For nearly 100 years, Grand Rapids business has been Chamber business, and Chamber members have volunteered their time and energy to making their community "A good place to live, work and do business."

182

In 1976, the Chamber of Commerce moved into its present quarters at 17 Fountain NW.

More than 100 years of service to customer needs

American Laundry & Cleaners, Inc. was founded April 4, 1881, by Adrian Otte, a French emigrant from the Netherlands. In the 1880s, stiff collars and cuffs were the fashion, but Grand Rapids had no laundry that could clean them and neither did most other American cities. Local laundries sent the detachable cuffs and collars to Troy, New York, where they were cleaned and returned.

Otte, then 23, was working for a cigar maker but decided to start a laundry. Having no funds, he persuaded a friendly hardware merchant to trust him for the purchase of a stove and copper boiler. Later he is quoted as saying, "I lost $16 the first week, but from then on it was all up-hill. There were four of us, three employees and myself. We picked up washings ourself on a bicycle. We did the work the old-fashioned way, by women rubbing the clothes on washboards. We hadn't a bit of machinery until 1884." Asked how the name American was derived he stated, "We had to have a name and America had been good to me, so I thought that was as good a name as any."

Otte's brother John joined him in 1887 and continued a member of the firm until his death in 1911. Today it is owned by his grandson, John P. Otte Jr., the second president of the century-old company.

The founder was a man of vision and considered a "radical" in the infant industry. In 1900, he designed and installed the first air conditioning system in the country for the benefit of his workers. Employee accident insurance, group life insurance, vacations with pay, coffee breaks and other benefits were provided long before such labor-management relations were to become standard.

In the days when Grand Rapids was known as the Furniture Capital of the World salesmen for furniture companies traveled for weeks at a time and encountered difficulty obtaining laundry service when out of town. American Laundry inaugurated a plan whereby any salesman could mail his soiled laundry to Grand Rapids, advise where he would be the next week, and his clean clothes would be waiting for him upon arrival. Typically many of these customers would meet salesmen from other cities who learned to take advantage of the "parcel post" laundry. As a consequence the company developed customers all over the United States who had never been in Michigan.

At the same time, the company developed a system of agencies throughout the state. At one time there were over 200 of them who sent and received laundry work by rail in wicker hampers. The furthest of these agents was 300 miles north.

It was not until 1915 that the company entered the dry-cleaning business, an industry then in its infancy. Today dry cleaning accounts for half of the business. With the advent of the home washing machine much of the commercial laundry business suffered, a trend accented by the wash-and-wear fabrics. Consequently American diversified its operations to include commercial laundering for hotels and hospitals as well as the shirt and uniform rental fields.

Through acquisition of other firms in recent years American Laundry & Cleaners is presently the largest of its kind in Michigan. Acquisitions included Paris Cleaners in Kalamazoo, Michigan; Suburban Cleaners; and Cole Laundry & Cleaners, among others in Grand Rapids. There are at this time fourteen routes and ten drive-in stores serving Battle Creek, Kalamazoo and areas within 30 miles of Grand Rapids.

John P. Otte Jr., the current president, notes that he has a small 3″ by 5″ notebook in which his grandfather kept all the corporate records and payroll statistics for 200 employees back in the early 1900s. Today, two large computers and mountains of computer records are required to operate the business. Otte notes, "we can't live with the computers, but we couldn't do today's business without them."

In 1881, the staff of American Laundry posed in front of the newly established business. Washerwomen soaked the clothes in tubs of hot, soapy water, then bent over to scrub them by hand on various kinds of corrugated washboards.

"The longest-running ground floor opportunity in town"

Amway Corporation came into being in 1959 with a single product, a unique marketing concept and the persistent dream of two men, Jay Van Andel and Rich DeVos, from Grand Rapids, Michigan. Today, Amway Corporation is one of the largest direct selling companies in the world. The story of that dramatic growth is the history of Amway.

DeVos and Van Andel, friends and business partners since their high school days, had, by 1959, been operating a successful food supplement distributorship for ten years. But they dreamed of something better—a business opportunity open to *anyone* who wanted to work hard enough to achieve success. They believed that people everywhere, from every background and walk of life, should have the chance to achieve financial security and personal freedom through a business of their own.

That belief found expression in the unique Amway Sales and Marketing Plan the two men created. Based on repeat sales of exclusive products and an incentive system designed to reward the distributor in direct relation to the amount of time and effort expended, the plan offers a comprehensive business opportunity for independent-minded entrepreneurs.

The initial product was a liquid all-purpose cleaner called Liquid Organic Concentrate (L.O.C.). It was an immediate success and set the pattern for many Amway products. The original item, the unique marketing concept and the dream

of the two men merged into an idea whose time was definitely at hand. In November 1959, Amway was incorporated. Van Andel's basement served as the office, and the warehouse was in the DeVos' basement next door.

Distributors were so responsive to both product and concept, however, that the business soon outgrew the available space. In 1960, Amway took over a former gas station and garage in Ada, Michigan. Expansion at the site began almost immediately, and the local contractor called in to perform the work has yet to leave the Amway complex.

Growth was rapid, but it had to be to keep up with the demands of the ever-expanding distributor organization. By 1960, the original distributor group—centered primarily in the Midwest—had spread across the country. Then, in 1962, Amway opened for business in Canada, and other countries soon followed. There are now a million Amway distributorships worldwide.

Today, Amway offers more than 350 products bearing the Amway name, plus more than 2,000 additional brand-name items through its Personal Shoppers Service. Most of the products that bear the Amway name are manufactured in its own plant at Ada or in the plants of Nutrilite Products, Inc., in California.

Amway's office, warehouse and manufacturing facilities continue to expand on the original 300-acre site in Ada. A $10 million Research and Development Building, with

24 separate research laboratories, is evidence of Amway's commitment to product innovation.

Amway also owns the Mutual Broadcasting System (the world's largest radio network), the Amway Grand Plaza Hotel and a Caribbean resort and seminar center on Peter Island, as well as other corporate properties and holdings.

Amway's sales figures reflect its rapid growth. In its first year of business, retail volume was $500,000. In fiscal 1981, consolidated revenues of Amway Corporation and its affiliates and subsidiaries were in excess of $1 billion, and estimated retail sales were in excess of $1.4 billion.

Clearly, much has changed in the world of Amway. But perhaps more important are the things that haven't changed. The "100% Amway Satisfaction Guarantee" still stands behind every Amway product. The Amway Sales and Marketing Plan is essentially the same, too. There have been a few improvements over the years, but the central idea remains the same—success is there for anyone who will work hard enough to achieve it.

Most important of all, DeVos and Van Andel—whose shared dream made it all possible—are still making it all possible. As chairman of the board and president of Amway respectively, they still actively guide the fortunes of the corporation and remain dedicated to providing an opportunity for self-improvement to millions of people the world over.

Amway Corporation headquarters in Ada, Michigan.

184

An age of excellence returns to Grand Rapids

The Amway Grand Plaza Hotel, Grand Rapids, Michigan.

Since 1865, a hotel has stood on the corner of Pearl and Monroe streets. The metamorphosis from Sweet's Hotel, a small wood and brick building with a handful of employees, to the present Amway Grand Plaza Hotel, one of the finest hotels in America, is marked by faith in Grand Rapids and service to the public.

In 1902, J. Boyd Pantlind bought Sweet's Hotel and enlarged it with several additions of his own. But the rising popularity of the furniture expositions prompted him to build an eleven-story hotel with 550 rooms. The new Pantlind cost a total of $2 million and covered an entire city block when it opened on January 1, 1916.

The Amway Hotel Corporation, a subsidiary of Amway Corporation, purchased the Pantlind and hired two Grand Rapids firms to effect the change. DeWinter Associates directed the project, and Dan Vos Construction Company reconstructed the city's landmark hotel at a cost of $24 million. The reconstruction is the first stage of a two-phase project that will cost over $60 million.

The second phase, presently under construction, is a 300-room, ultramodern 29-story tower to open in the fall of 1983. An eight-channel simultaneous translation service is planned for the tower along with an 8,800 square foot ballroom, four meeting rooms, a swimming pool, a gourmet restaurant, riverside restaurant and 5,200 square feet of shops in the motor lobby.

The first touch of elegance guests notice in the restored hotel is the antique sunburst sculpture from a Venetian palace, the many crystal chandeliers and more than 7,000 square feet of gold leaf that has been applied to the ceilings in the mezzanine, lobby and ballroom.

All the old world charm and graciousness of that bygone era have been recreated in accurate detail at the Amway Grand Plaza Hotel. Continental service—including a concierge and 24-hour room service—is provided. Every guest room is furnished with period-style headboards, coffee tables, armoires, dressers and chairs. The casegoods, in keeping with Grand Rapids tradition, were custom designed and locally manufactured.

Restaurants within the Amway Grand Plaza Hotel are many and varied. Tootsie Van Kelly's is an old-time saloon with a raised balcony and performance area. Tootsie herself is the featured singer and focal point of this informal meeting spot.

The 1913 Room is formal, with elegant Continental dining and velvet accents. The Lumber Baron Bar (named in honor of Grand Rapids' history) has a club-like atmosphere, taking its interior theme for the quiet, after-hours men's clubs of the early 1900s.

The Monroe Cafe is a light and airy res-

taurant with a menu as refreshing as the atmosphere. The Rendezvous Lounge, adjacent to the Lumber Baron Bar, is a lobby bar with a people-watching atmosphere, as is the Inner Circle Bar, a second lobby bar featuring a variety of cappuccino drinks.

The quality of the service, and the food, is of primary importance, providing service for a large banquet with the same attention given to a dinner for two.

The Amway Grand Plaza Hotel has hired over 690 (450 full-time) employees, annually pumping about $6.5 million into the local economy through payroll alone.

Since Amway announced its intention to open a superior downtown hotel, business in the central city has skyrocketed. Not only has an age of excellence returned to a luxury hotel, but to the entire downtown area as well.

"The Amway Grand Plaza Hotel is helping to turn Grand Rapids around," says Amway co-founder Jay Van Andel. His partner Rich DeVos adds, "Grand Rapids and the Amway Grand Plaza Hotel are going on record as serious contenders for major Midwestern conventions."

The Amway Grand Plaza and the adjoining city-owned Grand Center are aggressively vying for convention business previously funneled to Detroit and Chicago. With a combined 37 meeting rooms, 119,000 square feet of exhibit space, plus a kitchen capable of catering to 10,000, the Grand Plaza and Grand Center are indeed competitive.

More than a hotel "where excellence is served," the Amway Grand Plaza is a tangible example of the city's renaissance as well as a focal point of community pride.

185

At work for nearly a century

Americans spend more than one-third of their lives sitting—at school, at recreational events and in the workplace. Is it any wonder, then, that the American Seating Company has, for almost a century, provided seating responses to each generation's needs?

Founded in 1886 with 50 employees, as the Grand Rapids School Furniture Company, the firm (which today employs more than 1,500 people) produced the "combination" desk which provided a desk top and bookbox for one pupil with the seat and back for the pupil ahead. This revolutionary unit was an immediate success, and two years later the company had grown to 350 employees.

In 1887, the company expanded into the first of many diversified markets with the first noiseless, automatic, self-folding seat for opera houses, halls and other meeting rooms. As early as 1893, the School Furniture Company produced tilt-back opera seats and wood-slat folding chairs. With the introduction of baseball, the grandstand became a standard product, with early stadium installations in Boston, Baltimore, Pittsburgh, Cleveland and Cincinnati.

Thirteen years after its founding, the company became the American School Furniture Company, uniting eighteen of the largest public seating firms in the country. The firm was incorporated by the 1920s under the name American Seating Company, reflecting its diverse markets.

During those busy days, orders for theatre and recreation seats became as common as those for school furniture, and the company began to take on the diversified image it enjoys today.

Prior to the Depression the company began a public education program to build awareness of the need for good seating posture. That forward-thinking position has continued into the present with the introduction of BioChair, ergonomically designed seating for the office, and Centrum-3, a luxurious auditorium chair with an articulated-back design.

World War II saw the company's business operation shift to defense production. When the war ended, the demand for school and recreation seating found American Seating strongly functioning in these markets again.

At the same time, American Seating began to develop what is today the premier line of seating for the bus and light rail markets. New materials and manufacturing techniques were rapidly changing the face of American Seating.

In the 1980s, American Seating continues to grow and diversify. In the traditional markets of school and recreational seating, the firm's reputation is unequalled for innovation and product quality. Virtually every major civic center, performing arts facility and stadium in the United States and many international locations feature products from American Seating.

Universal Bleacher in Champaign, Illinois, produces the most advanced automatic recreation seating in the world, with platforms capable of retracting in seconds to allow multiple usage of indoor stadiums and ice rinks as exhibit halls—a definite advantage in economic times when

municipalities must maximize facility utilization.

The Centrum-3 auditorium chair line represents a contemporary solution for luxury mass seating. An ideal choice for corporate auditoriums or meeting facilities, as well as some public spaces, Centrum-3 features sophisticated design, fabric and finish options, and unique comfort features which reflect American Seating's century of public seating skills.

In the transportation seating market, the firm is again at the forefront. Highly effective manufacturing and productivity combine with the finest in engineering and product innovation to continue the forward-thinking tradition. Many design and manufacturing "firsts" for this operating division assures that the company's transportation seating remains the specified favorite.

American Seating's foundry—a highly automated facility—produces foundry products for its own operating divisions and markets wood-burning stoves.

The emerging office products industry—systems and contract furniture—continues to establish American Seating as the most diversified furniture and seating manufacturer in Grand Rapids.

Today, American Seating, after almost a century, remains committed to quality, integrity and product innovation, and is dedicated to fulfilling each generation's needs with new and improved seating and furniture for changing and expanding markets.

The BioChair (left), designed by Hugh Acton and introduced by American Seating in June of 1980, represented the company's most recent ergonomic seating product. The Centrum 3 Chair from Office Systems (below) is designed to integrate with the information management environment.

A wrecking ball knocked at the door and opportunity answered

In 1857, John Bertsch and Isaac Cappon built a tannery in Holland, Michigan, with John's $450 and Isaac's 85 acres on Black Lake. Because the Civil War created an urgent demand for leather, the tannery was expanded and a shoe factory added. In 1909, the partners sold their company to Armour and Co. of Chicago.

John bought the Studley and Barclay Co., a mill supply business, on Campau Square in 1906. He was joined by his son, C. Harley, and his son-in-law, Arthur Ayers. John, with George Metz, also built a large tannery in North Park where they constructed 75 houses in the village for employees and their families. John had now become a successful industrialist and active civic leader. He believed in the future of Grand Rapids as a thriving business and industrial community.

He was planning a new building for his mill supply company which was to be named Barclay, Ayers and Bertsch Company. About this time, the San Francisco earthquake occurred and John specified that the new five-story building on Bond Avenue should be constructed of reinforced concrete able to withstand earthquakes and other natural disasters.

C. Harley Bertsch served as president of Barclay, Ayers and Bertsch during the years when every dimension of the industrial world was witnessing extraordinary changes. The industrial supply business responded to the accelerating needs of its customers and leather harnesses, leather water buckets and blacksmith tongues and anvils were replaced with pipe, valves and fittings. Having the right supplies at the right time with the right prices meant being in a business that not only reflected current needs but anticipated the new developments.

In 1953, C. Harley's son John W. Bertsch and his wife, Margaret, purchased Arthur Ayer's interest when he retired. John became president and brought exuberance and a refreshing approach to sales and management. Inventories were expanded in pace with increasing sales and changes in engineering technology. He made the first major renovation in 50 years at Barclay, Ayers, and Bertsch Company by modernizing the office and its equipment. The week it was completed the City Commission approved funds for a dramatic urban renewal plan beginning on Bond Avenue. All the buildings were to be demolished. What earthquakes had not accomplished, the wrecking ball did and the virtually impregnable building fell.

The wrecking ball gave the company an opportunity to take a giant step forward. A handsome building, designed to serve with maximum efficiency, was built at 1655 Steele Avenue SW. At this time, Barclay, Ayers and Bertsch Company, which had

321 Bond being torn down in 1965 to make way for City Hall (above). Owners and office staff in original office of Barclay, Ayers and Bertsch Co. around 1916 (below). Standing left to right: Ayers, C. Harley Bertsch and John Bertsch. Seated left to right: unknown, unknown and Miss Pearl Cooper at the typewriter.

developed a tradition of service and trust, became one of the best known industrial supply houses in Michigan. John W. Bertsch and his wife, Margaret, became sole owners of the company.

In 1966, John R. Bertsch, a graduate of Duke University with a degree in engineering and business administration, joined his father in the company.

The space program had produced highly technical engineering concepts which were adapted in manufacturing in many fields and influenced the improvement of many items used in industry. John R. had the training he would need for the greatly sophisticated products now bursting into the market.

In 1975, the company built a branch in Marquette and celebrated its 100th anniversary. Recently, another branch opened in Midland, and a major addition and railroad spur have been added to the Barclay, Ayers and Bertsch Steele Avenue plant in order to keep in step with customers' requirements. There also has been a steady stream of service improvements with automation, product specialization and the

necessary expertise of personnel in engineering techniques.

Barclay, Ayers and Bertsch still retains the friendliness of a family store. Over 26,000 items are included in its computer-controlled inventory. They range from the basics—such as hose—to highly automated control and instrumentation valves, pumps, and a complete range of pipe and fittings including mild carbon steel through the highest grade alloys.

In 1980, John R. Bertsch became president, and under his vigorous leadership, the company is continuing to grow. The courage, intelligence and vision shown by his great-grandfather have come full cycle into the fourth generation.

A key factor to company success is the people who work there. Mutual respect, recognition of responsibility and competence have resulted in long-term service records for a majority of employees.

"An institution is the lengthened shadow of one man," Emerson wrote in "Self Reliance." Barclay, Ayers and Bertsch Company has an ever-growing profile of service and integrity through four generations.

187

Invention, innovation and acquisition paced Bissell growth worldwide

Anna and Melville R. Bissell.

It all began in a small Grand Rapids crockery shop in 1876. Today, Bissell operations span the entire free world with manufacturing and distribution centers in Canada, France, Switzerland, England, Ireland, Australia and six U.S. locations.

As in its beginning, new product development and marketing maintain the company's leadership in the housewares and home-care field. Continued diversification into new companies and new fields lead and pace Bissell's growth and assure corporate economic stability in changing times.

According to company president, John M. Bissell, sales in the recessionary year of 1981 were the highest in its history. Again new product development led the way. After many months of design and product testing, Bissell introduced the first faucet-connected "steam-type" carpet cleaning machine available to consumers on an ownership rather than rental basis. Called the "Bissell Carpet Machine...It's Magic," it is now one of the top selling products in the housewares field.

Early in 1982, the company returned to its roots with the introduction of the Bissell Double Action carpet and floor sweeper. As in Bissell's first sweeper, patented June 6, 1876, the new Double Action Sweeper improved upon the gearing design of all other sweepers to produce a sweeper that outperforms any other sweeper in the world.

Anna and Melville Bissell owned a small crockery shop in Grand Rapids in the 1870s. Shipments of their merchandise arrived packed in sawdust, and sweeping up the sawdust was a major problem. Anna complained. Even a newfangled item called a carpet sweeper couldn't handle the job.

Just like any other dutiful husband of 1876, Melville Bissell promised to do something about it. But unlike many other dutiful husbands, he had the mechanical skill to accomplish the task.

In those days the shippers of china and glassware weren't about to change from sawdust packaging to suit the Bissells, so Melville invented a better carpet sweeper. It worked. It picked up sawdust with ease and anything else sweepable that happened to have fallen on the carpet or the wooden floor.

Like many inventors, the Bissells at first didn't realize what they had. But first one crockery shop customer, then another, and then another, asked Anna where she had obtained the carpet sweeper she was using since it looked as though it performed with excellence.

So the Bissells put together a small work force to assemble the Bissell Carpet Sweeper in the loft over the crockery shop, then got on the train with samples. They visited many major cities and some smaller ones, calling on hardware and other retailers to try to persuade them to stock and sell the new device.

The price was $1.50 per sweeper, and Anna proved to be an accomplished salesperson. Her first day in Philadelphia, for example, she outsold her husband in orders. They made an excellent team. He the inventor, the mechanical and production expert—she the marketing and sales person, friendly, personable and persuasive.

By 1883, the Bissell's and their combined talents had seen their fledgling company grow to the point where a new factory was needed to keep pace with all the orders. The crockery shop was cast aside in favor of the new and exciting venture.

In March 1889, Melville Bissell died of pneumonia at age 45. Anna assumed the responsibilities of chief executive officer, established new guidelines on trademarks and patents and moved the Bissell Carpet Sweeper to the international markets.

Anna Bissell ran the Bissell Company until the 1920s. Women the world over Bisselled their carpets and floors free of dust and lint, of dog hair and breadcrumbs, and the company's growth continued. Even Queen Victoria endorsed the Bissell machine for use in her homes. Anna Bissell died in 1934 at the age of 88.

Today Bissell employs more than 1,200 persons worldwide and manufactures and sells more than 600 different products. The various factories manufacture Bissell carpet sweepers, vacuum cleaners, carpet and floor cleaning machines for home, business and industry as well as manufacturing cleaning powders and liquids for floors, carpets, upholstery and bathrooms. The products are also sold under the names of leading retail store chains and direct selling and mail order companies.

In addition, Bissell manufactures bath mats and safety treads in Grand Rapids. These products are from Bissell's Slip-X Division.

Bissell's Venturi Division manufactures and sells the famous TarGard cigarette filter and other products related to smoker health as well as a new disposable gel-filled toothbrush for travelers.

Their Atlantic Precision subsidiary in a separate Grand Rapids manufacturing facility produces warming trays for the housewares field.

The Penn Champ Division of Bissell in Butler, Pennsylvania, manufactures and sells a multitude of liquid and solid products for sale under the labels of major U.S. mass merchandisers.

Bissell's Frostline Division manufactures snow shovels for the hardware and mass merchandiser trade.

The Bissell Graphics Division prints and sells business forms, industrial tags, labels and computer paper. This division comprises three separate subsidiaries—

John M. Bissell, grandson of Melville and Anna Bissell, founders of Bissell Inc. (left). Bissell's current headquarters office and plant (above). The crockery shop (below) where Melville and Anna Bissell put together their first carpet sweeper.

Michigan Tag Co. and Imperial Business Forms, Inc. in Grand Rapids, and Atlas Tag and Label, Inc. in Neenah, Wisconsin.

The company remains privately held. John M. Bissell is the grandson of Melville and Anna Bissell. Unlike his grandmother, John Bissell has an MBA from Cornell University. He was first corporate controller and then vice president of marketing before being elected president in 1971.

"The foundation of the company—the carpet sweeper—remains as the base that will keep Bissell solid and growing," he says. "It is a new kind of market these days, with more and more families in the position of both husband and wife having careers and bringing home paychecks." And that's just fine with Bissell Inc.

"The ease and convenience of the Bissell Carpet Sweeper are ideal for the busy family of today," notes Bissell. "Family time together is precious. With both spouses having careers outside the home, maintaining carpets and caring for general floor upkeep is a job that should be made quick and easy."

Bissell Inc. thinks it is well positioned to serve the new marketplace. And although Bissell doesn't stress the point, the hand powered carpet sweeper is even easy enough for a man to use—whether it's his family job or because his wife is out of town at a business meeting. Anna Bissell would have liked that.

189

"We mean business" heritage began back in 1866

Just a few months after Lee surrendered to Grant, thereby ending the Civil War in 1866, a young man named Conrad Swensberg decided to open a bookkeeping, penmanship and arithmetic school in Grand Rapids.

Sixteen students entered that first classroom and were instructed by Swensberg. During the next 25 years, the venture prospered and Grand Rapids Business College became one of the best-known business colleges in the state.

Certainly, Swensberg had no idea that his vision of a business education school would develop during the next century into the largest private two-year college in Michigan, serving more than 4,000 students.

In 1891, Swensberg's business college came under the direction of Parrish and Klingensmith, men whose high ideals and excellent teaching abilities were not enough to compensate for their lack of management skills.

By 1892, Swensberg's college was declining, and a man named McLachlan started a business university that was to surpass the original college by the turn of the century. Then in 1910, a 25-year-old teacher named M.E. Davenport assumed responsibility for the struggling Swensberg school, and by 1924, had developed it into an institution with an enrollment matching that of McLachlan Business University.

Davenport acquired the McLachlan school that year and the two merged to become Davenport-McLachlan Institute, a solid organization whose effectiveness and credibility through the next quarter of a century and beyond would be measured by the success of its graduates.

Davenport was a pioneer in the field of education and believed strongly that cultural values and experiences designed to prepare students to "make a life" depended first upon their ability to "make a living." The Davenport philosophy of education was one of practical training in preparation for something in particular.

To implement this new educational concept, Davenport established the Grand Rapids College of Applied Science in 1936, and he hired Dr. Paul Voelker, former Olivet College president, to run it. That same year, the school was granted a charter as a non-profit, degree-granting institution of business.

Growing rapidly with its emphasis on specific training which fits students for employment upon graduation, the college acquired the 67-acre Edward Lowe estate in 1939 and was renamed The University of Grand Rapids. By the outbreak of World War II in 1941, it counted 407 students.

In addition to carving a new academic path, the university achieved national recognition on the athletic fields as well. George "Potsy" Clark, former coach of the world champion Detroit Lions, directed the football team, and his leading assistant was a young All-American center from the University of Michigan named Gerald Ford.

In 1945, after the Lowe estate was sold to Aquinas College, Robert W. Sneden joined the Davenport Institute staff as an admissions counselor. He was promoted to executive vice president in 1952 and assumed the presidency upon the death of Davenport in 1959.

The development of the college during the 18-year Sneden presidency was filled with milestones, from the changing of its name to Davenport College of Business in 1964 to the new campus at the top of Fulton Street hill in 1968.

At Founder's Day ceremonies marking 100 years of business education for Davenport College in 1966, Minority Leader of the House of Representatives, Gerald R. Ford, spoke of the many contributions made by the institution during the preceding century. Over the years, Davenport College evolved from a proprietary organization to a nonprofit, two-year institution governed by a public board of trustees. And in 1976, it received accreditation from the North Central Association of Colleges and Schools.

Then in August of 1977, Donald W. Maine was named president. Subsequently the Center for the Study of Emergency Medical Services and branch campuses in Lansing and Kalamazoo were acquired. Continuing Education centers were established in several western and central Michigan communities, and Davenport College made arrangements to host a baccalaureate program through Detroit College of Business. Now the sixteenth oldest independent business school in the country and currently serving more than 4,000 students, Davenport College continues to "mean business."

It all started when young Swensberg wrote the first chapter at the close of the Civil War in 1866. It's quite a heritage.

Davenport College's Warren Hall (right) was once the home of lumber-baron Thomas Stewart White and family. The English Tudor mansion was completed in 1908 at a cost of $250,000. The special occasion reception room, formerly the living room, honors founder and former President M.E. Davenport. Davenport College measured the effectiveness of its typing and transcription classes (above) by the business career success of its graduates.

Experience and variety enhance quality design reputation

A Romanesque, red-brick church on Grand Rapids' southeast side, completed in 1911, still stands today, a brick-and-mortar tribute to the father and son, Johannes and George Daverman, who designed it for this "city of churches." The twin-towered sanctuary of First Christian Reformed Church, the "trunk church" of its denomination, is but one of several houses of worship displaying the Daverman touch.

Dwellings, schools and churches were the roots of Daverman Associates, founded in Grand Rapids as J. and G. Daverman Co. in 1904. It is one of the oldest ongoing architectural firms in Michigan.

Churches and dwellings no longer are at the top of the Daverman priority list. The firm has expanded considerably and now does a wide variety of architectural, engineering and planning work for shopping centers, retail stores, factories, warehouses, office buildings, correctional facilities, hospitals, senior citizens complexes, public buildings, airports and educational institutions.

Examples of most may be found in Greater Grand Rapids. That fact prompted a reporter to write: "No matter where you live in the Grand Rapids area, you are probably in sight of, or at least within walking distance of, a structure designed by Daverman Associates."

In no way has the firm limited itself to just Grand Rapids. Its work may be found in many other cities in Michigan, in several states and in faraway places like Saudi Arabia, Nigeria and Jamaica, places the father and son team which formed J. and G. Daverman never would have dreamed designing for.

But the firm's present quarters in the Furniture Company Building are a far cry from the one-room office the two original partners shared in the old Porter Block Building in the core city back in 1904, the building that was home to the business for more than 35 years.

Another move to larger quarters came in 1952, not too many years after George's sons, Herbert and Joseph, both architects, and his nephews, Robert and Edward, both engineers, joined the firm. The new home was on Grandville Avenue on the city's southwest side, with several suites of offices and work areas for more than 75 employees.

By that time a much larger staff was needed. J. and G. Daverman had acquired new assignments nationwide. Engineering was becoming an integral part of the design process and formed part of a comprehensive service offered to new clients.

In the early 1960s, Grand Rapids, like many other cities, began urban renewal projects in and about the core city. Daverman Associates, its new name as the company grew, played a vital role designing

Skylighted atrium of the Furniture Company Building.

buildings for other companies and also new offices for themselves at the corner of Monroe Avenue and Lyon Street. The building bears the name of a major tenant, Michigan Consolidated Gas Company. Other Daverman projects in the Vandenberg Center renewal include Old Kent Bank & Trust Co., the United States Post Office, the Grand Rapids Press, the State Office Building, Calder Plaza Building and the Convention/Entertainment Center.

Fifteen years later, Daverman Associates again moved to larger quarters, the Furniture Company at Ionia Avenue and Fountain Street, once the home of a major Michigan furniture store.

The Daverman creativity and expertise was put to great use in remodeling the multi-level structure and joining the two "arms" of the U-shaped structure to form a skylighted atrium, a showspot in the renovated Monroe Center, Grand Rapids' central business district.

Its new home is just a block from where Johannes and George founded the business.

Today, Daverman is a member of Systems Planning Corp. of California, a national family of professional service companies engaged in architecture, engineering, planning and construction management.

The Grand Rapids-based Daverman Associates has its own branch offices in Petoskey as well as in the states of Texas, New York, California and Florida. It has 175 employees and its annual volume of business tops $7 million. Veteran employee Jay Volkers is now president of Daverman Associates.

To see just what a variety of projects this firm has produced in Grand Rapids since the days it designed First Christian Reformed Church in 1911, take a look at Kent County International Airport, Kent County Juvenile Center, Steelcase, Inc., Kent Skills Centers, Davenport College, Raybrook Manor, Grand Rapids Water Filtration Plant, Creston High School, Woodland Mall and Pine Rest Christian Hospital.

Those, just for starters. The list is long.

191

Architects concerned with designing happy people places

In 1962, after a brief period teaching architecture at the University of Michigan and working in a number of architectural offices, Marvin DeWinter returned to his hometown to start his own architectural practice. His objective was not to be the biggest or to design the flashiest buildings but rather to design and create buildings and environments that were happy people places. Whether it was a home or a place of work, he wanted to create places of beauty that people could enjoy and that would stand the test of time.

DeWinter Associates was originally established as a sole proprietership and remained relatively small, building a reputation over the years for designing buildings that had a distinctive quality and that would still look contemporary and function well decades after they were built.

In 1977, Marvin DeWinter was selected to design the Gerald R. Ford Presidential Museum to be located on the west riverbank in downtown Grand Rapids. This project, and soon afterward, a much larger project, the design of the Amway Grand Plaza Hotel—immediately across the river from the museum—has had a dramatic effect on the growth and revitalization of downtown Grand Rapids. These two projects, together with an earlier conversion of a riverfront warehouse into prestigious law offices, have contributed significantly to the growth, maturity and prestige of Marvin DeWinter's architectural practice, which in 1979 was incorporated and expanded to include a number of associates.

Marvin DeWinter holds both graduate and undergraduate degrees from the University of Michigan, is certified by the National Council of Architectural Registration Boards, is a director of the Grand Valley Chapter of the American Institute of Architects and has served continuously since 1972 on the American Arbitration Board. DeWinter has traveled extensively throughout the United States and Europe, and he has participated in a number of international seminars and conferences on urban planning. Over the years he has been active in a multitude of civic and religious organizations and at one time or another served on church boards, school boards and college alumni boards.

William Vanderbout, a graduate of the University of Michigan, is also certified by the National Council of Architectural Registration Boards and is currently serving on the National AIA Committee on Architecture for Justice. He is a member and past president of the Grand Valley Chapter of the American Institute of Architects, has been a charter member and past president of the Construction and Specification Institute and for the last ten years been a guest lecturer at the Grand Rapids Junior College.

Gretchen Minnhaar, a graduate of Lawrence Institute of Technology, also holds a master's degree in architectural design from the Universidad de Rosario, Argentina and a master's in business administration from Florida Atlantic University. Minnhaar is a member and past director of the Grand Valley Chapter of the American Institute of Architects, has served on the Michigan State Construction Code Commission and is presently serving as trustee for the Kendall School of Design. She has been a guest lecturer at many universities, participated in a number of international seminars and conferences on urban planning and co-authored the book *Women and Success*.

Today, DeWinter Associates offers clients professional services in the area of architectural design, landscape design, space planning and interior and graphic design. The firm also provides feasibility studies and offers project financial control as well as construction management.

In the twenty years that DeWinter Associates has been serving its clients in the Western Michigan area, its two primary objectives have been the pursuit of excellence in design and of professionally serving its clients' needs. This cornerstone of its practice has enabled it to gain a reputation for creative design combined with the highest level of professionalism. The diversity of its practice attests to this—a practice that has never been identified with a particular building type but which has proven itself at being equally proficient in the design of libraries, museums, medical offices, shopping centers, general office buildings, hotels churches and residential, educational and industrial facilities. All of these facilities have been designed with a concern for the people who use them and an attempt to create environments that help people to be happy.

Amway Grand Plaza Hotel (above). Gerald R. Ford Presidential Museum (below).

Rolling out the barrels since 1893

DeWitt Barrels started in the spring of 1893 when Peter DeWitt with his two sons, Peter and William, began making and repairing wooden barrels and kegs. This work, also known as cooperage, was a skilled trade that was often passed on from father to son. In those days, wooden containers were used in nearly every industry. Barrels were used for the transporting and storing of food products, drugs and nearly any liquid that had to be shipped. There were also light weight barrels, known as slack barrels, that were used to ship dry goods. Often coopers (men who worked with barrels) had to accompany the barrels to the customer to assist in sealing the barrels after they were filled.

It wasn't until shortly before World War II that steel drums were introduced. The need for these containers was brought about by a growing chemical industry and the expense and difficulty of hiring coopers. The light weight, or slack, barrels were replaced by fibre drums—reinforced cardboard containers. These two types of containers have continued to dominate the industry right up to the present day.

In the midst of all these changes, the world was shaken by World War II. DeWitt Barrels was selected as a defense supplier, making barrels for bullets. Due to a lack of help, German prisoners of war were used to make the barrels. The prisoners were held in Allegan and were brought in daily by truck. Working for DeWitt Barrels, must have agreed with them. One morning, while the truck was making the trip up from the prison camp, a prisoner fell off the truck; instead of trying to escape, he kept asking directions and finally found his way to DeWitt Barrels, claiming he didn't want to lose his job.

Immediately following the war, the employees of DeWitt Barrels affilliated with the United Furniture Workers of America (UFWA), Local 415. The AFL-CIO union continues to represent the men of DeWitt Barrels. The spirit of co-operation between employer and employee has helped DeWitt Barrels keep going without any work stoppage—even under the most adverse conditions.

On Saturday May 18, 1974, arsonists set fire to DeWitt Barrels. The plant was a total loss. On Sunday, as the ashes were smoldering, employees showed up on their own time, offering their assistance. With their help, on Monday, DeWitt Barrels went back to work—without a building—keeping the customers supplied with containers. Even as they worked, a new building was erected around them. Today, after a couple of additions, DeWitt Barrels has a modern facility supplying its customers with the finest in re-conditioned steel, fibre and plastic drums. The future of the industry may be in the poly-drum, an all plastic container, which has the advantages of being completely recyclable and lighter in weight than steel. But the flexibility of DeWitt Barrels, and the DeWitt family will keep them a leader in the container industry.

Civic involvement has always been a major concern for DeWitt Barrels. By donating time and services to local projects, they help make their community a better place to live. Projects like the Grand Rapids Arts Festival, Old Kent River Bank Run and parades have benefitted from the generosity of DeWitt Barrels. The DeWitt family personally involves themselves in organizations such as the Chamber of Commerce—local, state and national—the Grand Rapids and Michigan Jaycees, the Grand Valley State College Foundation and the Catholic Human Development Center.

DeWitt Barrels is, and has been from its inception, a family business. The business was passed from father to son and operated as a sole proprietorship until 1976 when the business was incorporated. Today, the business is run by Peter DeWitt and three of his sons, Michael, Peter and Timothy, making them the fourth and fifth generations of DeWitts at DeWitt Barrels. With recent land purchases and expansion of its fleet, the DeWitts are looking with great expectations to the future and growth with Grand Rapids.

The first three generations at DeWitt Barrels (left to right): Peter DeWitt (son), Peter DeWitt (father and founder), Neil DeWitt (grandson), Peter DeWitt (grandson), and William DeWitt (son) (above). Drivers and their teams at DeWitt Barrels in 1912 (below).

193

Reflections of contemporary American history and government

The Gerald R. Ford Museum

The Gerald R. Ford Museum is situated on a six-acre plot that for hundreds of years had been a meeting and trading place for the constantly moving American Indian tribes who inhabited west Michigan. Today, Ah-Nab-Awen Bicentennial Park—a memorial to the original inhabitants—fronts the museum building and separates it from the Grand River.

The museum's mirrored windows look out upon and reflect the city where Gerald R. Ford grew up. Although very few of the downtown buildings and businesses have been left unchanged, the basic values and character of Grand Rapids and the people remain about the same. The city and its inhabitants are an integral part of the museum presentation.

The Museum began as a dream of the people of Grand Rapids to honor Gerald R. Ford, their representative in Congress for 25 years and the 38th president of the United States. Shortly after the presidential election in 1976, the Gerald R. Ford Commemorative Committee was formed. Under the leadership of its first chairman, Carl H. Morgenstern, the building site and architect were selected, and a grant was received from the state of Michigan for site acquisition. In the fall of 1977, Jordan Sheperd became Chairman of the Commemorative Committee and directed the design, construction and furnishing of the museum. It is now administered by the National Archives and Records Service of the General Services Administration.

Assisted by a state of Michigan grant, contributions from the county of Kent, the city of Grand Rapids and hundreds of private donors, the Commemorative Committee accomplished its goal on September 18, 1981, when the Gerald R. Ford Museum was dedicated and given to the people of the United States.

Dedication ceremonies and the weeklong celebration preceeding it were attended by thousands of Gerald R. Ford's admirers, including President Ronald Reagan, Vice President George Bush, the prime minister of Canada, the president of Mexico, the minister of foreign affairs for Japan and the former president of France, Valery Giscard D'Estaing.

The Ford Museum tells the story of the life and times of Gerald R. Ford. Within the context of Ford's own background and public life, museum visitors find a wealth of information on contemporary American history and government. A tour of the museum begins in the first floor auditorium with the viewing of a 28-minute movie entitled *Gerald R. Ford: The Presidency Restored*.

On the second floor, the 15,000-square-foot exhibition area presents the story of Gerald R. Ford's life and his career of public service. In this spacious setting of hand-rubbed oak, Belgian linen and jewel-like cases, are Richard M. Nixon's August 9, 1974 letter resigning the presidency and Gerald R. Ford's subsequent pardon of Nixon, discussions of major domestic and international issues during the Ford administration, a look at the special role Mrs. Ford played in the White House and three video presentations on Congress, the vice presidency and the 1976 campaign. Of particular interest is a full-scale reproduction of the Oval Office decorated just as it was during President Ford's term of office.

Other major displays include "Three Days in the Presidency," a minute-by-minute outline of presidential crisis-management during the 1975 Mayaquez incident; "How Our Laws Are Made," a cartooned schematic exhibit depicting the labyrinthine legislative process and a multi-screen slide show, "An American Celebration: The Bicentennial" with photographs from nearly 100 photographers and an original score performed by the University of Michigan Symphony.

Visited by over 100,000 visitors during its first two months of operations, the Gerald R. Ford Museum has become a major point of interest in western Michigan.

First of its kind in the United States

Visitors and residents of the West Michigan region, especially newcomers, wonder how Grand Rapids became the "Furniture Capital of the World." Many have heard that Grand Rapids had the ideal natural location because of its proximity to the river and forest lands of the region, but only a few have been aware of the other force behind Grand Rapids' growth as a world leader in the furniture industry—the quality of craftsmanship fostered by the furniture makers here.

The artistry of design, the quality of materials and the exceptional attention to detail established Grand Rapids' furniture leadership more than one hundred years ago. It is this Grand Rapids' combination that continues to assure the region's status as a world center for the manufacture of fine furniture.

As early as the 1880s, the Grand Rapids region was considered to be the "Furniture Capital of the World," and manufacturers recognized the need to join together to protect their reputation. Thus, in 1881, the Furniture Manufacturers Association of Grand Rapids was born to "promote and protect the welfare of the furniture industry in the city of Grand Rapids and vicinity; and to promote and protect the welfare of all persons engaged in any capacity in the furniture and woodworking industry in Grand Rapids or in its vicinity."

Today, many residents of West Michigan think of the Grand Rapids furniture heyday as part of the past. They assume that it has slowed because the industry is no longer as visible as it once was (no longer needing the semi-annual markets here—instead using showroom locations in major cities across the country and in other nations). But the fact is that the Grand Rapids furniture industry is a billion-dollar business in both residential and business furniture production.

Currently, the Furniture Manufacturers Association of Grand Rapids is actively promoting and protecting the welfare of its membership by providing services such as public relations activities, training courses, specialized surveys and technical information distribution. With 100 years of heritage behind us and a bright future ahead, Furniture Manufacturers Association is continuing to serve its "recognized for quality" members.

MEMBERS

Alexis Manufacturing Company
Baker Furniture, Inc.
Bennett Wood Specialties
The Brothers Forslund
Budres Lumber & Dry Kiln
Charlotte Chair Company
Colonial Mfg. Co.
Davidson Plyforms, Inc.
Grand Rapids Dowel Works
Hekman Furniture Company
H.L. Hubbell Company
Ideal Seating Company
Irwin Seating Company
Johnson Furniture Company
Kindel Furniture Company
Klise Manufacturing Company
Mastercraft Furniture Company
Herman Miller, Inc.
Morgan Manufacturing Company
Mueller Furniture Corp.
Nucraft Furniture Company
S.E. Overton Company
Ply-Curves, Inc.
Rose Manufacturing Company
S. F. S. Corp.
St. Johns, Inc.
Sligh Furniture Company
Stow/Davis Furniture Company
Superior Furniture Company
T A D D Ind. Inc.
Trend Clocks
Valley City Plating Company
Van Keulen & Winchester
West Michigan Furniture Company
John Widdicomb Company
Worden Manufacturing Co.
Zeeland Wood Turning

ASSOCIATE MEMBERS

V.S. Barnes Company
John K. Burch Company
J.&H. Cutting, Inc.
Guardsman Chemicals Inc.
Hekman Contract
Keeler Brass Company
Landscape Forms, Inc.
Monical Machinery Company
Jack Peterson Sales Company
Rose/Johnson, Inc.
Steelcase, Inc.
Ted Thompson Sales
W.P. Williams Company

A log jam on the Grand (left). Millions of logs have become furniture during the 150 years of furniture manufacturing in Grand Rapids, circa 1900. Skill, talent and experience are required to produce "Grand Rapids Quality" furniture (below). Hand Carver, circa 1940.

195

Thirty years of progress through innovation

History teaches that two things are necessary to start a successful business: a good idea and the right timing. On June 12, 1952, a small group of Grand Rapids businessmen had an idea and realized the time was right to offer insurance and financing for a very young mobile home industry. Foremost Insurance Company was formed as a result of the idea and started business in a one-room office with eight employees.

Edward J. Frey, then president of Union Bank, and Richard E. Riebel, now president of Foremost Corporation of America, were among the founders of Foremost and became pioneers in assisting the growth of a new form of American housing.

The mobile home industry had its start in Michigan and northern Indiana. Virtually all mobile homes were manufactured within a 150-mile radius of Grand Rapids. As a result, major Grand Rapids banks became the national hub for financing mobile homes. Then—as today—insurance was the key to credit availability in housing.

Frey and Riebel saw the need for consistent and dependable mobile home insurance and Foremost filled that need. At its inception, Foremost was licensed to write physical damage insurance in Michigan only and had one account, Union Bank. By the end of 1952 there were eleven people on the payroll, and the company had $956,119 in assets with $850,265 in net written premium.

This was significant growth considering there were no specialized forms or policies

for insuring mobile homes at that time. Using the innovation that has been the mainstay of the company, Foremost people modified coverages of an automobile policy to fill the specific needs of mobile home owners, dealers and lenders.

Within two years, Foremost needed more space and moved to 67 Barclay, an unoccupied parish house owned by the Christian Reformed Church. Office space there was double that of the initial office in the Federal Square Building.

In the five years between 1952 and 1957 Foremost experienced rapid growth. Innovative insurance writers specialized insurance coverages and services for all those involved in mobile home sales. The company worked with lenders to encourage their entry into mobile home financing, and acting as a catalyst between mobile,

home dealers and financial institutions, Foremost became an integral part of the industry.

From the beginning, each person and every organization in Foremost's distribution channel was considered a valuable customer—the dealer, agent, financial institution and policyholder. Foremost people, products and services facilitated the growth of the mobile home industry and thus advanced an affordable lifestyle for millions of Americans.

By 1957, Foremost was well on its way, growing from an original eight employees to 44 employees and from assets of $956,119 to $3.5 million. During the same year, the company moved next door to 49 Barclay, which had three times the space, and R.E. Riebel became president. Under his personal direction and guidance, the growth and prosperity of the company was accelerated. By the end of Riebel's first year as president, Foremost had seven branch offices across the country and was licensed to sell insurance in 35 states.

In 1961, Foremost moved to a new office building with 20,000 square feet of space. As the company grew into its larger office facilities, it expanded into other areas. Besides involvement in all phases of the mobile home industry, Foremost introduced the first policy in the nation specifically designed for travel trailers. By the end of 1966, Foremost assets had reached $28.5 million. There were 3,500 insurance agents selling Foremost insurance in 49 states.

By the mid-'60s, Foremost regional offices were located in Indianapolis, Indiana; Clearwater, Florida; Overland Park, Kansas; Harrisburg, Pennsylvania and Walnut Creek, California. Each regional office operated as a huge fully staffed separate business center.

Business was increasing so rapidly by 1969 that the company outgrew its East Beltline office. Well over 150 home-office employees moved to 28th and Kraft and into another new building with three times the space.

During the five-year period from 1967 to 1971 Foremost aggressively entered one of the fastest growing markets in the country recreational vehicles. Specialized policies and coverages were developed for the owners of snowmobiles, motor homes, travel trailers, boats, motorcycles and all-terrain vehicles. The decision to enter the RV insurance market was a wise one. By 1973, Foremost wrote $37.4 million in RV premium alone.

Foremost Corporation, Foremost Insurance Company's parent holding company, was incorporated in 1967, with Foremost Insurance Company as its principal subsidiary. In 1971, Foremost Corporation changed its name to Centennial Corporation. The following year, Centennial Corpo-

Centennial Park (top) was 260 acres of hundred year old farm land and orchards when ground breaking by Cascade Township officials, R.E. Riebel and Edward J. Frey (right of Riebel) took place in 1968. Foremost's first office (above) was located in the Federal Square Building on the corner of Pearl and Ionia. The building was originally constructed in 1900 as a YMCA.

ration made a public sale of its common stock, which was traded nationally over-the-counter. By 1973, Foremost Insurance company premium writing reached an all-time high of over $224 million.

During Foremost's first 21 years the company learned, innovated and grew. It became the benchmark by which other mobile home insurance companies measured their performance. But then came 1974 and 1975—tough years for the nation, for the mobile home industry and for Foremost. In the face of severe adversity, Foremost people created even stronger programs to overcome adverse market conditions.

In 1978, in order to better meet the challenges of the future, the holding company changed its name from Centennial Corporation to Foremost Corporation of America. Among other steps taken to ensure growth and increase productivity, Foremost consolidated its five regional offices into three larger key marketing zones in 1979. Three zone operating centers allowed maximum automation to increase processing efficiency. The consolidation resulted in cost savings, a higher level of marketing and claims service, as well as upgraded produc-tivity levels.

Currently, new insurance products and services are being researched and developed to meet the ever-changing needs of the marketplace. These new products, along with established insurance products, are the key to future corporate development and growth.

In addition to Foremost Insurance Company, Foremost Corporation of America holds several other subsidiary companies in the Grand Rapids area. They include Foremost Life Insurance Company, Foremost Financial Services Corporation, Foremost Home Brokers, Inc. and Foremost Real Estate Company.

Foremost continues to be a good neighbor while developing their 260-acre business, residential and recreational community on the southeast side of Grand Rapids at the corner of Kraft and 28th streets. Located in Centennial Park are the headquarters of Foremost Corporation, the Marriott Hotel, Sebrite Corporation, IBM, Guardsman Chemical and future sites for other successful firms.

Centennial Park's Gatehouse and Meadows condominiums feature distinctive exterior architecture which blends with the surrounding meadows, orchards and woodlands. The Golf Ridge condominium development is the newest residential community in the park. Health and recreational facilities include the Charlevoix Club and Meadowood Activities Center which features an athletic club, a nine-hole golf course and tennis courts.

From a small beginning with eight employees and one account, Foremost has grown to nearly 1,500 employees nationwide, with over 500 people in the Grand Rapids area alone. Foremost Insurance Company, the major subsidiary of Foremost Corporation of America, has over one million policies currently in force and is represented by 11,000 insurance agents from coast to coast. The company has more mobile home insurance policies in force than any other insurance company in the nation. At year-end 1981, the assets of Foremost Corporation of America reached approximately $475 million.

The factors that contributed to past success—superior products, industry specialization, a broad range of services and creative people—will allow Foremost to continue planned growth through innovation now and in the future.

Foremost's home office complex—Centennial Park—is a well-designed business, residential and recreational community.

People enhancing the quality of community life through area automotive facilities

With about 10,000 employment opportunities, currently, GM is the largest employer in the Grand Rapids area. Over the years, the GM facilities have shouldered great responsibility for community growth and economic well-being.

It has been observed that, "These Grand Rapids plants are among GM's most efficient, and the reason is the workforce—people here want to do a good job."

The feeling of being involved and that people are important, dates back to 1936 when *Fisher Body Metal Fabrication Plant,* largest and oldest of the four facilities, established operations at 36th Street SW. The high caliber of workforce available was the motivating factor in choosing the area.

As the forerunner of all Fisher Body metal-fabricating plant layouts, Grand Rapids Fisher Metal Fab has been recognized as the finest of its kind in the Fisher Body Division of General Motors.

Major metal components for all General Motors automobiles are produced by the facility. Most notable of these include: doors, rear fenders, trunk lids, roof panels and floor pans. In addition to these body components, the Metal Fab plant designs and builds the majority of the dies, welding fixtures, mechanical devices and manufacturing aids used in production.

Since the first automotive body parts were shipped in 1936, six expansion programs on the 88-acre site have increased the floor space to 1.8 million square feet. When operating at capacity, the plant, each week, ships an average of 325 railroad cars and 80-trucks loaded with components to General Motors assembly plants. Over 300,000 tons of steel are processed each year.

The *Rochester Products Division Plant* traces its history back to 1943 when Saginaw Steering Gear Division of GM merged with the Irwin-Pedersen Arms Company. Their product, the M-1 carbine rifle, was manufactured for the U.S. government in the old Macy Furniture factory on South Division Avenue.

With the rifle contract completed, the facility was revised to produce fuel injectors for military diesel engines. By January 1, 1944, the operation was reorganized, moved to its present location at Burlingame Avenue and Burton Street and renamed Diesel Equipment Division.

Design, development and mass production of high-technology precision components for gasoline, diesel and gas turbine engines represent its major contribution to industry. By 1981, products manufactured included 95 parts for GM and competitive vehicle manufacturers, plus 104 parts in diesel and gas turbine engines used around the world. Over the years there have been fourteen expansions accumulating 1.6 million square feet and occupying over 91

The silhouettes depict "people importance" in the GM workplace. Left to right: Fisher Body Trim Fabrication Plant, Fisher Body Metal Fabrication Plant, Rochester Products Division Plant.

acres. Capacity for diesel engine fuel injectors reached the one million mark annually in 1981. Capacity for hydraulic valve lifters, which began in 1947, reached an annual volume of 125 million units by 1981.

Two important events occurred in 1981: the consolidation of Diesel Equipment Division with Rochester (N.Y.) Products Division and the completion of the 300,000 square-foot Coopersville Plant, located 22 miles northwest of Grand Rapids. Beginning in 1982, full-volume production of the throttle body injector was located in the *Coopersville Plant.*

Throttle body injector production, first introduced in 1979, reached the four-million annual-capacity mark by 1982.

What is now the south unit of the *Fisher Body Trim Fabrication Plant* was purchased in 1950. It was opened in 1952, making forward fuselages for the Republic Aircraft F-84 Thunderbird, a jet-propelled fighter plane used in the Korean conflict. Nearly 600 of the fuselages were built when, in March of 1954, plant production was converted to trim fabricating. By 1955, the facility began making interior trim for the 1955 Chevrolet.

The Trim Plant suffered the most from the downturn in the automotive industry in the mid- and late 1970s. While employment was still down in 1980, the 1981 spring introduction of GM's J-car—and subsequent new smaller models in 1982—brought employment at the plant back to normal. Both the J and X cars were introduced to meet foreign competition head-on as well as to meet public demand for high quality and fuel economy.

By 1981, the Trim Plant made all of the back and cushion trim sets and some interior door trim for the Pontiac, Chevrolet, Buick and Oldsmobile J cars. They also made the interior trim for the Buick Skylark, Chevrolet Camaro, Monte Carlo, Impala and Caprice.

Fifty-three acres encompass the site of the Trim Plant, with 800,000 square feet of floor space. More than 900 sewing machines are used in making interior trim parts. Twelve million yards of roll material goods are used annually with approximately 2,600 miles of thread per day used in the sewing operation.

One of the greatest motivating factors in the Grand Rapids area GM plants has been the feeling that the individual is important. Along with this "priority of people," evolved the *Quality of Worklife* process known as QWL which represented teamwork—people pooling their efforts to reach a common goal, whether in manufacturing, quality assurance or union and management. Whether inspectors or assemblers, janitors or grinders, sewers or welders, personnel specialists or engineers, QWL means pulling together to find the best possible solution to the problem at hand. And, in turn, becoming the benefactors within a more productive organization.

Problem-solving groups of employes in the plants meet weekly, on company time, to solve problems occurring in their areas. The quality of worklife was enhanced by putting the decision making where the knowledge was found. It involved much training and time to put into effect. By 1981, all of the GM plants were involved with the QWL process, producing a "generation of new ideas" and great hope for the quality of industrial worklife in Grand Rapids.

As an important economic force in the area, the four facilities made expenditures for employe payrolls, supplies and services totaling about $450 million in 1981. From the beginning, high standards of quality and workmanship have been maintained at the plants through the cooperative efforts of employes utilizing their time and individual talents. Equally important has been the concern and involvement of dedicated employes with the quality of community life—giving their time as well as their financial support.

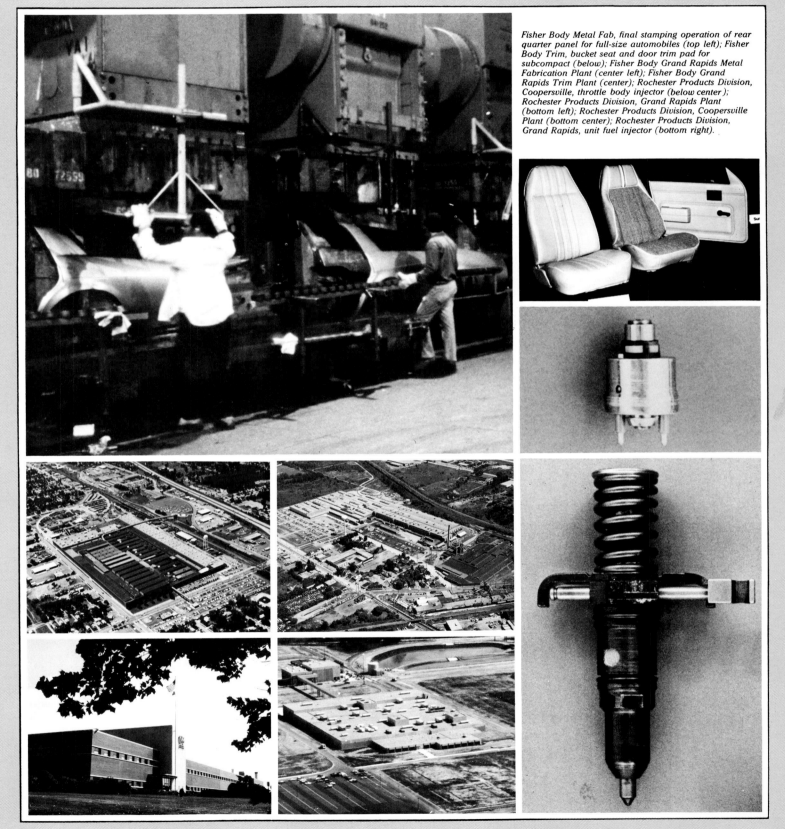

Fisher Body Metal Fab, final stamping operation of rear quarter panel for full-size automobiles (top left); Fisher Body Trim, bucket seat and door trim pad for subcompact (below); Fisher Body Grand Rapids Metal Fabrication Plant (center left); Fisher Body Grand Rapids Trim Plant (center); Rochester Products Division, Coopersville, throttle body injector (below center); Rochester Products Division, Grand Rapids Plant (bottom left); Rochester Products Division, Coopersville Plant (bottom center); Rochester Products Division, Grand Rapids, unit fuel injector (bottom right).

199

Preserving and communicating the history of Grand Rapids

On February 18, 1858, John Ball and 22 other Grand Rapids pioneers called on their fellow citizens to join them in forming an Old Settlers Society for the county. Three years before issuing that call, Ball had led another group in forming the Grand Rapids Lyceum of Natural History. Neither organization survived, but their successors stand as proof of the community's continuing determination to preserve its heritage and traditions.

The Lyceum became the Grand Rapids Public Museum, a repository that would eventually attract more than 250,000 visitors annually to see its outstanding historical exhibits.

The Old Settlers' Society, initially restricted to people who had lived in the county in 1837 when Michigan became a state, established a fine collection of reminiscences, scrapbooks, photographs and drawings that were deposited in the Grand Rapids Public Library. When the Old Settlers Society saw its number diminishing as senior members "stepped from [its] ranks and crossed the dark river to be seen no more on this side," its remaining members changed the name to the Old Residents' Association and opened membership to anyone over 35 who had lived in the Grand River Valley for 25 years.

The new group continued to collect local information and to hold annual outings until it disbanded in 1967. By then, the Grand Rapids Historical Society, founded in 1894 and reorganized in 1950, had taken over much of the responsibility for preserving historical records, presenting public programs and encouraging historical research and publication.

When the Ryerson Library (now Grand Rapids Public Library) opened in 1904, the Society deposited its archives in the Michigan Room where they are still housed. Over the years the Historical Society has been an active and enthusiastic participant in events such as the 1926 Louis Campau Centennial, the 1976 American Bicentennial and the Grand Rapids Sesquicentennial celebrations. It was responsible for reprinting Albert Baxter's popular *History of the City of Grand Rapids,* and it currently publishes the *Grand River Valley Review,* a magazine of West Michigan history.

Joining the Historical Society in preserving and studying the many facets of local family history is the Western Michigan Genealogical Society. Since its inception in 1954, the Society has worked to build the public library's genealogy collection, donating hundreds of books and contributing countless volunteer hours to research and indexing projects. In addition, the Society conducts regular workshops and publishes a quarterly magazine, *Michigana.*

In recent years, Grand Rapids city commissioners have recognized the increasing interest in local history and have created the Grand Rapids Historical Commission and the Historic Preservation Commission. The Historical Commission, created in 1962, has published *The Story of Grand Rapids,* edited by Z.Z. Lydens, and the *Pictorial History of Grand Rapids* by Lynn Mapes and Anthony Travis. The Historical Commission also supervises the activities of the city historian—a position that it was instrumental in establishing in 1978, making Grand Rapids one of the few American cities employing a full-time professional historian.

The Historic Preservation Commission was created in 1971 in response to the growing desire to preserve older buildings, sites and neighborhoods. It recommends historic landmarks to the city commission for official designation and then oversees the process to ensure that historic integrity is preserved. Grand Rapids now boasts nearly 30 historic landmarks ranging from the 2,000-year-old Norton Indian Mounds to the turn-of the-century Heritage Hill district. There are now several hundred Heritage Hill Association members dedicated to preserving the area's historic ambience.

In 1988, Grand Rapids will celebrate its 150th year as an incorporated municipality. Thanks to its many historical organizations and institutions, its citizens will have a more complete picture of who they are and what their city is and has been. John Ball and the other early settlers would be pleased.

The Calkins Law Office is Grand Rapids' oldest building. Restored by the Public Museum with the assistance of numerous organizations and individuals, it is an example of the community's appreciation for its heritage.

A tradition of excellence since 1914

Woodrow Wilson was president in the fall of 1914 when Grand Rapids Junior College opened its doors for the first time and enrolled a total of 49 students who attended classes at Central High School.

The board of education, upon the recommendation of the University of Michigan, established the junior college as a two-year school that would provide a broad liberal arts education for citizens living in the Grand Rapids metropolitan area.

Grand Rapids Junior College has undergone many changes since then, but the standard of academic excellence on which the college was founded continues to be the level of distinction sought in every program and service offered students today.

In its 68-year history, Grand Rapids Junior College has served more than 160,000 students. The total number of persons participating in regular classes, workshops and special seminars exceeds 30,000 annually, which makes Grand Rapids Junior College the second largest college in western Michigan.

In response to the educational needs of the community, the college has developed programs in the liberal arts, pre-professional and occupational curricula. These curricula provide students with the first two years of four-year degree programs or prepare them for immediate positions in business, industry or public service.

Grand Rapids Junior College could be described as several colleges within one. The day college and the continuing education division combine to increase the number of educational alternatives available for students of all ages, on- and off-campus throughout the year.

The continuing education division of the college offers a wide variety of programs. These include traditional academic courses, workshops and seminars, and related services in an attempt to more completely and effectively serve the educational needs of students.

By offering these programs and services on- and off-campus, during the evening, and on weekends, Grand Rapids Junior College provides an important alternative to students who are employed or have other responsibilities and are not able to attend classes during the day.

Another established tradition at the college is the demonstrated quality and dedication of its teaching faculty. The faculty has been and continues to be one of the major strengths of the college.

Grand Rapids Junior College is recognized nationally for maintaining a high standard of excellence. Credits earned at the school are readily accepted for transfer to major four-year colleges and universities as students pursue degrees in such fields as medicine, engineering, education and law.

The College has developed a comprehensive student services program to assist students in their efforts to achieve academic success. These free services include academic and personal counseling, tutoring, career exploration and job placement.

From its original site at Central High School, the college moved to its convenient downtown location in 1925. Since then the campus has expanded from one building to a total of ten, seven of which have been constructed since 1970.

The newest addition to the campus is the beautiful new Student Community

Center which opened at the beginning of the 1981-82 academic year. The 60,000 square-foot building houses most of the offices and programs providing student services. The building also features a number of conference rooms which are available for community use.

The total college experience at Grand Rapids Junior College includes many opportunities for social as well as academic growth. Students are encouraged to participate in a variety of organizations such as the Student Congress, the Black Student Union, Native American Club and the Latino Student Club. A variety of athletic programs and competitive intramural programs are also available for men and women.

Throughout the academic year, the college sponsors a number of cultural events and activities for students and the community. The best known and most popular of these events is the Great American Talk Festival which has become one of the largest and most successful lecture series on any college campus in the country. Held each spring, the series features six nationally known celebrities who visit the campus on consecutive days.

Another attractive feature of the college has been its ability to offer low cost tuition rates. As part of the Grand Rapids Public School system, the college is partially funded by local property taxes and offers residents of the district additional savings in tuition costs.

The tradition of excellence that has been the hallmark of Grand Rapids Junior College since 1914 is the key to the continued success of the college as it serves the community now and in the future.

Practical experience has always been an integral part of the Grand Rapids Junior College tradition of excellence (above). For 68 years, pre-professional, occupational and liberal arts curricula have prepared students for positions in public service, industry and business—as well as for further education (left).

201

Concern for community guided newspaper's growth

In 1892, Grand Rapids was a bustling metropolis of 63,000. There were electric streetcars, major railroad lines and electric arc lights on giant towers.

Stores and homes were heated with wood and still lit by gaslight. Sweet's Hotel on Canal Street let rooms for $2 a night, the John Ball Park Zoo was just a year old, and the furniture industry was booming.

On September 9 of that same year, a 28-year-old Canadian, George C. Booth, ventured to Grand Rapids to buy the *Morning Press,* a four-page daily that sold for a penny a copy.

Booth was new in the newspaper business. Born in Ontario, he had operated a foundry in Windsor until he married Ellen Warren Scripps, whose father owned the *Detroit News.* Scripps talked Booth into taking over as business manager of the Detroit paper—an experience that led to Booth's purchase of the *Morning Press.*

Newspapers of the day were not known for their restraint and objectivity. But Booth, whose father had been a well-known religious writer, changed all that. Booth believed a newspaper should be reliable, intelligent and restrained in its content, and that its main concern should be the welfare of the community.

Three months after he bought the *Morning Press,* Booth bought out one of his competitors, the *Evening Leader.* By 1897, his newspaper, now called the *Evening Press,* had a circulation of 22,000—more than double the combined circulation of its two predecessors.

Booth's newspaper started business in a two-story building on Pearl Street, near the bridge. Then Booth returned to Detroit to continue running the *Detroit News,* and later he founded other newspapers in Michigan.

The *Evening Press*—which didn't change its name to the *Grand Rapids Press* until 1913—operated out of its original building until the great flood of 1904 washed through the first floor and basement.

Two years later, the newspaper moved to new headquarters at 20 E. Fulton Street, the first all-concrete building in the city and one of the first in the world.

The *Press* was the first in a chain of newspapers put together by George Booth. Booth Newspapers included the *Kalamazoo Gazette, Saginaw News, Ann Arbor News, Jackson Citizen-Patriot, Muskegon Chronicle, Bay City Times* and *Flint Journal.*

By the mid-1950s, there were only two major newspapers left in the city, the *Press* and the *Grand Rapids Herald.* The *Herald* was a morning paper with a Sunday edition, and the *Press* remained an afternoon paper published Monday through Saturday.

Founded in 1884, the *Herald* boasted a long line of notables who had worked as editors and managers, two of whom became U.S. senators.

William Alden Smith was vice president of the *Herald* from 1888 to 1906 when he went to Washington, D.C., as a senator. He was followed by Arthur H. Vandenberg, who also became a U.S. senator.

The *Press* and *Herald* competed tooth-and-nail throughout the first half of the twentieth century. The *Press* finally won the battle when advertising revenues dropped for the *Herald,* and in 1958 Booth bought out its old competitor.

Booth ran the *Herald* as a morning paper for nearly a year before a newspaper strike forced the company to give up. The last issue of the *Herald* was published March 29, 1959.

By the mid-1960s, the *Press* had outgrown its building on Fulton and erected its present structure at Michigan Street and Monroe Avenue NW in Vandenberg Center.

In late 1976, in the largest newspaper transaction in history, the *Press* and Booth Newspapers were sold to Samuel I. Newhouse, owner of a communications conglomerate headquartered in New York.

As a cause-oriented newspaper, the *Press* consistently has shown concern for better city government in the tradition of its founder. The newspaper was an early leader in boosting better roads and West Michigan tourism, in seeking better care for the mentally ill and in supporting urban renewal. It sounded a lonely alarm in the early 1970s on the threat of PBB contamination of Michigan farms.

With nearly 600 full- and part-time employees, the *Press* celebrated its 90th anniversary in 1982 with a daily circulation of more than 130,000 and a Sunday circulation of more than 160,000.

In the early 1950s, (top) linotype operators worked in the old Press *building on Fulton Street. By the early 1970s, electronic equipment had replaced linotype machines. As late as the 1950s (above) the* Press *and the* Herald *were neighbors on Fulton Street.*

Needs of industry created a new supplier company

In the mid 1930s, industrial manufacturing in Western Michigan was expanding at an ever increasing rate. Because manufacturing plants cannot operate without adequate tools, equipment and supplies, two men—Roy R. Wenger and Joseph A. Hager—decided to form a closely held corporation to fill the needs for goods and services of these various manufacturing facilities. On June 1, 1936, Grand Rapids Supply Company began operations in rented space at 47 Market Avenue SW in Grand Rapids. The combined office and warehouse was probably not more than 1,250 square feet.

In the early days, one of the founders would go out and make calls on the various manufacturing plants while the other "minded the store." This arrangement went on for about a year with the utilization of some part-time and temporary office help. In July of 1937, they hired their first full-time regular employee. That person was Robert E. Cribley who today is president of the corporation. In those days everybody worked six full days a week. Many evenings were spent doing paperwork, building shelving and arranging stock on the shelves.

The first product the company supplied was a cutting tool manufactured by Greenfield Tap and Die Corporation in Greenfield, Massachusetts. The first order the company received was for Greenfield threading tools. The order was from Keeler Brass Company in Grand Rapids. Available cash was in short supply, and it was necessary to ask Keeler Brass for payment of the invoice so the company in turn could pay Greenfield for the tools.

In 1938, E.L. Switzer, who was a manufacturers representative, put some cash into the company and became president. He was inactive in the day-to-day business but acted primarily in an advisory capacity until his death in 1947. The company was successful in fulfilling the needs of industry and in 1938, Arthur D. Grover joined the company as an outside contact man to help Wenger and Hager. During this time, Cribley answered the phone, prepared purchase orders and sales orders, typed invoices and dictation and did receiving, shipping and janitor work. The bookkeeping was done by Hager.

Also in 1939, William M. Klaassen, who is still with the company in a purchasing capacity, joined the organization as it continued to grow. After the addition of another person or two, it was necessary for the company to seek larger quarters, and a former department store on the corner of Grandville Avenue and Wealthy Street was purchased in 1940. In 1942, along came the Second World War and while the need for products and services remained basically the same, the company went into full-scale support of war-tool manufacturing. This required control of the critical items needed in production. Duty assignments were changed around so that priority items could be directed into channels where they were critically needed. Manpower was also in short supply as some employees were called into military service. To help this situation, women were employed in the warehouse—an almost unheard of practice at that time.

Hostilities ended in 1945, and the conversion to manufacturing consumer items began. The demands and needs of industry increased and it was necessary to utilize the entire two floors and basement of the old department store. At the same time, the acquisition of adjoining land and old buildings was begun in anticipation of future expansion.

Shortly after the death of Wenger in 1965, it was decided that new facilities were needed to accommodate a larger inventory and to improve efficiency. In October 1968, after the completion of its "privately financed urban renewal project," the company moved into its new building which contained 6,000 square feet of office and over 300,000 cubic feet of warehouse space.

In 1977, a branch was established in Muskegon, Michigan through the purchase of Towne Supply Co. Today, Grand Rapids Supply Company employs 55 people, and continues in its ever expanding role of filling the needs of industry in all of Western Michigan.

The Grand Rapids Supply Company started in business in June 1936 in this building at 47 Market Avenue SW (above). Grand Rapids Supply Company moved to its second home in 1940 (right).

From varnish to know-how in all areas of coating and furniture finishing

Grand Rapids' nickname, Furniture Capital of the World, means more than fine wood and intricate details. It means quality coatings and finishes, too, such as those produced by Guardsman Chemicals, Inc.

Founded in 1915 by former railroadsman, telegrapher and self-described "jack-of-all trades" Wallace E. Brown, the Grand Rapids Varnish Company had first-year sales of $50,000 and one customer, a small furniture manufacturer.

By 1981, Guardsman operated eleven facilities in ten cities, employed over 700 people and recorded sales of more than $67 million. Its customers included some of the world's largest corporations. And although Guardsman still produces varnish—it also produces lacquers, enamels and related finishing products for wood household and office furniture, wood paneling, kitchen cabinets and a variety of other goods, as well as technologically advanced coatings for metal office furniture, appliances, metal shelving and other products.

Guardsman also manufactures and markets a number of wood care products and packages aerosol and non-aerosol goods—both its own products and those of household, commercial and automotive manufacturers.

In 66 years, the company grew from a small business on Godfrey Avenue SW, in Grand Rapids to a corporation whose know-how gained international recognition.

Shortly after opening his company, Wallace Brown recruited his brother George, an authority on varnish formulation, and Joseph A. Hager, renowned throughout the South for his marketing skills. By 1925, business increased to the point that Grand Rapids Varnish Company built a lacquer production plant on Steele Avenue SW, in Grand Rapids. Though en-

larged and modernized, the plant still operates.

The company also began a research and development program in 1925 and introduced enamels and quick-drying lacquers. This program sparked the company's ongoing commitment to research.

In 1927, the company began to produce metal coatings, making one of its first sales to Terrel Equipment Company—today's Steelcase, Inc., the world's largest metal office furniture manufacturer and still a Guardsman customer.

As many Grand Rapids furniture companies failed during the Great Depression—or moved South in later years—numerous wood finish manufacturers also failed. But because metal coatings accounted for nearly three-quarters of Grand Rapids Varnish Company's sales, the company made it through these difficult times. Guardsman even added a two-story enamel production facility to its Steele Avenue plant during the depths of the Depression.

The company also added a resin manufacturing plant in 1937. And it trademarked the name "Guardsman" on its finest products—foretelling its name change 25 years later.

In 1943, founder Wallace Brown passed away, and the company's helm passed to Howard C. Lawrence. Joseph Hager assumed the office of vice president.

During World War II, Grand Rapids Varnish Company products and personnel gained national recognition. The company produced finishes for military housing, gliders and weapons. And Joseph Hager served as a paint, varnish and lacquer consultant to the War Production Board and the Smaller War Plants Corporation. De-

Construction progressed on the company's enamel manufacturing facility (above), "Plant No. 3." Steele Avenue research facility (date unknown). In 1947, Guardsman wood finishes (below), manufactured at the Steele Avenue plant, were delivered to local paint stores.

spite war-related manpower and supply shortages—and rising costs—business boomed, and the company added a third floor to its enamel production facility.

After the war, Grand Rapids Varnish Company developed five marketing classifications: Furniture, Appliances, Metal Fabrications, Trade Sales and Specialized Finishes. The company also began to supply furniture manufacturers with stains, fillers, sealers and topcoats.

Marketing of "Guardsman Cleaning Polish" began in 1945 through furniture manufacturers and retailers. Known today as Guardsman Furniture Polish, it is carried in many grocery, hardware and lumber supply stores.

Offices and labs moved to a brand new building, across the street from the Steele Avenue plant, in 1947. Corporate offices remained until 1980, when Guardsman opened its new headquarters building on Lucerne Drive, SE, in suburban Grand Rapids' Centennial Park.

Witnessing the continued southern flight of Grand Rapids wood furniture companies during the 1940s and '50s, Grand Rapids Varnish Company of North Carolina opened in 1953. And by 1960, the company added a warehouse, studio, offices and a manufacturing plant.

Joseph Hager succeeded Howard C. Lawrence as president in 1961, and he reaffirmed the company's commitment to research and sales growth through expansion and acquisitions.

After the National Paint, Varnish and Lacquer Association designated Grand Rapids Varnish Company products as "chemical coatings," and the company recognized varnish was only three percent of its sales, it became Guardsman Chemical Coatings Company in 1963.

"Acquisition" became the theme for Guardsman during the 1960s and '70s. Through the purchase of several regional finishes and coatings manufacturers, Guardsman was able to service customers in all parts of the United States. And by establishing research and development facilities at several new locations, the company built a reputation for custom finishes and coatings development in a broad range of industries.

To help increase production of its furniture polish line, Guardsman acquired American Aerosols of Holland, Michigan, in 1969. Not only could Guardsman now package its own polish products, it could also package other companies' products.

Keith C. VanderHyde assumed the presidency in 1970, and the company continued to expand and diversify. By 1975, Guardsman no longer solely produced coatings and finishes, so it dropped the word coatings from its name and became Guardsman Chemicals, Inc., its present title.

Once again entering a new market, Guardsman opened the Southwestern Division at Orange, California, in 1976. This operation became the Pacific Coast Division, serving one of the nation's largest metal, wood furniture and forest products markets.

In 1977, Guardsman purchased Joseph Parmet Co., Inc., manufacturer of One-Wipe® Dust Cloths, the nation's top-selling treated dust cloth. And in 1979, Guardsman moved One-Wipe production to Grand Rapids.

Entering the 1980s, Guardsman continued to strengthen its national distribution beginning on the West Coast. In 1980, Guardsman acquired both the Technical Research Company of Seattle and Harper's Stain and Lacquer of South Gate, California. Adding to its furniture finishing capability, Guardsman purchased the Furniture Gravure Company of Richmond—a manufacturer of cylinders used in printed finishes.

Recent Guardsman innovations include the formulation of environmentally safe, medium high-solids metal coatings—one of the nation's first. Research continues with high-solids metal coatings, as well as with waterborne wood finishing products. These new products will allow manufacturers to reduce solvent emissions common in the finishing and coatings industry—and reduce emissions more economically than trying to clean the air before it's returned to the atmosphere. Future plans call for the development of finishes for metal-coil coatings as well as electrostatic finishes for wood.

Indeed, Guardsman will continue to bring its know-how out of the lab and onto the production line.

205

Chemists conduct experiments (above), early in 1937. The company's resin manufacturing plant (below), as it appeared in the winter of 1942.

Over 100 years of family tradition

The Groskopf family was a part of the wave of European immigrants that came to America in the mid-1850s. The parents with their three young sons, August, Henry and William, made the long journey from Germany and settled in Detroit. It was there that young William was apprenticed to a leather working firm and gained the knowledge that would later serve the family so well. The Groskopfs moved to Grand Rapids where the brothers opened their trunk and leather goods store in 1881. The first small Groskopf Brothers' Store was on Lower Canal Street near today's Justice building. William, the youngest of the three, was 26 when they first went into business.

In the "good old days" of the late 1800s, Groskopf's used William's expertise and hand made most of the trunks and leather goods they sold in their store. The factory for these goods was on the second floor of the building, right above the store. Groskopf advertisements from the period boast all-leather trunks in the popular dome shape retailing for just $3.50 and $7.50.

A few years later the firm moved to 19 Canal Street, and August and Henry left the company for other fields. To help offset their absence, young Ada Groskopf began working in her father's store in 1900. After the move to Canal Street, William closed out production and specialized in retailing fine leather goods and luggage. The Canal Street store was flanked on one side by the Seigel Jewelry Company and on the other side by the Kent State Bank that stood on the corner of Canal and Lyon. All these properties were sold to the Pantlind family, and the 750-room Pantlind Hotel was built there in 1913.

When the Groskopfs left Canal Street, they moved to Monroe Avenue where they spent the trying days of World War I and the boom days that followed. After more than 30 years in the family firm, William Groskopf retired and handed the business over to his son, R. William, and his daughter, Ada, who had been working in the store since she was 15. William not enjoying the leather goods business, left the firm soon afterwards and went on to other endeavors. At a time when most men believed that a woman was incapable of running a business, Ada Groskopf used her excellent business ability to bring the firm successfully through the Great Depression and World War II when materials and merchandise were extremely scarce.

Ada's nephew Claude Heth joined his aunt in the firm in 1937, and in 1940, when other companies were folding in the face of World War II, Groskopf's expanded to carry the fine line of imported and domestic gifts for which they are famous.

In 1965, the company incorporated, and Mr. Heth became its first president. He and his two sons, Jeffrey and John, led the business through a period of expansion, including the opening of the Eastbrook Mall store in September of 1976 and the new Grand Village Mall store in October 1980. The downtown "mother store" has remained on Monroe Avenue and is part of the recently opened new Monroe Center Mall.

In January 1982, Claude Heth retired and his son Jeffrey became the new president of Groskopf's and John became vice president of the firm. Both are dedicated to the second 100 years of bringing the city an extensive line of fine luggage and leather goods and an unusual selection of better gifts.

At age 97, Ada Groskopf is watching her father's great-grandsons carry the family firm into its second century in Grand Rapids.

William Groskopf, founder, c. 1890 (top). Ada Groskopf was considered a pioneer for women in business in the Grand Rapids area (above). In the first Groskopf store (below), luggage was manufactured above the store.

Their first job was engineered on the kitchen stove

During the heart of the Depression, in 1932, J.B. Haviland, a young chemical engineer, founded a small research and testing laboratory in Grand Rapids. With the assistance of his wife, their first job was engineered on the kitchen stove. From that small beginning grew Haviland Enterprises, today one of the largest independent distributors of chemicals in the Midwest.

Over the past 50 years, annual sales have risen from $13,000 to more than $35,000,000. With a product inventory that now numbers in the thousands of tons. The original testing laboratory has grown into a three-company corporation whose divisions supply industrial and agricultural chemicals, consumer products and pollution control systems to customers here and abroad.

Haviland's first half-century has been distinguished by financial stability, development through diversification, customer loyalty, staff dedication and the company's commitment to the well-being of its workers. At Haviland Enterprises there is no mandatory retirement age. The company values the expertise of older employees, and several top executives who were with the company before World War II are still with the company today. J. B. Haviland, the founder, has been and remains chairman of the board.

Continuity of leadership has been matched by continuous growth. In the '30s,

Haviland began compounding chemicals for the industrial market. In the '40s, faced with automotive industry slowdowns, J.B. Haviland, who grew up in a farm family, was quick to recognize the potential of the agricultural chemical market. Haviland's agricultural products attracted farm customers throughout Michigan. The expanded packaging, warehousing and tank storage facilities of the 1950s provided more efficient services at lower prices. The '60s saw an unprecedented growth rate of 325 percent. Through a steady and dedicated pattern of innovation and expansion in the '70s, Haviland Products achieved its greatest increases in sales and market penetration.

Over the past decade, Haviland has become an acknowledged leader in resource conservation through pollution control. The Environmental Research and Engineering Division develops chemical processing systems designed to meet specific pollution problems. In addition, the division markets specialized chemical compounds enabling the electroplating, water treatment and electronics industries to eliminate pollutants in accordance with environmental protection laws. The automated systems remove metal contaminants from wastewater and have been hailed as a major step toward the solution of industrial waste problems.

Haviland Enterprises, being family

owned, has three Haviland sons in key corporate positions. Headquartered in Grand Rapids, the corporation maintains its own delivery fleet and operates major complexes including tank farms and warehouses in Grand Rapids and Kalamazoo. Other key facilities for distribution—including sales offices—are strategically located in Muskegon, Acme, Hart, Blissfield, and Watervliet, Michigan. The fully computerized operation offers high-speed order processing, on line inventory data, and up-to-the-minute credit analysis.

The Haviland Agricultural Chemical Company distributes a complete line of agricultural chemicals and farm equipment throughout the Midwest.

Wheaton Chemical Company markets an array of cleaning solvents, bleaches and fabric softners. Wheaton Chemical also markets laundry, drycleaning and energy conservation equipment.

Haviland Products, the largest company, has four divisions. The Consumer Products Division markets a full line of swimming pool accessories and chemical supplies, as well as contract packaging services utilized by many prominent companies for private label programs. The Manufactured Products Divisions markets proprietary compounds, researched and developed by Haviland, which are used in the plating, electronics and metal-processing industries. The Industrial Division packages and distributes basic chemical commodities to all major chemical markets and maintains one of the country's largest inventories of acids, alkalis, alcohols, amines, metals, ketones and solvents for custom blending to buyer specifications.

Chemical production is an exacting business, calling for rigid standards and allowing little margin for error. Haviland's testing laboratory, operating as part of the Environmental Research and Engineering Division, monitors product purity and assures customers, through careful testing, that strict standards of quality control are achieved.

The Environmental Research and Engineering Division is Haviland's most rapidly growing division, totally devoted to the research and development of new products sought by industry for a variety of technical applications. In a market where requirements are constantly changing, Haviland's research group takes pride in its ability to offer practical solutions to current chemical problems.

For the past 50 years, Haviland has been growing at an annual rate of more than twenty percent. And as the company charts its course for the decades ahead, J.B. Haviland, its founder and board chairman, expresses the philosophy that has guided his company from the beginning, "The future belongs to those who believe in it."

207

A privately owned company, Haviland Enterprises has several family members on its board of directors. Seated: J.B. Haviland (left), Mildred Haviland (right); standing: E. Bernard Haviland (left), James Haviland (center), and Paul Haviland (right).

A 130-year-old Grand Rapids tradition continues

Houseman's beginnings reach back to the city's lumbering days. Julius Houseman, who emigrated to the United States from his native Germany, arrived in Grand Rapids in the 1840s and began manufacturing work clothes for the lumberjack trade. When his cousin Joseph settled in Grand Rapids in 1852, the two men formed a partnership, opened a Monroe Avenue clothing store, and a Grand Rapids mercantile institution was born.

There were other partners in the early years—first Albert Alsberg, a Houseman cousin, and later Abraham May, who subsequently became a competitor.

Julius Houseman also left the business to pursue other interests. He ran for political office, serving as alderman, mayor of Grand Rapids, state legislator and United States congressman. Deeply involved in the civic and financial affairs of the rapidly growing city, Houseman was long one of Grand Rapids' most prominent citizens.

Joseph Houseman, who was widely known for his efforts as a conciliator between settlers and the local Indian tribes, remained with the business that grew as the city grew.

By 1883, there were two new partners, Edward Donnally and Eugene W. Jones, both longtime Houseman employees. There was also a new store, described by a newspaper of the time as a "superb mercantile palace, every department being furnished and fitted regardless of expense." The opening of the new Houseman, Donnally and Jones was a gala occasion. The storefront was brilliantly lit with electric lamps, and crowds of visitors came to witness what the newspaper called "an important event in the history of the city's commercial enterprise."

Joseph Houseman died in 1908, but his son Henry maintained the Houseman family's association with the store. The family tradition continued as Henry's sons—Felix, Joseph and Maurice—were brought into the business, each one assigned to work on a different floor. Felix left, but Joseph and Maurice remained, and in 1957 they incorporated the business as the Houseman Clothing Company. Today, Maurice Houseman Jr., is the president of a company whose attention to service and quality remains the same as it was during his great-grandfather Joseph's day.

After moving the store's downtown location three times, Houseman's presently occupies the same site on which Joseph and Julius opened the original Houseman's. There is also a branch store at Woodland Mall in Grand Rapids.

Modern merchandising techniques have changed the retailing business, and Houseman's has moved with the times. The first significant change came when the Housemans eliminated their manufacturing operations to devote all their efforts to retailing. For many years, Houseman's sold men's and boys' clothing only. It wasn't until 1927 that the store began stocking women's apparel. Today, women's wear accounts for more than half of Houseman's annual sales volume, and the boys' department is gone.

What hasn't changed is Houseman's fine selection, described in 1883 as "probably the largest line carried by any one house in the state." Maurice Houseman Sr., as a young man, was put in charge of the third-floor coat department. His efforts established Houseman's selection of women's coats as the finest in the area.

An alteration department has been a Houseman service since the very beginning. Nearly a century ago, a Houseman salesman boasted their custom fitters would make a "splendid figure of a poor-shaped customer." Modern customers are perhaps better shaped than those of the past century, but Houseman's continues the longstanding tradition of expert alterations.

Over the years, Houseman's grew into one of the city's leading downtown businesses, and the store remained as a Monroe Avenue business anchor during downtown's years of decline and decay. The store's continuing commitment to a healthy, revitalized downtown has not wavered, and its president, Maury Houseman, plays an active role in the Downtown Development Corporation.

Those efforts have not gone unnoticed. On the occasion of Houseman's 125th anniversary, the Michigan Senate, recognizing Grand Rapids' oldest clothing store, adopted a resolution which said, in part, "Such longevity says many things, not only about the good business sense of the proprietors and the quality of goods and service, but of community loyalty, faith and vitality. The 125 years that Houseman's has stood in downtown Grand Rapids have been marked by many changes. It is due in part to the hard work of all those associated with Houseman's that Grand Rapids is once again in its ascendancy....So many years of excellence are indeed deserving of praise and recognition."

Houseman's clothing store as it appeared in 1867 to the carriage trade of that era.

208

Backed by generations of experience

The four-story Spenser Duffy Furniture Exhibition Building (below), originally designed as a furniture showplace, has been restored to its original beauty and now houses Israels. The stained glass windows and stone columns, (inset), provide an elegant entrance for the downtown showroom.

Israels Designs for Living, established in March 1959, is an extension of founder Ray R. Israels' ancestry. His great-grandfather had established a successful merchandising organization in the Netherlands in the mid-nineteenth century. He passed his expertise on to his sons, who in turn formed individual merchandising corporations. Johan Israels, Ray's father, established an excellent reputation in his industry in Zutphen, Gelderland, the Netherlands. His foresight in the early twentieth century led him to move his firm to the New World. He and his family established their home-furnishings enterprise in Canada. His talents were passed on to his youngest son, Ray R. Israels, who was employed by the T. Eaton Company of Toronto, Ontario, as a designer to develop the new furnishing techniques. December 15, 1941, Ray Israels joined the Royal Canadian Air Force and served on the European front for five years. When the world returned to normal, it was time for Ray to think about a place to build his family heritage. After much searching, he selected Grand Rapids, the furniture capital of the world.

Israels' corporation was formed in Grand Rapids in March 1959. Ray R. Israels and his wife, Harriet, had strong beliefs in family involvement and established the enterprise with all four children—Joyce, Robert, James and Pamelia—as working partners. The first establishment was set up in the Kentwood suburb. The business developed, and as the early '60s demanded sophistication and new ideas, it was inevitable that the firm would move in many directions as well as to many locations.

The firm's first move was to the Murray building in the heart of Grand Rapids. In the new location, the family worked together with the children learning the ancestral trades at an early age. The corporation was geared to the design trade, fortified by the Grand Rapids Furniture Making Guild. With the design aspect in mind, the corporation grew rapidly, and its second move was to the Barclay Company addition, a lumber baron's development.

The family worked hard together, responsibilities developed for each of the younger members of the family. In the mid-'60s, individual extremities of personal taste and design called for the corporation to develop a personable attitude in its merchandising. The 25-room Pugh estate was decided on as corporate headquarters for merchandising and designing. As the corporation's volume continued to grow, "Israels" became synonymous with quality and reasonable prices. Warehousing grew from one location to several locations and became a problem for operating efficiency—forcing another decision. It was apparent that another direct retailing program needed to be formed by the company.

The corporation took a step toward an adventure in direct furniture sales and interior design. The business was moved to the historic Spencer Duffy Furniture Exhibition Building in newly renovated downtown Grand Rapids. The entire five-story building was designated as a furniture show place and was restored to its original majesty.

As the business grew, the partners established themselves as an essential part of the corporation with all the family members becoming officers. Robert R. Israels became president, James Henry Israels, vice president and Joyce and Pamelia Israels, secretaries. Israels' merchandising attitude was built to serve the public by educating them to new environments. "Israels Designs for Living, Inc." continued on the move with growth in many directions—in kitchen planning, home building, remodeling, interior and exterior

drawings, expanded contract and office concepts, and the retailing of merchandise and services pertinent to the customer's mode of life.

Israels has expanded itself once again, taking in many competent designers and professional staff. Through the direction of Robert Boersma, treasurer, John Arends, director of Israels' service network, and Susan E. Moushon of the design department, the company has expanded in design and retailing capabilities.

As the corporation serves the Grand Rapids public in retailing fine furniture at reasonable prices and in personalized design services, the Israels family will continue to be personally involved in all aspects of the corporation. The quality of Israels' family growth and service will help reestablish Grand Rapids as a giant in the furniture industry.

209

Company legacy of "working harder" evolves attitude of "working smarter"

One cold winter night in the early 1890s a group of men, shootin' the breeze around the pot-bellied stove in Miner S. Keeler's Middleville, Michigan, dry goods store, listened intently to a story about the fortune to be made in brass products. "Well, the boys around the stove listened to all this and became quite excited," explained Miner in his memoirs. "Every town was bidding for industries and this seemed like a wonderful chance . . . we were all anxious to boom the town and it ended in forming the Middleville Manufacturing Company."

The panic of 1893 hit the fledgling brass company hard. As Keeler recounted, "One day, I remember, there were six or seven firms in Rockford, Illinois, that folded the same day and they were all owing our company." And so, under receivership, with no buyer in sight, the court ordered the company to be sold.

Out of the dashed hopes of the Middleville Brass Company emerged the Keeler Brass Company purchased in 1893 for $12,500. The infant company (KBC) struggled for survival during those first three years. "One thing I can remember very distinctly," Miner related, "everytime that I turned the corner to go down to the plant, I would grit my teeth and say, I will get you yet."

Miner experienced full well the wisdom in the words, "Once you put your hand to the plow, don't look back."

It wasn't long before Keeler's brothers,

Isaac and George, recognized that a move from Middleville to Grand Rapids was essential. The little brass foundry on Godfrey and Martha streets prospered. Soon punch presses were added so that wrought furniture pulls and cast pulls could be manufactured. And that was followed by a revolutionary new product—robe rails, which were bars that stretched along the back of an automobile's front seat and were used for the storage of robes that kept backseat passengers warm in winter.

Automotive and furniture hardware flourished before and after World War I. The Keeler Building on Division and Fountain streets was built in 1914 as a furniture exposition center. Early in 1919, KBC began experimenting with various types of screw-making machines. But it wasn't until 1921, with an initial investment of $75,000 for machinery, that one of the most modern screw-making plants in America was established—producing over 350,000 screws daily. The August 5, 1922, *Grand Rapids Herald* acclaimed this feat, "Without the aid of human hands!"

The Great Depression years caused KBC to forge ahead in technology culminating in the development of the stainless steel sheetmetal handle which was produced for Studebaker and Ford—carrying KBC through Hoover's period of reconstruction.

World War II found KBC still a small company, but rapid growth soon followed. Zinc alloy die castings began to replace stainless steel and brass. In 1951, Keeler in-

vested heavily in die casting and finishing facilities, and the present-day Stevens Street plant is dubbed "the most modern zinc die casting plant in the world."

Further acquisitions, building and expansions occurred under the leadership of Miner S. Keeler's son, Isaac S. Keeler, and his grandson, Miner S. Keeler II. Several decades of business finds KBC today with nine plants in west Michigan and plants in Jamestown, New York and Pico Rivera, California.

Having merged in the summer of 1979 with Babcock International Incorporated of Trumbull, Connecticut, three generations of family leadership drew to a close. Almost half of the KBC product line today is automotive trim—hood ornaments, nameplates, hubcaps, taillight assemblies and sideview mirrors. Keeler is the largest manufacturer of hardware for America's furniture industry, presently marketing almost 15,000 hardware items. A newcomer, the Consumer Product Line, markets decorative accessories and is penetrating home electronics, office equipment, computer, word processing and giftware markets. Keeler's products can be found in homes and autos throughout the world.

The Keeler legacy of hard work, which began on that cold winter night almost 90 years ago, has been passed to Leslie A.L. Garvie, current president. Garvie pledges to build on that legacy a company attitude of "working smarter" to produce a quality product at a competitive price.

The original Keeler Brass Company located in Middleville, Michigan, was purchased in 1893.

Graduating America's designers for over 50 years

David Wolcott Kendall, the furniture designer after whom Kendall School of Design was named, is considered by many to have been the greatest furniture designer of his age. Some have said that he left a greater impression on the field of furniture than any other designer of his time.

After his death, his widow, Helen M. Kendall, provided in her will for the founding of a school to be known as the David Wolcott Memorial School of Design. The school was incorporated in 1928 and on the first day of March, 1931, the old Kendall homestead, located at 145 Fountain Street, opened to a class of 35 students.

From the start, artistic training at Kendall stressed instruction along traditional lines. The first director, Edgar R. Somes, discouraged the teaching of modern art and art fads. The original two-year course of study included classes in drawing from still life and from models. Detailed study in the major areas of illustration and design was conducted in the second year.

By 1937, the school had made a specialty of teaching furniture design, and many students were drawn to the school from the families of local Polish and Dutch furniture craftsmen.

The school flourished in its early years, but with the coming of World War II, Kendall fell on hard times, and many potential students were drawn into military service. By 1944, the school had reached an all-time low enrollment of only six students. Many former Kendall students served in the armed forces as illustrators and artists on art sections of squadron newspapers and as sign painters or cartoonists.

The school survived, however, and after the war was over the influx of veterans studying on the GI Bill boosted the school's enrollment to new highs and set the trend for future development. Within a twelve-month period, enrollment skyrocketed from six to 146 and led to an increased faculty as well as a larger number of course offerings.

In 1947, the school's name was shortened to Kendall school of Design. The curriculum was further increased and the school began to offer training in wider areas of design.

In 1948, further growth resulted when the small Gilbert School of Design was incorporated into Kendall. This enabled Kendall to include a third year of instruction in its program, and soon afterwards a commercial and advertising program was added to the illustration, furniture design and interior design courses.

Under the 23-year tenure of President Lawrence O. Mailloux (1952-1975), the school underwent many changes. A concerted enrollment effort swelled the student population to over 400.

The continued growth in the size of the student body finally proved too much for the old Kendall homestead. In 1961, the school purchased the Kenneth Welch home at 1110 College Avenue NE. Classes were originally held in the home itself, but within a few years the East and West Buildings were completed and in use. (Some classes continued to be held at the Fountain Street location until 1967.)

In 1976, under President Phyllis I. Danielson, the curriculum again underwent extensive revision. In 1978, Kendall began to offer an Associate of Fine Arts Degree for the first time. And in 1979, the school was granted the right to confer on its students a Bachelor of Fine Arts Degree. In April 1981, the school was recognized as a fully accredited four-year institution of higher learning by the North Central Association of Schools and Colleges.

Kendall currently offers nine major areas of study: advertising design, environmental design, fine arts, furniture design, graphic arts, illustration, interior design, television communications and industrial design.

Throughout the many years of its existence, Kendall School of Design's philosophy remains the same: educate men and women for careers in the visual arts by instilling the fundamental principles and skills of drawing and design, by teaching the students to think clearly and creatively and by developing their ability to translate their ideas visually.

David Wolcott Kendall at the drawing table watched over by his ever-present friend.

211

A tradition of quality

In 1898, John Knape, then a Grand Rapids machinist, saw good possibilities in a chainless bicycle he named the Clipper. History didn't verify his judgement on that occasion, but the company he founded had many significant achievements over the ensuing decades.

Where company founder Knape sought to serve the consumer outside his home, today's Knape & Vogt Manufacturing Co. has linked its fortunes to home interiors. The company is Number One in the country in wall-attached decorative shelving. Very well-liked words at Knape & Vogt are "Do it yourself," because the company's sales growth tracks closely with the increase in annual spending by those home owners who use their own labor—plus the products available at retail—to beautify their homes. Linking the company's fortunes to home modernization has been an important factor in employment stability.

One of the company's most important assets is its strong customer base. Name a retailer who caters to the do-it-yourself consumer and almost surely you've named a Knape & Vogt customer. This includes the largest hardware chains and buying organizations, home centers, nationally known department stores and merchandisers.

The company estimates there are 35,000 retail outlets for its home decor products, which may be twice as many outlets as its nearest competitor. In addition to shelving, the KV product line includes closet rods, clothing carriers, sliding towel bars, and other commonly used hardware items.

Drawer slides also comprise a well-established product line. Many of these are sold through retail outlets, but the majority of them are marketed through builders' hardware distributors or direct to certain casework manufacturers and cabinetmakers.

Their history relates to Knape & Vogt's change in emphasis over the years. Today's company is primarily, although not exclusively, oriented toward consumer products sold at retail. (In its early days the consumer hardware market received little or no attention at all.)

Founder John Knape's bicycle was less than a resounding success due to the advent of the chain-drive coaster brake, which enabled other manufacturers to produce better-riding and safer cycles. However, this was not as unfortunate as it sounds because Knape turned his skills as a machinist in other directions. Soon he was making specialty machinery and tool and die products.

In 1904, his brother-in-law, Englebert J. Vogt, joined him. They grew as a partnership and in 1918 incorporated the firm as Knape & Vogt Mfg. Co. In the 1920s and 1930s, there was a gradual transition from machinery products to specialty hardware for Grand Rapids and for the nation's furniture manufacturers. It was in these years that drawer slides became an important product line.

Another increasing opportunity was in hardware for store display fixtures and showcases. This was the birth of KV shelving hardware. Although in those days, the consumer market was very small and the term "do it yourself" certainly did not have today's meaning.

World War II brought about a major change in emphasis for Knape & Vogt, as it did for many other companies. At the start of the war the company discontinued virtually all of its civilian product lines and turned to contract work for military needs. Glider wings, shell cases and bandolier clips were among the components made in the company's plant on Richmond Street.

The housing boom that began after veterans returned to civilian life provided a fertile sales territory in the late 1940s. Donald J. Knape, now president, recalls that he was one of seven or eight salesmen recruited in those postwar years. At the time it was a major expansion move because the sales organization previously consisted of the then president, Frederick J. Vogt, and one salesman, Herman J. Brink.

Undoubtedly, Mr. Knape observes, the do-it-yourself boom originated because veterans and other young marrieds couldn't afford to pay for professional work, but equally important was the fact that manufacturers developed better, simpler, more handsomely finished products which could be used even by those of less than average mechanical ability.

Knape & Vogt was among the companies which simplified the do-it-yourself work. In 1967, management made a corporate decision to focus primarily on the consumer market, although continuing to serve original equipment manufacturers and the builders' hardware field. Today more than 30 company representatives call on all major merchandisers. The company estimates that it serves 85 to 90 of the 100 largest retailers of home modernization products.

What are the reasons for the company's growth and success? Emphasis on quality and service, plus a consistent policy of reinvesting profits in modernizing plant and equipment, are cited by Knape as among the more important ingredients.

"Our quality emphasis started in 1898 with the Old World Standards of our founder, and today it also reflects American know-how," Knape observed. "When you come down to it, quality results from a personal attitude even more than

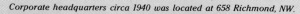

Corporate headquarters circa 1940 was located at 658 Richmond, NW.

from use of expensive materials or production equipment. If you have superior men and women on the production line and in the office, as we do, they themselves live up to the highest standards."

The executive added: "Quality applies to many things besides products. At Knape & Vogt, we also achieve quality in such individual tasks as fulfillment of delivery promises or prompt answering of inquiries. Whether an individual employee ever deals directly with a customer, the quality of his work has a bearing on the company's overall success."

As to the importance of financial strength, it is noteworthy that over 60 percent of net income has been reinvested in the last ten years. Reinvestment in plant and equipment in those years has totaled $15,700,000, and the company's facilities—including Grand Rapids headquarters—have an insurance/appraisal value exceeding $46,000,000. That averages out to $53,000 per employee. "The best level of craftsmanship is possible only when the worker is backed with such an investment," declared Knape.

Other than Grand Rapids, KV has three production facilities. A plant in La Mirada, California, was purchased in 1972 and gives the company full capability to serve West Coast customers, including the western stores of national chains. A wood processing plant in Benton Harbor, Michigan, was acquired in 1970. The company built its first Canadian manufacturing plant in 1966 in Rexdale, near Toronto. The plant has been expanded several times and now has virtually all the capabilities of U.S. operations. Canadian sales have shown an excellent growth rate.

"There are do-it-yourselfers in all states, so our products are nationally distributed," Knape said. "The do-it-yourself market consistently moves ahead when other segments of the economy tend to falter. That is why we regard our long-term growth opportunities as among the best available to any company."

The company's return on stockholders' investment over the past nine or ten years exceeded the median for the 500 largest industrial companies, as reported by *Fortune* magazine.

Common stock in the company became publicly held in 1961. The stock is traded in the national over-the-counter market. Members of the Knape family retain a substantial interest in the firm as shareholders and on an operating basis.

"Our stockholders, employees, customers and suppliers comprise four groups of almost equal importance," Mr. Knape summarized. "We're grateful that all have contributed to the company's growth, and we expect to continue to grow with their enduring support and cooperation."

New corporate headquarters is located at 2700 Oak Industrial Drive, NE. Completed in 1965, this modern office and manufacturing facility (above) consists of more than 300,000 square feet. Example of decorative shelving systems (below), for the do-it-yourself market.

213

An integral part of Grand Rapids for 120 years

Adolph Leitelt was born in 1833 in Kratzau, Bohemia, and came to Grand Rapids at age 21. In 1862, he and a brother Edward established a blacksmith and machine shop called A. Leitelt & Brother at 5 Erie Street near Canal (approximately where the present Justice Building is now located). By 1867, they had added a foundry and were using the name Valley City Iron Works. It was an iron and brass foundry, forge shop and machine shop where steam engines, waterwheels and flour and sawmill machinery were built. Eventually, they added a boiler shop and began to make boilers and to fabricate structural iron. The company became dealers in pipe, pipe fittings and mill supplies.

Edward left the business in the early 1880s and in 1891, the business was incorporated as Adolph Leitelt Iron Works.

Upon Adolph's death in 1897, the business was operated by the Leitelt family with Adolph Jr. serving as president until his death in 1906, followed by his sisters Mathilda T. and Rosetta C.

In 1912, the company designed and built, for the Grand Rapids Veneer Works, a heavy platform supported by four rotating corner screw columns which raised and lowered a load of lumber. The invention became the first lumber lift installation in the country. Another such lift was built for Leitelts' next-door neighbor, Bissell Carpet Sweeper Co., and remained in service for over 50 years.

The original lift designs were later refined and became recognized throughout the lumber and woodworking industry. To augment the lumber lift, Leitelt developed a line of transfer cars, sub-cars, turntables and car pullers. Today Leitelt lumber-handling products are found throughout the country. The screw lift principle has been applied to industrial platform lifts, railroad lift bridges and to stage and orchestra lifts. The first stage lift built by Leitelt is still in use in the Welsh Civic Auditorium.

The company also designed and built hydraulic and belt-driven cable elevators and became well known in the elevator industry. Leitelt was one of the charter members of the National Elevator Manufacturer's Association and remained active in that organization until the elevator division was sold in 1966.

In 1919, the company was sold and reincorporated under its present day name of Leitelt Iron Works. The new owners were headed by David C. McKay who served as president until 1936 and Fred H. Meyer as general manager, eventually became president and served in that capacity until 1951. The foundry, forge shop, pipe department and the mill supply division had been—or eventually were—closed or sold. The remaining company consisted of the machine shop, fabricating shop, lumber handling and elevator divisions. Leitelt's primary business became the manufacture of lumber handling equipment and elevators, general machining and fabricating, repair work and the building of special machinery and equipment.

Business was good until the Depression hit. The company struggled through that period, emerging with a debt that it could not repay until 1950.

In 1951, Glenn W. Sackett, succeeded Meyer as president, and he served until his death in 1958. Thomas A. Steel then served as president until he retired in 1966. He was followed by Peter H. Decker who served as president until he retired in 1972. Currently, Herbert W. Weidenfeller is president.

In the early 1960s, the downtown urban renewal project forced the plant to relocate. And by 1963, a new 90,000 square foot plant, located on north Turner Avenue had been completed. The plant includes fully equipped fabrication and machine shops with high bays (each with Leitelt built overhead cranes) and bigger machine tools enabling the company to receive, repair, build and rebuild larger and heavier machinery and equipment.

Although many interesting machines, special equipment and fabrications are still being designed and built for power plants, hydroelectric dams, steel mills, industrial plants and municipalities around the country, service and repair are now the company's primary business. Many customers throughout the state depend on Leitelt Iron Works when a breakdown occurs or a repair is needed in their equipment.

Leitelt has established a reputation of "high quality workmanship and fair dealing with its customers and employees." The company looks with pride and satisfaction on its long history of contributing to the growth and prosperity of Grand Rapids.

ADOLPH LEITELT IRON WORKS
GRAND RAPIDS, MICH.

The Adolph Leitelt Iron Works in 1915 produced elevators, lumber lifts, boilers, smokestacks, special machinery, steam forgings and heating, factory and mill supplies (above). Workers at the Adolph Leitelt Iron Works posed in front of their company sign in the late 1800s (below).

214

Where the spirit of 'Why Pay More' made one-stop shopping a way of life

The Meijer story began almost by accident not quite half a century ago, when a 50-year old Dutch immigrant gave up his dream of raising chickens on a small farm near Greenville.

Hendrik Meijer had been a barber in the little town since 1912, the year his fiancée, Gezina, joined him in America. His shop was a regular stop for farmers and railroad men. But when the Depression hit, money for haircuts grew scarce. Meijer tried to supplement his income with a few head of dairy cattle. Gezina milked the cows, while the children, Johanna and Fred, peddled bottles of milk door to door.

A year or two before the Great Crash, Meijer had built a new building next door to his shop. He wanted some rental income for his old age, but by 1934 he still couldn't find a tenant for the space. With no rent coming in, he couldn't meet his mortgage payments. Business in the barber shop dwindled, and the bottom dropped out of milk prices.

Someone suggested Meijer see if one of the grocery chains might rent the building for a store. "No one wanted it," he recalled. "At that time there were 22 groceries in Greenville, and they were hanging on by their fingernails."

At least they were hanging on. With a little credit, desperate men across the country were setting up shop. People had to eat, didn't they? The barber was running out of alternatives, so he used his credit to get an order for $328 worth of groceries and traded his ten-dollar violin to a plasterer to finish the vacant building's interior.

Meijer had heard customers in his barber shop talk about the big new stores they'd seen in Grand Rapids. Supermarkets were revolutionizing the grocery business even as Meijer set up his first displays. These barn-like markets did away with service and credit and—with their lower overhead—shaved precious pennies off prices. Meijer vowed to compete with them on their own low-priced terms. He put baskets in the front of the store and invited customers to help themselves. With Fred at his side, he searched out the best buys on potatoes or peanut butter, and the little Thrift Market, as it was called, was on its way to becoming a supermarket.

Meijer had an instinct for mass merchandising years before the phrase was coined. He catered to his customers with a

Hendrik and Fred Meijer in 1960 (above) and the Meijer Thrift Market, Greenville, in 1936 (below).

zeal and honesty that was infectious. When he died 30 years later, the enterprise he so desperately embarked upon in 1934 had undergone a metamorphosis.

A second store, and then a third, followed in neighboring towns. The first Grand Rapids store opened in 1949. It was "Meijer's Supermarkets" by then, although Fred and his wife, Lena, still wrote all the ads in their Greenville kitchen. The offices and warehouse were moved to Grand Rapids in 1952 when the company's sixth supermarket was opened at the intersection of Michigan and Fuller.

The "Why-Pay-More" commitment to low prices had come to town, but the transformation remained incomplete. In 1962, with Fred now guiding day-to-day activities, the company undertook its greatest gamble since that first order of groceries back in 1934. At the corner of 28th Street and Kalamazoo Avenue, Meijer opened the first Thrifty Acres—a self-service discount department store "With the Hometown Touch." These were the days when "discount" was often synonymous with second-rate. Meijer gave the word a new definition. With 100,000 square feet of floor space under one roof, Thrifty Acres sold lettuce and dresses and lawn mowers, food and general merchandise in great quantities at low prices—and all through the same battery of cash registers.

It was the debut of one-stop shopping. The foundation had been laid for a shopping experience Grand Rapids would soon share with neighboring cities in Michigan and beyond, a foundation built on the sober virtues of the Dutch and the unsinkable optimism of a middle-aged barber.

215

A tradition of innovation and service

Today, Michigan National Corporation Banks comprise a statewide financial organization with 365 banking offices and 120 automatic teller machines, serving more than 2.5 million customers. Total assets are in excess of $6 billion. This combination of offices and assets makes Michigan National the second largest banking institution in Michigan and the 36th largest banking organization in the country.

The founder of Michigan National Banks was Howard J. Stoddard, who was sent to Michigan in 1933 as a representative of the Reconstruction Finance Corporation. His assignment was to help rebuild the banking structure of Michigan in those troubled times.

In 1940, after seven years of establishing new banks and liquidating older, less sound institutions, he went into banking for himself. Backed by several wealthy industrialists. Michigan National Bank was formed by the acquisition of six banks lo-

cated in Grand Rapids, Lansing, Battle Creek, Charlotte, Marshall and Saginaw.

Michigan National Bank in Grand Rapids came about through the acquaintanceship of Howard J. Stoddard and Joseph H. Brewer, president of Grand Rapids National Bank. By 1939 Stoddard had obtained a majority position in the bank. The bank then merged with Grand Rapids Trust Company to form the new National Bank of Grand Rapids. In 1940 the National Bank of Grand Rapids was one of the six banks purchased by Stoddard and his backers to form the nucleus of Michigan National Bank. Headquarters for the new bank then and now are in Lansing, Michigan, with assets over $1.7 billion. Today, the Grand Rapids Office, headed by John B. Baum, senior vice president, is a center for commercial banking as well as trust and international services.

Howard J. Stoddard was an innovator in a world dominated by conservative banking

practices. Shortly after World War II, Michigan National Bank introduced drive-in banking, using a patented push-out money drawer designed by the Wickes Corporation of Saginaw. Michigan National Bank was also the first to offer Saturday banking and soon became known as "The Saturday Bank." In the 1950s, when mobile homes were gaining popularity, Michigan National was among the first to offer financing of these homes and soon had the largest portfolio in the country. Under Stoddard's leadership, Michigan National was among the first banks offering credit cards to its customers in the mid-1960s.

Stoddard was also among the first to advocate state-wide branch banking even after Michigan law was changed in the 1940s to restrict branching. This restrictive law forbade branching except for within 25 miles of the main office. This meant that Michigan National Bank, Grand Rapids, which Stoddard brought into being, could

The elegance of yesterday and the newest features of banking efficiency and convenience come together in Michigan National Bank-Central's Grand Plaza Office. Virtually no effort has been spared to authentically restore this landmark building, as part of Grand Rapids' on-going Renaissance.

Upon entering the bank, you will be immediately aware that you have entered a very special place. The high, 27-foot ceiling demands attention as you see two chandeliers against the striking and ornate gold-leaf inlay of the ceiling. This is the original ceiling, dating from 1915, refurbished and preserved. Roll-top desks of both the cylinder and scurve styles are made of walnut and mahogany. These turn-of-the-century masterpieces have been painstakingly restored to their original, lustrous beauty in keeping with the walnut interior of the building. The result is a unique museum piece of the late Victorian period which must be visited to be fully appreciated.

not branch since, technically, it was a branch of the bank headquartered in Lansing. While this situation persists for the Grand Rapids Office, the over-all problem was solved by forming a holding company, which in turn could acquire affiliates. As a result, Michigan National Corporation was formed and subsequently acquired the Central Bank, N.A., Grand Rapids and First National Bank of Wyoming, as well as other banks throughout Michigan.

The Central Bank was founded in 1934 and was located at the corner of Monroe and Pearl streets. Its president was Howard C. Lawrence. By 1937 the bank's growth in services required additional operating space. The move was then made to 65 Monroe, where the headquarters remained until 1976 when the headquarters were moved again to their present location in the Waters Building.

Central Bank, N.A. provided one office throughout its early years. It wasn't until December 1956 that the first branch was opened—the start of an expansion that continues to this day.

During this period of expansion through branching, Central Bank, N.A. became affiliated with Michigan National Corporation, and by 1976 had assumed the new name of Michigan National Bank-Central. The period also marked an impressive rise in bank assets through an aggressive branching effort. Assets in 1974 were at the $48 million level; in 1976 they were at $69 million. By 1978 that total had attained the $100 million mark. Today assets are in excess of $150 million. Michigan National Bank-Central serves the Grand Rapids area with 21 offices fulfilling individual and commercial banking needs.

Past presidents of Michigan National Bank-Central and its predecessor, the Central Bank of Grand Rapids include: Howard C. Lawrence, 1934-1935; Leon T. Closterhouse, 1935-1954; C. Lincoln Linderholm, 1954-1974; and Robert H. Becker, 1974-1976. Howard Stoddard's son, Charles C. Stoddard, became president in 1976 and chairman in 1980.

Michigan National Bank-Wyoming, headed by Richard H. Jones, president, rounds out the Michigan National presence in Kent and Ottawa counties. This affiliate bank has eleven offices including three in the Holland/Zeeland area. Assets for this third arm in the Grand Rapids area are in excess of $60 million.

All told, Michigan National Corporation Banks has 33 offices in the greater Grand Rapids area, plus Michigan Money Automatic Teller Machines, four of which were the first drive-in units in the area. Michigan National has always been committed to serving the financial needs of the community; it will continue to grow by maintaining its tradition of innovative banking.

The Grand Rapids Michigan National Bank Building was built in 1926 by Owen-Ames-Kimball Company. It was the architectural marvel of its time and was built for the Grand Rapids Trust Company. The architecture is modern Romanesque with early American and particularly early Michigan influence. It is 12 stories high, with the top two floors presenting a receding skyline. The face of the building cream-mottled terra cotta and the base is of Coldspring granite. A full size Indian gazes down from the corner of the building. The entry way is framed by two columns over which are carved two wolverines holding shields showing rapids, pine woods and men in canoes. In other areas pine trees and cones and the heads of small animals are used as decoration.

The weather ball was added to the building in 1967 and has become a Grand Rapids landmark. The colors of the ball indicate weather condition with red for warmer, blue—cooler, green—no change, flashing—precipitation.

217

The 125-year saga of the Jackoboice family business

Joseph Jackoboice arrived alone in Grand Rapids in 1853 and in 1856 established a machinery business that has continued for 125 years through five generations of the Jackoboice family.

Information on his early life is limited. Joseph Jackoboice was born March 16, 1824, on the Prussian-Polish border in the 1800-year-old town of Kalisz. After living for some time in his native land and later in Germany, he immigrated to America at age 28, a decision perhaps hastened by the 1848 Revolution. He came to Grand Rapids when it still had a population of less than 4,000.

With an education, financial resources, a knowledge of several languages and a skill in his trade, he was able to establish a company. It bore his name and occupied space in the loft of a small building on Mill Street near the riverbank in the area that is now downtown. The fledgling firm directed its first efforts towards the manufacture of steam engines, sawmill machinery and general millwork. In 1862, the modest operation moved to the northwest corner of Monroe and Michigan streets (then known as Canal and East Bridge) an area described as "Germantown" by Charles E. Belknap in his *Yesterdays of Grand Rapids* because of the blacksmith shops, forges, ironworks and Germans dominating the scene. The Rasch House, an early Grand Rapids hostelry, also occupied the site. (Among its owners was Frances Rasch who, in 1859, married Joseph Jackoboice.) In later years the Clarendon, the Charlevoix and, finally, the Rowe Hotel—now the Olds Manor—found favor at this corner.

The population of the city in the mid-1860s was approximately 15,000 when the Jackoboice factory was moved to the west bank of the Grand River near the terminus of the interurban bridge. The small firm utilized waterpower as an energy source and continued in the traditional product and service lines. Among recollections related by Edward J. Jackoboice, is the memory of the river and canal being used for a swim by some workers at the end of a warm day.

The story of the business during this period is limited to wisps of family conversations heard by George A. Jackoboice Sr., who at the time was not privileged to hear or concerned enough to remember.

Meanwhile the family of Joseph and Frances Jackoboice flourished at their residence on Broadway Avenue NW, where later the convent of St. Mary's Church would be built. They were chartered members of the pioneer Catholic parish.

In 1880, the company assumed a new dimension with its move to the neighboring southwest corner of Front and Douglas streets where a building, once known as the German-English Schoolhouse, served as

Edward J. Jackoboice, 1864-1935 (left). Joseph Jackoboice, 1824-1899 (right).

the Jackoboice factory for 75 years. The 115-year-old landmark survives as the oldest and last of the original Front Street buildings. Badly damaged by two fires, it was demolished in 1982.

J. Jackoboice combined the name of the business with the more descriptive "West Side Iron Works" and boldly lettered it on the facade.

In 1875, there were no other structures south of the school in the same block. The influence of the German-English School Association lingered until 1880 when finances directed its demise. Alois, Julius and Robert Rasch conveyed title to Joseph Jackoboice who soon adapted the building to manufacturing. A third floor was introduced for pattern storage; the ticket office disappeared, and the stage vanished. Prosaic industry followed. Lathes, planers, milling machines, drill presses, forges and work benches replaced blackboards and school desks, and men in overalls toiled where pupils once studied. Jackoboice patented a lumber recording device to measure board feet cut from logs in sawmills and was perhaps the first in the West to manufacture a band saw which found favor in furniture and wood-working trades.

Edward J. Jackoboice, the son of Joseph, joined the firm after serving his apprenticeship. Father and son combined their talents for the manufacture of steam en-

gines and also introduced a line of saws in addition to arbors, boring and shaping machines. Fire escapes also were designed, fabricated and installed on many old Grand Rapids structures.

After a brief retirement Joseph Jackoboice died in 1899. His achievements were recognized in the various histories of Grand Rapids by authors Baxter, Chapman, Conrad and Lyden, by various trade journals and by the local press. The Polish ethnic exhibit in the Grand Rapids Public Museum acknowledges his role as a pioneer.

Edward J., the son of Joseph and father of George A. Jackoboice Sr. and Edward W. Jackoboice, assumed active management. His zest for machinery included a steam-propelled pleasure craft, the *Comet* on the Grand River and this venture was a prelude to personally designing and constructing a steam-powered automobile in 1897 that is believed to be the fourth such vehicle in Grand Rapids.

Involvement with the automobile manufacturing business was considered and dismissed. At that time the wood-working machinery market was more attractive because of increasing demands by emerging automobile body builders for wooden framework.

In trend with the good-roads program for the travel-minded nation, in pursuit of a

more relaxed life style and in the desire to journey, Edward developed a line of road maintenance machines that merited acceptance by highway departments nationally. Meanwhile, the West Side Iron Works was sold to a major Chicago concern, the terms of which prohibited continuance in a similar competitive business. The product line remained in Grand Rapids in substantial measure, however, when family friend and business neighbor, Carl Tannewitz, added similar band and rip saws to his manufacturing line at the Tannewitz Works.

The era of the West Side Iron Works had ended but another venture began, and it preserved the continuity of the family machinery tradition. Known since 1922 as the Edward J. Jackoboice Company, the firm was incorporated in 1931 as the Monarch Road Machinery Company with George A. Jackoboice Sr. as president; Edward W. Jackoboice as secretary-treasurer; and Helen J. Jackoboice as vice-president. (Ruth succeeded as vice president after the death of Helen in 1936). Frances followed a career in executive capacities with the city, county and state departments of social services.

Underbody truck scrapers were then in demand for the maintenance of gravel roads. The Jackoboice-patented reversible machine coincided with state laws requir-

George A. Jackoboice Sr., president of the Monarch Road Machinery Company (top), with a steam engine used to power the fourth automobile in Grand Rapids, built in 1897 by Edward J. Jackoboice. Edward J. Jackoboice, father of George A. and Edward W. who founded the Monarch Road Machinery Company and developed many items of highway maintenance equipment (above). Edward J. Jackoboice (driver and owner of car) (below), Paul J. Hake (brother-in-law of Edward Jackoboice in passenger seat front) and Edward Rasch (cousin of EJ) in back seat.

ing all such units to travel in the direction of traffic. For a few years the main highway system from Indianapolis to Sault Ste. Marie was patrolled by Monarch scrapers.

Edward J. Jackoboice who was the transitional figure and the major influence in moving from wood-working to road machinery, died in 1935.

In the years that followed, Edward would have been proud to acknowledge that the products of his generation were replaced by items representative of a more sophisticated technology.

The onslaught of World War II altered established Monarch patterns of business due to material scarcities, allocations, and the necessity of coping with federal agencies.

Although hydraulic methods had been adapted to underbody truck scrapers as early as 1925, the increasing popularity of this power medium was given impetus by the war. The market surged beyond the capacity of the facilities and personnel even though augmented by 46 firemen who found part-time employment at Monarch until the armistice in 1941. By 1954, the company needed more room for expansion and moved to Michigan Street where it now occupies 125,000 square feet of office and manufacturing space.

Monarch products are concentrated in precision power hydraulic pumps, valves, cylinders and systems for a variety of mobile and industrial applications.

Monarch also operates a Canadian subsidiary and an assembly facility in the Netherlands. Monarch controls are exported to approximately 25 countries.

The present officers are George A. Jackoboice Sr., president; John S. Jackoboice, vice president; Edward James Jackoboice, secretary; George A. Jackoboice Jr., treasurer; and Thomas J. Jackoboice, director of international operations.

Like a tapestry woven over the years, with knots and tufts on the underside representing the toil and labor of generations, so the Monarch Road Machinery Company and its pioneering antecedent family companies have produced achievements for all to see and have survived the turmoil of wars, economic cycles, the march of five generations, product and market changes, and the opportunities and challenges of an ever-changing world.

On the occasion of the Sesquicentennial Anniversary of Grand Rapids, the Jackoboice philosophy was splendidly expressed on the Tree of Dates:

> Dedicated to all members of the Jackoboice Family, Past, Present, and Future, whose pioneering, faith, and perseverence in Grand Rapids since 1853, may merit distinction for what has been accomplished, and what is yet to be fulfilled.

219

Over 125 years serving the
construction trade of West Michigan

In 1834, Mr. William Morman left England for the New World. Landing in New York, he worked and walked his way to Grand Rapids, Michigan, arriving on June 6, 1836. He farmed until 1857, then started a lime burning operation on the banks of the Grand River to make building bricks. At that time 6,000 people lived in the village of Grand Rapids.

From this beginning, the Morman Company tradition of quality, value and service has continued in an ever upward spiral. A son, Samuel, was born in 1858 and became a partner in 1880. Six years later, upon his father's retirement, Samuel became the sole proprietor and from that time on the company has been called S.A. Morman & Co.

Since in Grand Rapids all construction stopped during the bitter winter months, Sam Morman decided to expand his line to keep his men busy during that part of the year when they couldn't make or sell bricks. Thus coal became a major part of his business during the '20s and was a real help during the 1930's Depression, when most construction came to a standstill and coal sales kept the building supply firm afloat.

The principle of employee involvement is inherent in S.A. Morman & Co. During the Depression the firm didn't lay off a single worker. The work force was called together and told "We either lay off two truck driv-

ers, or we all get by on a little less." The employees met and decided that they would each take less, rather than have two men without work.

World War II brought an upswing in the company's business with the receiving of several government contracts for supplies to build war plants. Among others, the firm supplied building materials for Haskelite, the Grand Rapids plant that built wooden wing-frames for the gliders that flew across the Rhine.

The product line kept increasing and by now the company sold coal, brick, cement, plaster, windows, sewer tile and furnished materials for most of the downtown and residential construction in Grand Rapids.

Sam Morman had a knack for business and started several. One business that he and several other men started was American Box Board. Morman served this company as vice president and then spent many years as chairman of the board. American Box Board later became a part of Packaging Corporation of America (now a unit of Tenneco).

When Sam Morman was 90, he sent his chauffeur inside his house to get something off his dresser and then stole his own car. Returning after a 45 minute drive, he was incensed to find that many of the Morman Co. employees were out with the police

searching for him. A spry and active man, he had just wanted to see how the new fluid transmission in his Buick worked. Possessed of a quick sense of humor, he would often joke that he was living on "borrowed time and my heirs money."

In 125 years, S.A. Morman & Co. has become a leader in the supply of finish hardware (door locks, hinges, closers, etc.) hollow metal doors and frames and specialty items to the nonresidential construction trade in West Michigan.

It has been a tradition for the firm members to be active in the community and for years many have served on boards, including United Way, Chamber of Commerce, YMCA, Hospital, Red Cross, Church, Assoc. for the Blind, Rotary and others.

The company is currently incorporated and is employee owned with the Board of Directors and Stockholders all from within the employee group.

After Mr. Morman's retirement in about 1927 the management helm was assumed by his son-in-law William B. Steele. William Steele is the man responsible for the company growth into hardware and hollow metal. William Steele retired in 1962 and the presidency was filled by his son-in-law, John C. Baxter, and when he retired in 1977 John Baxter's brother Harry M. Baxter assumed the C.E.O. position.

Employees posed in front of S.A. Morman yard office, c. 1900.

Founded on a willingness to work

"Every man can have his own life to lead, if he is willing to work and willing to dream," was Earl H. Beckering Sr.'s philosophy. And commitment to that idea has made the Beckering family a leader in the heavy construction industry in West Michigan.

Beckering emigrated from the Netherlands to this country at age nineteen and made his home in Grand Rapids. He worked as an expert cabinetmaker but was more interested in building. In 1932, he made his dream a reality when he established the Beckering Construction Company.

Beckering was devoted to his church and community. His religious beliefs were part of his business life. He stood for what he believed in, and he fostered strong family bonds. As a traditional patriarch, he kept Beckering Construction a family business.

Earl H. Beckering Jr. began working in his father's construction company at age sixteen as a truck driver during his summer vacations. He received his training in architectural engineering from the University of Michigan and earned a degree in construction engineering from the Chicago Technical College.

Earl Jr. took control of the company in 1954 and quickly enlarged the scope of its operations. Not one to stay hidden in a walnut and teak office, Earl Jr. has always been a familiar figure on the company's construction sites. He is known for his handshake agreements, his word of honor and his involvement in community affairs.

In 1963, Earl formed a partnership with Kenneth Harmsen, changed the name of the working company to Pioneer Construction Company and became allied with the Associated Builders and Contractors Merit Shop. The buildings Pioneer has constructed dot the West Michigan countryside—each a proud statement of Pioneer's dedication to its craft.

Earl Jr.'s professional commitment to quality workmanship and excellence in construction has led him to state recognition for his efforts. On a state basis, he is past president of Associated Builders and Contractors and also of the Builders Exchange of Grand Rapids. Currently, he is on the national board of directors for Associated Builders and Contractors.

His commitment to the community is further evidenced in his strong participation in community functions; for over a decade, he has been on the board of directors for United Way, is on the board of directors for the Salvation Army and is actively involved—as well as being a past president of—Rotary International.

Sereta Morten Beckering, Earl's bride of 1942, is a well-known personality in the cultural life of Grand Rapids. She is active on the Grand Rapids Symphony Orchestra Board of Directors and on the Kendall

The Grand Rapids Marriot Hotel was completed by Pioneer Construction in 1980 (above). One of the first of its kind in the area, Riverview Center combines the best of old and new Grand Rapids. The old R.C. Allen building on the Grand River was completely renovated and remodeled by Pioneer Construction in 1979 into a modern office complex (below).

Hospital Guild of Butterworth Hospital. Earl and Sereta are patrons of the Grand Rapids Civic Theatre, Grand Rapids Art Museum and the Grand Rapids Opera.

Earl Jr.'s son, Thomas E. Beckering, and Kenneth's son David Harmsen, joined the company about 1968. Currently, David's responsibility is in the field of operations.

Tom joined the management team of Pioneer in 1972 after receiving his degree in business administration. High energy best describes Tom's style of business. A quick and forward thinking individual, Tom recognizes alternatives and solutions to problems that may stymie other firms. And, as many construction firms suffer through a slack economy, Pioneer is able to keep its people working and contributing to the community.

Tom brought new vitality to the company by creating the development division that has been responsible for such innovative projects as Riverview Center, Plaza Twenty One and Anchorage Marina.

The officers of Pioneer Construction Company firmly believe that strong commerce in the building industry creates a solid base for community growth. This belief and their philosophy of "willingness to work and willingness to dream" enabled Pioneer to become one of the largest construction firms in West Michigan and leaders in the field in every sense. The company motto "We build with Pride" was established by Earl Beckering Jr. because in his words, "We will proudly live with everything we build for the rest of our lives."

221

Protecting lives and property since the turn of the century

Frank E. Stevens was a furniture man, and J.A. Ziesse was an engineer. On a spring day in 1903, these two friends combined their talents to begin a new business venture and Phoenix Sprinkler and Heating Company opened its doors in Grand Rapids.

Business was good from the start. Although the automatic sprinkler industry was competitive, the company earned a reputation as a first-class mechanical contractor. Starting with its first automatic sprinkler installation at the Grand Ledge Chair Company in 1903, the company grew rapidly.

In 1917, Phoenix Sprinkler and Heating Company installed its first Dow Chemical automatic sprinkler contract. As Dow grew to be one of the largest chemical enterprises in the world, Phoenix was called on again and again to install new systems to protect plant expansions. When the Midland facility became known as the world's largest single sprinklered installation, Phoenix took great pride that it had been a major contributor to that project.

The Ziesse family bought out the Stevens' interests in 1940, and Karl took over the presidency when his father died in 1942.

With World War II in full gear, Phoenix became a major military contractor. Karl directed its operations during those hectic but exciting years, and the company was called upon to provide plumbing, heating, water main and sprinkler fire protection systems for military facilities in Columbus, Ohio, and Fort Custer, Michigan. These two projects required a workforce of as many as 600 people, a sizeable increase from the six men who cut pipe by hand on the company's first automatic sprinkler project.

After the war, the company established a modern pipe fabricating shop on Graham Street allowing all pipe to be shipped by rail. Until 1966, however, the office and engineering staff remained at the Campau Avenue location.

In 1964, the company name was changed to Phoenix Contractors, Inc. to describe more fully the scope of the company's operations. By this time the company had already absorbed the Pulte Plumbing and Heating Company and had broadened its geographic base.

Its operations were expanded also, in order to meet the needs of a changing world. As a pioneer in power piping, PCI was responsible for the installation of three Consumers Power projects including the B.C. Cobb plant in Muskegon and the John C. Weadock plant in Essexville, Michigan. The latter facility at one time had 150 Phoenix steamfitters on the job welding large diameter piping for an eight-story, coal-fired boiler.

In the late '60s the Environmental Protection Agency began an extensive program of wastewater and sewage treatment plant construction and modernization. Phoenix adapted again to meet these new challenges and by June 30, 1981, had completed, or had under contract, 90 major projects ranging in size from $200,000 to $10 million.

Today, the Steel Pipe Fabrications Division of the company is developing as a recognized national supplier of large diameter steel piping for this same wastewater industry. Growing with the times, Phoenix now has the capability to handle the piping needs of industrial and institutional giants—a far cry from the simpler demands of 50 years ago.

Robert C. Bodine Jr. brought a new perspective to PCI when he purchased it from former President J.E. Keller in 1976. Based on his experience with many of the world's largest mechanical contractors, Bodine directed the creation of new divisions important to the company's continued growth. The largest of these was the Special Hazards Division which addressed itself to the fire protection needs of modern power plants throughout the United States. Projects from that division were undertaken from Nevada to West Virginia and New York and prompted PCI to open offices in Taunton, Massachusetts, and Cincinnati, Ohio.

Phoenix fire protection systems use a variety of methods to assure complete protection of nuclear- or fossil-powered generating stations, chemical process plants and airplane hangars. Methods like deluge water spray, dry chemical, carbon dioxide, foam and Halon, a combustion prohibitor, have all been employed effectively.

An extensive system was installed at Cook Nuclear Plant in Bridgeman, Michigan, in conjunction with Hodgman Manufacturing Company. At the facility, all transformers are protected with a Water Spray Deluge System which was perfected by Phoenix. And the exterior of the turbine building is protected by the Exposure Water Spray System. A carbon dioxide system protects many of the internal sections of the facility including the containment cable tunnel quadrants, cable vaults, computer room and diesel generators.

Additional specialized systems are in use throughout the plant offering state-of-the-art protection for sophisticated machinery, equipment, instruments and records. A massive project such as the Cook Nuclear Plant is a difficult undertaking, even for a

J.A. Ziesse (left) and Frank E. Stevens (right), the original founders of Phoenix Sprinkler and Heating Company, in their 1910 office.

company of Phoenix's size and reputation. But Phoenix rose to the occasion again as it has for almost 80 years.

Over the past decades Phoenix has contributed to the construction of many Grand Rapids area landmarks: Herp's Department Store, American Seating, St. Mary's Hospital, George Welsh Civic Auditorium, the new State Office Building, Steketee's Department Store and the original Pantlind Hotel, just to name a few.

Phoenix installations in bakeries have protected food manufacturing processes. In schools, they have assured comfort and health for children. In public buildings, office structures and clubs, Phoenix installations have given silent, efficient service.

Furniture stores, the auto industry and allied plants have been served in many ways by Phoenix. Wherever piping has been needed, and for whatever reason, Phoenix has been there—fabricating, installing, protecting.

Industry has come to depend on Phoenix Contractors. Institutions such as schools and hospitals trust the workmanship. Government relies on its sound reputation. And businessmen appreciate the service.

Recently, the company established Phoenix Systems and Installation (PSI) which specializes in many of the ongoing boiler-system needs of area businesses and institutions. Prompt professional service and the reputation of Phoenix Contractors have made it a fast growing division and a permanent part of the corporate structure.

Phoenix Contractors, Inc. employs 275-350 persons around the United States from its modern corporate headquarters and manufacturing facility at 1345 Monroe Avenue NW, as well as its Farmington, Michigan, facility.

People make the difference at Phoenix Contractors, Inc. A broad-based organization of professionals has given Phoenix the reputation of a "can-do" company. Mechanical, fire protection and civil engineers are actively involved in all stages of the construction process to assure that jobs are done right, completed on time and within budget. Having good people throughout the company is the reason Phoenix has survived and flourished in its competitive, changing industry.

Mindful of its civic responsibilities, Phoenix encourages its employees to take an active role in community associations and events. An ongoing training program for Phoenix employees stresses the need for continued quality, the same quality that has allowed Phoenix to be an active employer in the local area for almost 80 years. The company began with a policy that a customer must be satisfied that any Phoenix job is a job well done, and nothing in the company's history of steady growth has changed that.

The Phoenix Sprinkler and Heating Company (above) as it appeared in 1913. The present corporate headquarters and manufacturing facility (below) for Phoenix Contractors, Inc.

223

Since 1850, Michigan's oldest jeweler

In 1850, William Preusser, a skilled watchmaker, came to Grand Rapids from Detroit and started a jewelry and watchmaking business. Preusser Jewelers is still going strong; it is today the oldest continuously operating business in Grand Rapids and the oldest jewelry store in Michigan.

There were about 5,000 people living in Grand Rapids when Preusser arrived and set up his store in the Luce Block at the corner of Ottawa and Monroe. Preusser rented the building for $90 a year and stocked it with a reported $10,000 in merchandise. William and his son Albert were regarded as fools for putting in such a large stock. They were told that "people here want pork and beans, not knickknacks for jewelry." Grand Rapids was still an Indian trading center when Preusser opened his business. And when the Indians came to town to collect their government payments, some of them slept in the store basement. Also in Preusser's basement were two fire engines, stored there by the city in 1853 for a yearly fee of $10.

After William Preusser succumbed to wanderlust and moved to Fond du Lac, Wisconsin, he left his son Albert to manage the store. Albert, who operated the business for 69 years, played an active part in the city's development. He was appointed the official city timekeeper by the Common Council, and the clock that he used is still displayed at Preusser's. Later, when the new city hall with its magnificent clock tower was constructed, Albert Preusser was

called upon to wind the clock daily and provide regular maintenance.

Preusser Jewelers has had several owners and several locations in downtown Grand Rapids. From the original Luce Block site, the business was moved to 136 Monroe where it remained for 63 years. Then in 1919, Albert moved the business to 63 Monroe. After his death a corporation was formed consisting of William Johnson and Henry Merkle, both of whom had worked for Albert.

The 1930s brought the Great Depression, and it was not unusual for someone to try and sell a sterling teaset for food money. People were disposing of valuables rather than buying them. The jewelers did a lot of waiting for customers and tried to keep busy with the few repairs that came in.

In 1934, the corporation was succeeded by the partnership of William Frey, Fred Geller and Henry Merkle (who also served as store manager). The business was then moved to 6 Sheldon SE.

The partners wished to maintain the store's long tradition by retaining the Preusser name, but there was some question about the family's wishes. Albert Preusser's daughter, Mrs. Annie Hodenpyle, wrote to Henry Merkle, reassuring him that she had no objection to continuing the business under the Preusser name, adding that, "Father was always very fond of you."

Preusser Jewelers remained at the Sheldon Street location for eighteen years. During that time Fred Merkle, who began at

Preusser's as a clerk hired by his father, was accepted as a partner, and Fred Geller and William Frey withdrew. When the senior Merkle died in 1948, his son Fred became sole proprietor, and in 1952, the business was moved to its present site at 16 Monroe NE, opposite Monument Park.

Today, the business is managed by Marian Merkle-TerKeurst. TerKeurst became associated with Preusser's in 1946 when she joined her husband, Fred Merkle, in the store's operation. She became a full partner in 1959. Widowed twelve years later and subsequently remarried, she has been the store's manager and proprietor since 1971.

The store continues to carry fine jewelry for a clientele that tends to be conservative in its jewelry tastes. Originally Preusser's sold only Swiss watches, the old-fashioned kind that great-great-grandfathers used to carry—key wind and key set—great watches, big as apples with a tick that could be plainly heard, but reliable as timekeepers. Those customers of more than a century ago would continue to be comfortable with the quality merchandise available today.

Preusser Jewelers represents an important part of the city's history and tradition. Its present owner, Marian Merkle-TerKeurst, is active in the growing effort to revitalize downtown. As a strong advocate of downtown redevelopment plans, she has her eye firmly fixed on the future of her business and her community's future as well.

Shipped direct from Germany, the clock was hung in the store in the late 1850s and was the first official timekeeper for the city (above). Still on the wall in the original Preusser's store, it continues to work well. William Preusser (in dark suit) with two of his salesmen (right), inside his store in 1905.

A century and a half of spiritual leadership

In June 1833, the Reverend Frederic Baraga, a Slovenian missionary laboring among the Ottawas at L'Arbre Croche, near the present Harbor Springs, Michigan, arrived at the rapids of the Grand River and offered Mass at the trading post of Louis Campau. Campau and a group of French fur traders had settled on the Grand in 1826. Baraga preached to the Indians and also served the French-Canadians at the trading post. In 1835, he left the Grand River area, returning to the Indians in the northern part of the peninsula. Later he would become Bishop of Marquette. His successor, the Reverend Andrew Viszoski, spent seventeen years in the burgeoning village—as missionary, and then as pastor. With the exodus of the Indians after 1836, he built up his parish among the white settlers. St. Andrew's Church, erected on Monroe Avenue in 1850, bears his patron's name.

During the next decades, Grand Rapids grew rapidly, and the migration of first Irish, then German, and later Polish immigrants to the western Michigan area brought numerous Catholic settlers. In 1876, Father Patrick J. McManus completed the present St. Andrew's Church on Sheldon Avenue. In 1883, the church became the cathedral of the newly established Diocese of Grand Rapids when the Most Reverend Henry Joseph Richter was made its first bishop. At its creation in May 1882, the new diocese contained 37 parishes, 36 priests, and seventeen parish schools. St. Mary's Parish (German) in Grand Rapids, was established in 1857. St. James, largely Irish, was formed in 1870, and St. Adalbert's (Polish) was organized in 1881.

The original Diocese of Grand Rapids had 38 counties and included the entire western portion of the lower peninsula and most of the upper eastern half. Today the diocese embraces eleven counties in Western Michigan. The Catholic population of the area is almost 150,000. There are 88 parishes and sixteen missions. There are 162 diocesan priests and 40 religious order priests, 747 Sisters and eight Brothers.

Bishop Richter died in 1916. Bishop Michael J. Gallagher was bishop from 1916 to 1918. Bishop Edward D. Kelly was bishop from 1919 to 1926. Bishop Joseph G. Pinten served here from 1926 to 1940, succeeded by Bishop Joseph C. Plagens 1940-43. Bishop Francis J. Haas was bishop from 1943 to 1953. Bishop Allen J. Babcock's tenure was from 1954 to 1969. Bishop Joseph M. Breitenbeck came to Grand Rapids in 1969. His auxiliary is Bishop Joseph C. McKinney.

The first teaching Sisters in Grand Rapids were the Brigidines from Ireland, who taught briefly at St. Andrew's Academy. In 1873, the Sisters of Mercy came but left in 1878 to work as hospital Sisters for the lumberjacks around Big Rapids. In 1876, the Sisters of Charity from

St. Andrew's Cathedral, Grand Rapids, Michigan.

Cincinnati came to staff St. Andrew's School and stayed until 1914 when the Sisters of St. Dominic took their place. In 1866, the School Sisters of Notre Dame came to teach at St. Mary's School, later opening St. James School, and still later St. Adalbert's, Sacred Heart and St. Isidore's Schools. Felician Sisters also taught in Grand Rapids.

The Sisters of Mercy moved their Motherhouse to Grand Rapids in 1914. The Dominican Sisters who first came to Michigan in 1877, cared for St. John's Orphan Home, opened Catholic Central High School in 1906, Marywood Academy in 1922 and Catholic Junior College in 1923 which became Aquinas College in 1945.

St. Joseph's Seminary opened in 1909 as a minor seminary, but was closed in 1980.

In May 1937, a new diocese was formed in central Michigan with Lansing as its see city, and in February 1938 the northeastern portion of the Grand Rapids Diocese was formed into the Diocese of Saginaw.

In 1971, the Diocese of Gaylord, embracing the northern portion of Michigan's Lower Peninsula was established. Each of these new dioceses reduced the size of the Diocese of Grand Rapids.

Although a century and a half brought many changes to Grand Rapids and west Michigan, the Grand Rapids Diocese continues to provide its parishioners with strong educational and spiritual leadership.

225

Largest accounting firm in Grand Rapids rooted in local history

Some say Frank E. Seidman started practicing public accounting in Grand Rapids because a local businessman talked him into it. Others say it was because he married a local girl who wouldn't leave Michigan. There's a little truth to both stories, but the end result has been good for Grand Rapids.

F.E. was a youngster when he came to America from Russia in 1900. Like many immigrants, he helped support his family by day and pursued an education at night. By age 21, he had earned a college degree as well as his CPA certificate from New York State, and he had begun a professional career. Continuing his night studies, he later earned a master's degree in economics.

During World War I, F.E. audited government contractors for the U.S. Aircraft Production Board. He came eventually to Grand Rapids to examine the financial records of furniture manufacturers who produced wooden airplane wings. F.E. wanted to return to New York when his assignment ended, but a local manufacturer, impressed with the young accountant, persuaded him to stay for at least six months. Meanwhile, he met and married a West Michigan girl who was unwilling to leave her beloved state.

F.E. settled in Grand Rapids and in 1919 opened a branch of the family accounting firm which his older brother founded in 1910. The same furniture companies F.E. audited became the backbone of the new office.

The end of the war brought new government regulations, taxes and opportunities for an ambitious accountant. Sometimes F.E. found himself at odds with Uncle Sam as he represented Grand Rapids businessmen in tax matters. His skills, however, helped bring the firm a reputation for tax expertise, business savvy and concern for local business—still a cornerstone of the firm's philosophy. By the 1930s Seidman & Seidman was an integral part of Grand Rapids. The firm expanded its services to business analysis and economic advising.

During World War II, Seidman & Seidman continued to advise clients and the public about the wartime economy, business trends and contemporary issues. F.E. was named chairman of the Michigan State Board of Accountancy in 1941, a post he held for almost ten years.

The 1940s brought some of the firm's and the profession's future leaders into the firm, including Raymond E. Knape, John J. Spinetto, David L. Wares and F.E.'s son, L. William (Bill) Seidman, who would later direct the firm's phenomenal growth. Bill Seidman joined the firm in 1946; like his father, he sought education at many levels, earning bachelor's, master's and law degrees. Active in the community, he was chairman of the first committee to study the feasibility of a four-year college in Grand Rapids. That college is now Grand Valley State Colleges—one of the city's proud achievements.

For many years, Seidman & Seidman remained a family firm. By 1957—47 years after its founding—the firm had only fifteen offices. But when Bill Seidman was elected to head the firm in 1968, the family operation gave way to a general partnership, and through unparalleled growth, expanded to twenty more cities in just a few years. Bill, who later became President Gerald R. Ford's chief assistant for economic affairs, retired in 1974. Bernard Z. Lee was elected managing partner—the first non-Seidman—and he accelerated the firm's growth.

Today, Seidman & Seidman serves clients through its 38 U.S. offices and in over 65 nations through its international affiliates. But ties to Grand Rapids are reflected in the Seidman Center, the F.E. Seidman Graduate School of Business at Grand Valley State Colleges and other landmarks and buildings the firm donated to the city.

The Grand Rapids office is the largest CPA practice in the city and is one of Seidman & Seidman's biggest, with tremendous growth achievements. Many Grand Rapids clients have expanded their businesses nationally and internationally. With its 23 partners and an average of 150 personnel, the office carries on the legacy of community service that is a Seidman tradition.

Seidman & Seidman's philosophy is unchanged: to provide highest quality certified public accounting, auditing, tax and management advisory services to its clients. The firm's total service involvement philosophy couples high professional standards with a commitment to community service. Much of that commitment is in Grand Rapids—a good place to live.

Company founder Frank E. Seidman c. 1948.

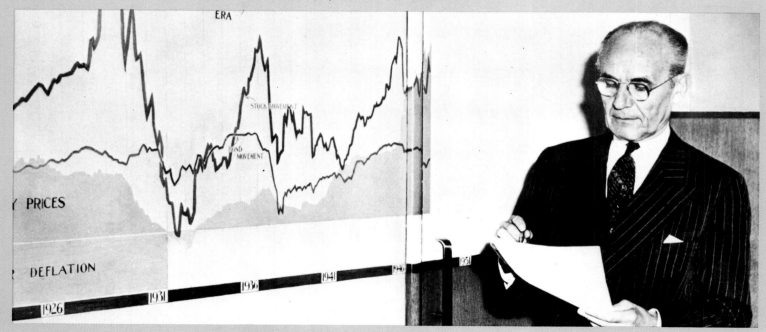

226

A model of cooperative effort

It was an association brought about by necessity, although few, if any, of the participants realized it at the time. In 1917, 27 Grand Rapids grocers joined together to purchase a carload of sugar. It was the first cooperative action taken by independent food retailers to fight the national chain stores that were threatening their very existence. They recognized that cost savings brought about by buying in carload lots allowed them to compete more effectively with high-volume operations.

The idea took hold and less than a year later, the group incorporated as the Grand Rapids Wholesale Grocery Company. That same year, they rented a small warehouse on Ionia Street. The loosely knit group became a warehouse cooperative enabling them to buy their merchandise in cost-saving quantities and to store the inventory in a central location.

Within seven years, Grand Rapids Wholesale Grocery Company had grown to 181 members. Even during the traumatic years of the Great Depression, the company continued to add members and to prosper.

By 1933, Grand Rapids Wholesale Grocery Company had outgrown its first warehouse and had moved to a larger facility. Just five years later, the company moved again, this time to a newly constructed and even larger building at 1501 Buchanan Avenue.

From 1937 until 1957, membership increased by more than 175 new retailers. During these two decades of sustained growth, the company's character changed from being merely a warehousing facility to being a full service financial, marketing and merchandising consultant.

Then in 1949, the company organized the first major collective sales program, bringing all member retailers together for a giant promotional push—the first of an uninterrupted series of fall sales that has continued to the present time.

In 1950, Grand Rapids Wholesale Grocery Company established its first wholly owned subsidiary—United Wholesale Grocery Company—to serve small, independent retailers whose volume did not warrant buying in large quantities. (Today, United Wholesale Grocery Company has ten branches located throughout Michigan and into Ohio.)

By 1954, the company had outgrown its "Wholesale Grocery" identity. It was now a formidable food marketing force seriously challenging the big regional and national chains in Michigan. The retailers too, had undergone a subtle change. Although still independent and competitive, they realized that more bound them together than what separated them.

At this time, they adopted the Spartan warrior as a unifying symbol for warehouse and retailers alike. The Spartan warrior

The Buchanan Street warehouse built in 1938 (above) proved adequate for the next twenty years although a second floor had to be added in the early 1950s. The independent grocer of the 1920s (below) offered fewer than 500 products compared to the 25,000 items in today's average Spartan Store.

epitomizes the lean, hard, disciplined spirit of the independent retailer, a man willing to join with others of his kind to defend what is his.

Three years later, Grand Rapids Wholesale Grocery became Spartan Stores, Inc., and construction was begun on a new 450,000-square-foot, semi-automated warehouse facility at 1111 44th Street.

1960 saw the beginnings of the Market Development Corporation, a subsidiary company that works with member retailers, helping them acquire good locations and operate profitable stores. Market Development also helps negotiate leases, arranges for zoning and financing and helps solve problems inherent in building and operating new stores.

Spartan Stores, Inc. deepened its market penetration into the eastern side of the state in 1962 with the purchase of the A.G. Tick Tock Company. Within five years, growth outstripped the capacity of the existing Detroit area warehouse, and a new 300,000-square-foot facility was built in Plymouth, Michigan.

In 1966, Spartan Stores purchased Produce, Inc., making high quality produce available to retail members. The next year, Spartan began building one of the largest private truck fleets in Michigan. (Presently, it numbers more than 140 tractors and 250 trailers.)

By 1974, Spartan Stores once again had outgrown its warehouse facilities. A giant six-building office and warehouse complex was built on 140 acres of land at 850 76th Street. The highly automated grocery warehouse features a central computer-controlled system of lanes and conveyors.

In 1979, two new wholly owned subsidiaries, Spartan Insurance Company, Ltd. and the Shield Insurance Agency were incorporated to provide specialized insurance protection to member retailers.

By 1982, Spartan Stores, Inc. had grown into the eleventh largest food wholesaler and third largest warehouse cooperative in the nation. Spartan also climbed to one billion dollars annually in sales. Today, one out of every six food dollars in Michigan is spent at a Spartan Store.

227

Innovation began world's largest manufacturer of office furniture

In the early 1900s, the poet W.R. Benét saw the office world as a million brains throbbing. Today there are not only more brains throbbing in the office world—there is electronic equipment also throbbing. And the combination is probably the biggest challenge office designers and furniture manufacturers have ever faced.

"When our company was founded in 1912, all you needed for a new office employee was a desk and a chair," says Robert C. Pew, chairman of the board and chief executive officer of Steelcase Inc. "Now it's not that simple. Most office people need privacy—usually in the form of a modular workstation which can be easily relocated. Often these workstations have provisions for electronic equipment, acoustical controls and furniture-mounted lighting—things our founders never dreamed of."

From the beginning, though, innovation was very much a part of Steelcase. Peter M. Wege found that by giving right-angle bends to sheet steel, he could make office safes as strong as iron ones, at lower cost. So he persuaded Walter Idema, and a handful of other stockholders, to join him in founding Steelcase (then Metal Office Furniture Company) to make fireproof office safes and office furniture.

David D. Hunting Sr., now vice chairman of the board, joined the company in 1914 and was involved with other Steelcase innovations. One of the most widely known was the first modular workstation designed by Frank Lloyd Wright and produced by Steelcase in 1938. Hunting worked with Wright in developing the unique desks and chairs, many of which are still in use today.

"Wright designed a three-level desk," says Hunting. "There was a surface for in/out trays, with storage below; a middle surface, sometimes with cutouts for business machines, and a bottom surface for storage. By changing the tops you could make different modular workstations."

It was Hunting himself who gave modular office furniture its second boost with the Multiple-15 Principle, developed after World War II when office space was at a premium. He persuaded the company to produce office furniture designed in multiples of fifteen inches instead of the odd sizes then available. Thus, six desks could fit into a space formerly required for five.

Next came office furniture in light colors, a Steelcase/Hunting innovation which brought interior designers into office planning. At first their primary interest was color and its effect on office morale. Later, as the computerized office evolved, their concerns expanded to include the planning of systems furniture, with its acoustical, lighting, wiring and other environmental provisions.

"Systems furniture creates a total office environment, is adjustable to changing office procedures and is the leading edge of office planning today," explains Fred A. Bell, executive vice president of corporate development. "We're constantly expanding our systems furniture manufacturing capability—not only locally, but also in our facilities in California, North Carolina, Georgia, Canada, Japan, France and West Germany."

Over the years, Steelcase has acquired subsidiaries in related fields; among them, Attwood Corporation of Lowell, world's largest manufacturer of die cast pleasure-boat hardware and an important source of Steelcase furniture components; and Vecta Contract of Dallas, widely known for its innovative office seating and tables.

Since its earliest years, Steelcase has grown from fifteen to 8,000 employees, with 6,000 at the Grand Rapids headquarters. Frank Merlotti, president and chief operating officer, says, "Opportunity for advancement, profit-sharing programs, pleasant working conditions and interesting work have created a compatible group. We know the importance of people because it is people who have created our success."

Steelcase officials state that the company's growth would not have been possible without years of reinvesting profits in facilities and equipment and the growth of the industry as a whole. "It's an exciting time to be in our kind of business," says Paul H. Witting, senior vice president of marketing. "When this company was founded, factory jobs far outnumbered office jobs. In recent years those figures have reversed and the office population continues to grow. And Grand Rapids, known as the furniture capital of the world because of its reputation for fine residential furniture, is now the leading producer of office furniture as well. Many of the country's major office furniture manufacturers are located in Grand Rapids. We're proud to be a part of it."

228

Steelcase three-level workstation in 1938, designed by Frank Lloyd Wright (top). Steelcase systems furniture workstation in 1981, with optional worksurface and panel heights (right).

A one-hundred year tradition of quality furniture

In 1880, two men—Russell Stow and Thomas Haight—invested $421.99 in machinery and tools and opened the doors to a new business, Stow & Haight Furniture. The plant was located on Front Street on Grand Rapids' west side and was dedicated to the manufacture of dining tables for national distribution.

George Davis purchased an interest in the company in 1885, and shortly thereafter the company was renamed Stow & Davis. Davis became president of the company and changed the course of its history when, in the 1890s, he directed the firm to begin manufacturing office tables. In 1910, Davis announced at the annual stockholder's meeting that, "Our line of office and directors tables is recognized by the trade as the best offered for sale in the country. I believe there is an excellent prospect for this firm in the development of special office and bank furniture." By 1917, Stow & Davis manufactured office furniture exclusively.

By 1930, Stow & Davis had been in business for half a century and was renowned for the manufacture of fine quality office and institutional furniture. It was during this period that the Kent Suite was first offered. It is the suite owned by former President Gerald R. Ford, and is the longest continuously manufactured design in Stow/Davis history. The firm was frequently commissioned to create special directors tables and suites for such industrial giants as General Motors, Michigan Bell Telephone, Union Carbide and numerous notable individuals, as well as the governors of several states.

Virtually all the furniture manufactured from the 1930s through the 1950s and into the 1960s was a product of Stow/Davis in-house designer, Giacomo "Jack" Buzzitta. Buzzitta was the only full-time designer in the entire office furniture industry during his early years with Stow/Davis.

The reputation as a quality manufacturer was further enhanced in 1947 with the founding of the Executive Furniture Guild of America. Stow/Davis was the manufacturing member of the guild. Furniture dealers and resource people from all over the country represented the remainder of the membership. Established as a non-profit association dedicated to relating art and science in the furniture industry to make working spaces more efficient, rewarding, beautiful and fun, the guild was primarily concerned with influences on spatial environments as they applied to of-

At the turn of the century, horse-drawn lumber wagons were used to bring supplies and finished tables to and from the train depot. The original Stow/Davis plant (bottom) on Front Street is still in use today. In 1918, the Gothic-style suite in the governor's office was furnished by Stow/Davis (below).

fice interiors and furnishings. Its activities had a major impact on the office furniture industry during the '50s and '60s.

Since 1968, Allen I. Hunting has been president of Stow/Davis. Through his leadership the past decade has seen another major leap in Stow/Davis history with the manufacture of highly innovative, yet functional and aesthetically attractive office furnishings. Independent designers such as Warren Snodgrass, Bert England and Robert DeFuccio have made their distinctive design personalities felt through the superior furniture offered by Stow/Davis.

The decision by Stow/Davis to manufacture open-plan systems in the 1970s saw another surge of growth surpassing all previous expectations. In addition to six plants that consist of over three-quarters of a million square feet, plans are underway to build a $10 million plant that will employ between 400 and 500 persons to manufacture a new line of office systems and furniture. The completion of this facility is scheduled for 1984.

Today, Stow/Davis personnel are approaching 600 in number. The Stow/Davis family is made up of highly skilled craftsmen who are dedicated to providing the highest quality furniture obtainable.

Stow/Davis products are serviced by a network of over 400 dealers located in principal cities throughout the United States and Canada.

A continuation of product quality, the highly skilled talent of Stow/Davis employees and the visionary foresight of the company's leaders can only result in a successful future for decades to come.

WOTV (WLAV-TV/WOOD-TV) — West Michigan's pioneer television station

In August 1949, the Midtown Theatre on Pearl Street in downtown Grand Rapids was jammed for west Michigan's first television program, two hours of speeches. A production crew and equipment was brought in from Detroit to launch WLAV-TV, Michigan's first out-state television station.

That one program was the only live, local television that west Michigan viewers saw for two years. WLAV-TV had no cameras and could only show films and slides at its transmitter building on 92nd Street SE, outfitted with what would now be called extremely primitive equipment. Network programs were brought to the station by a relay system that picked up off-the-air telecasts from Chicago. For most of the first year, the station's viewers (only about 3,500 sets when the station went on the air) saw few live telecasts, because the transcontinental relay system was not yet in service.

In 1951, WOOD, Grand Rapids' oldest and most important radio station, on the air since 1924, bought WLAV-TV, changing the call letters to WOOD-TV. Telecasting on Channel 7 from one studio in the Grand Rapids National Bank Building (now McKay Tower), WOOD-TV originated many live, local programs such as "Buckaroo Rodeo," "Jiffy Carnival" and "Chic Chat" that headlined local personalities such as Buck Barry, Carol Duvall, Eddie Chase and Gordon Kibby.

Since it's beginning, WOOD-TV was a primary NBC-TV affiliate. However, until there was an ABC-TV station in west Michigan, WOOD-TV also carried some programs from that network.

In late 1953, with a change of channel allocations by the FCC, the station began telecasting on Channel 8 from its new transmitter on Pettis Road NE. In early 1955, WOOD-AM-FM moved into their own building at 120 College, constructed to be used as a television-radio facility. With two studios, one large enough to handle a symphony orchestra, expansive programs were finally possible. With a program called "UNIT 8," WOTV went to remote locations (a difficult feat in those early days) to produce live programs around the area, including Miss Michigan Contests, races at the Speedrome, the Blossomtime Festivals at Benton Harbor, Annual Apple Smorgasbords from the heart of the fruit belt in Kent County and Annual Antique Auto Tours. "UNIT 8" was a weekly half-hour live remote. Wherever something special was happening, WOOD-TV was there to bring it to western Michigan viewers. An early innovation by WOOD-TV was the live telecasting of the Catholic mass each Sunday, originally from its large studio and eventually live from Saint Andrews Cathedral.

In 1957, Time Incorporated purchased WOOD-AM-FM-TV, bringing a new prestige to the operation of WOOD-TV. In 1971, Time Incorporated sold WOOD-AM-FM, but continued ownership of WOOD-TV. This caused a change in the stations call letters to WOTV. WOOD-AM-FM moved into their own quarters in downtown Grand Rapids a few years later.

From the beginning, news was one of the station's consuming interests and grew more important when Time Incorporated took over ownership. Currently with fourteen hours of local news each week, WOTV is west Michigan's only television station with a full hour of early evening news programming. During the Grand Celebration in September 1981, WOTV originated live programs all week, including the Gerald R. Ford Museum dedication, which was fed to many other midwest stations.

Through the years, the station has received many outstanding awards, including a Peabody Award, an Alfred I. DuPont Award and, recently, the Gabriel Award for the program "Father Mike, God Be With You," produced by Chet Matel after Monsignor Hugh Michael Beahan's death.

Willard Schroeder guided the operation as General Manager from 1951 until his retirement in 1978. Tom Girocco succeeded him until he moved to Time Incorporated headquarters in New York. On his departure in 1980, Marvin Chauvin became General Manager.

Antique Auto Tour (top). WOTV today (above). Buck Barry on "Thunder" (below).

"Tell us what you need" bank made city's early personal loans

The Union Bank founder's office (left), circa 1930, is still in use today. Union Bank's ten-story main office building (above), completed in 1967, was one of the first new residents of Vandenberg Center.

When John E. Frey opened the Morris Plan Bank of Grand Rapids at Ottawa and Monroe, one of the first things he did was make installment loans to individuals. And though the name of the bank Frey founded later changed to Union Bank and Trust Co., N.A.—the bank's philosophy didn't. Today, as in 1918, when people "tell Union Bank what they need," the bank responds with quality customer service. And Union Bank's history reflects this response to individual and community needs.

As "Grand Rapids Industrial Bank," a name reflecting the city's strong industrial base, the bank became the second state-chartered industrial bank in 1923.

In 1929, the bank became Union Bank of Michigan, just as America's whirlwind prosperity was wiped out by the Great Depression. Banks everywhere closed during the next few years, but Union Bank remained solvent and dedicated to its customers. In 1936, it was the first bank in the country to develop a national program to finance mobile homes, helping customers afford decent housing.

Prosperity returned in the 1940s, and Union Bank opened four neighborhood branch offices. By 1950, credit operations were merged into one central office for more efficient loan processing. And over the next ten years, the bank opened nine more branch offices.

In 1957, Union Bank entered the computer age and laid the groundwork for West Michigan's first complete bank data processing center. A complete Trust/

Estate-Planning Department opened in 1957, too, and Union Bank became Union Bank and Trust Co.

By 1960, Grand Rapids' central business district started to show its age. Union Bank quickly became involved in the city's renaissance as bank chairman, Edward J. Frey and other civic leaders raised funds for a planning study, later named the Grand Rapids Urban Redevelopment Program. The bank also was named the city's paying agent for $18 million in expressway bond issues. By 1965, plans had become action, and Union Bank began construction of its new headquarters building. The ten-story, $5 million Union Bank Building opened in 1967. With its neighbor the Frey Building, named for the bank's founder, the new Union Bank headquarters was one of the first new residents of downtown's Vandenberg Center.

During the same decade, Union Bank introduced free checking accounts for senior citizens, newlyweds and customers with balances of $300 or more. As bank competition increased, people demanded more financial services than ever before. Union Bank responded to those demands with its Ready Money™ line of credit and overdraft protection in 1963. And in 1966, the initials "N.A." were added to Union Bank and Trust Co. when the bank received its national charter.

Changes in Michigan banking regulations enabled Great Lakes Financial Corporation, a bank holding company, to form in 1972; Union Bank became its primary constituent

bank in 1973. In subsequent years, The Peoples Bank of Grand Haven and the First National Bank of Petoskey joined the corporation a few years later. Then, in 1981, Great Lakes Financial Corporation became Union Bancorp Inc.

Union Bank's early ventures into computerization helped introduce new, streamlined customer services during the '70s. Paperless processing of transactions, statement savings accounts and a central information file for more rapid loan processing were among new services offered. Then in 1981, the bank encouraged Grand Rapids residents to "Play The Keyboard™," Union Bank's 24-hour banking machine.

Union Bank's record of community involvement continued. Joining retailer, Meijer, Inc., the bank lighted *La Grande Vitesse,* the giant red-orange Alexander Calder stabile in Vandenberg Center. And in 1981, the bank welcomed American hostages home from Iran by displaying giant yellow ribbons downtown and distributing thousands of smaller-sized ribbons at branch offices. The bank also offered commemorative "All-America City" license plates after Grand Rapids won the title for the third time in 1981.

Ever mindful of founder John Frey's philosophy, David Frey, current Union Bank president, remains dedicated to quality customer and community service.

"Just tell us what you need," he tells customers. "And we'll treat you just as we'd want to be treated."

231

Work ethic binds employees in lumber, restaurant business

At the Universal Companies, things are done a little different from other companies. That's because Universal is 81 percent employee owned, and the employees take their ownership seriously.

Visitors to any Universal facility are often surprised to find the atmosphere more similar to a family working together on a mutually beneficial project than to a typical business office. Everyone clearly has a task to do and works toward completion of his task.

One reason for this attitude is Universal's strong belief in the work ethic. The company attracts personnel with similar views. Another reason is Universal's willingness to allow employees a measure of autonomy in their jobs. There is freedom to do the job any reasonable way as long as it gets done. As a result, tasks are accomplished quickly, efficiently and creatively. Still another reason is Universal's liberal profit-sharing plan that furthers personal involvement in the work and gives employees a firsthand look at how their efforts are directly beneficial to themselves and to their families.

Under such a system, a lot is demanded of the employees, but the employee gets a lot in return. Age, education, previous experience or other usual criteria for hiring and advancement mean far less than the desire to get ahead.

Typical comments from employees praise the structure: "The company treats me like a person." "The benefits are better than anywhere I've ever worked, and that makes me want to contribute more of myself." "It's like being self-employed, because you can see the rewards of your own endeavor."

It is this kind of feeling that helped Universal grow from a small lumber wholesaler into a large and diversified corporation with operations in several states and fiscal 1981 sales of $86 million.

The firm was launched as Universal Forest Products, Inc., in 1955 by William F. Grant (now retired). In 1959, Richard B. Lewis, now vice president for corporate services, joined the company. In 1962, Peter F. Secchia, the current chairman, joined Universal. And in 1964, William Grant Jr., now president of Universal Forest Products, became part of the company. These three men took control in 1971 and developed a number of marketing innovations and customer service concepts that led the company to dramatic growth and success.

The single most important development was the refining of the component lumber yard idea which was conceived in the late 1960s. Universal realized that with railroad services declining and interest rates soaring, customers could no longer maintain present sites or locate suitable new ones along rail lines. And, therefore, the custom-

Checking rafters at one of the lumber facilities of Universal Forest Products (above). The elegant 1913 room at the Amway Grand Plaza Hotel in Grand Rapids (right).

ers couldn't use full carload shipments of lumber. At the same time, many of these customers were finishing their own lumber using outdated machinery and inefficient labor.

The component yard, located along a major rail line, solved these problems. It enabled large amounts of lumber to be delivered, unloaded, trimmed or otherwise remanufactured and then resold in smaller lots. Such a yard also made an ideal place to manufacture conventional roof trusses and sections for the manufactured-housing industry. Later, to meet the growing demand for wood products that would stand up under a variety of weather conditions, the concept was expanded to include lumber treatment plants.

Thus, from one component yard in 1970, Universal Forest Products grew to twelve facilities in nine states by 1982.

Since construction is a cyclical business, Universal decided in 1976 to diversify. Partly because of Peter Secchia's interest in food service, the company expanded into

the restaurant business, creating Universal Restaurants, a wholly owned subsidiary. Today, the company owns thirteen Mr. Steak restaurants in three states, an Italian-American ristorante, two conventional steak houses, an elegant restaurant as well as a fun time saloon in the Amway Grand Plaza Hotel.

In 1977, Universal Properties was created to invest in land and buildings including restaurants. Also in 1977, The Universal Companies, Inc., was created as an umbrella for its various subsidiaries, thus setting the stage for future growth.

A commitment to excellence and to the community

David A. Warner, George S. Norcross and Siegel W. Judd joined in partnership on May 1, 1931. David Warner was a rugged individualist who, with his bride, had paddled a canoe from Grand Haven to Chicago on their honeymoon. George Norcross never attended law school; he gained admission to the Michigan Bar by reading law under a bankruptcy referee and a probate judge. Siegel Judd practiced law and worked as a stockbroker in Chicago and Grand Rapids.

The organization of a new law firm in the depths of the Great Depression was not as risky as it may now appear. The high incidence of business failures created the need for innovative approaches to financial reorganization. The members of the fledgling firm helped the Grand Rapids business and financial community to "pick up the pieces" as the economy began to regain its vigor. In the process, they gained experience in corporate law, bankruptcy practice and in the newly created field of federal securities law.

In those early years, life at the firm reflected the style of a bygone era. No matter how busy the partners were, they still paused each afternoon for tea. Young attorneys, in addition to their legal work, were expected to serve process and, on Saturdays, to operate the switchboard and open the mail.

As with all successful institutions, Warner, Norcross & Judd changed with the times. Composed of over 70 attorneys, it is Michigan's largest law firm outside Detroit. Almost every major law school is represented in the firm. Warner, Norcross and Judd attorneys, through the firm's specialized practice groups, engage in almost every area of civil practice, including all aspects of corporate and securities law, litigation before all federal and state courts and administrative agencies, federal and state taxation, employee relations, all aspects of commercial transactions and international law, as well as multidisciplinary work in employee benefits, real estate development, municipal bonding, estate planning and health law.

Warner, Norcross & Judd occupies three floors in the Old Kent Building, One Vandenberg Center, overlooking Calder's *La Grande Vitesse* in the financial and legal center of the city. The client reception area, decorated with photographs of Calder stabiles around the world, reflects the firm's community involvement and its commitment to excellence.

Contemporary styled offices are fully computerized for word processing and accounting. In addition, the library has computerized legal research facilties and is staffed by a full-time librarian.

Despite its modern quarters and equipment, Warner, Norcross & Judd maintains the values established by its founders. Like the founders, the present members of the firm are committed to the service of their community. Its attorneys have in recent years served as presidents of the West Michigan Opera Company, the Grand Rapids Symphony and the Grand Rapids Art Museum, as well as officers or trustees of all Grand Rapids medical hospitals. The firm regularly donates legal services to a number of charitable and civic institutions. The firm also includes among its number a past president of the Grand Rapids Bar Association and a past chairman of the Grand Rapids Chamber of Commerce. Several members of the firm have entered public life, including two congressmen and a former chairman of the Federal Trade Commission.

The year 1981 marked the fiftieth anniversary of Warner, Norcross & Judd, Grand Rapids' largest law firm. A half-century after its founding, Warner, Norcross & Judd maintains its original commitment to excellence in service of community and clients.

As it enters its second 50 years, Warner, Norcross & Judd is proud to have been a part of Grand Rapids' past and looks forward to participating in the city's future.

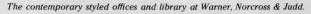

The contemporary styled offices and library at Warner, Norcross & Judd.

233

A unique office building with a colorful past

In 1856, Daniel Howard Waters arrived in west Michigan as an emigrant from New York. Armed with $1,200, he opened a packing and provision business in Grand Rapids which, during the Civil War, was extremely prosperous. Among many pursuits, he engaged in street contracting, and in 1870—holding patents for a mechanical wood-bending device—he founded the Michigan Barrel Company. However, he achieved his greatest financial success when he acquired vast upstate tracts of pine forests. As other lumbermen timbered at a fast pace, he retained his holdings intact. Over a period of years, the value increased substantially making him one of the most successful lumber barons of his day.

In 1883, he made his first downtown land acquisition; and by 1887, he had accumulated parcels that would become the site of today's Waters Building. Despite his wealth, he was noted for humanitarian works and, during the Panic of 1893, distributed provisions and clothing to the unemployed.

On March 17, 1894, he died in Florida. His obituary stated "In business, he was honourable and just and his word was ever as good as his bond. . .He was generous . . .tender hearted, sympathetic and. . .will be especially remembered by the poor."

His wealth passed into his estate and the hands of his three children. Mr. Klingman of Klingman Sample Furniture Co. interested the estate in constructing a major furniture showroom building. On July 12, 1898, the *Grand Rapids Herald* printed:

Few. . .who visited the last Grand Rapids Market entertained the idea that. . .three months later they would see an immense handsomely designed building erected for the exhibition of furniture. . .The Building. . .has been. . . completed as to permit. . .the use of the first three floors. . .which contain as fine a display. . .as. . .exhibited anywhere.

The Furniture Exhibition Company

threw open its salesrooms to public inspection. . .Hundreds. . .took advantage of the Company's invitation. . .An orchestra of six pieces. . .played throughout the evening.

The earliest known illustration depicts a building of five stories. The sixth floor was added due to the enormous demand for space. Constructed in record time (approximately 180 days) the building was one of the first to be built of precast, hollow-core iron columns with steel beams. The entire skeleton was prefabricated to dimension in Chicago and assembled on site. The building occupies a full city block and was advertised as "The World's Largest Building Devoted Exclusively To The Exhibition of Fine Furniture." Thoughout the national-furniture-market era, it housed samples of virtually every major furniture manufacturer.

After Daniel Waters' children died, ownership passed to the third generation. Despite their efforts to retain the Market in Grand Rapids, the opening of the Merchandise Mart and American Furniture Marts in Chicago inevitably led to a dwindling of exhibitors in the building. In 1956, those who remained were consolidated into "The Decorative Art Center."

In 1958, the building embarked on a new course. David Cassard was hired as manager to seek alternative building uses. Although the building's configuration was far from ideal for conversion, David Cassard recommended a redirection toward a multiple occupancy office building. On November 18, 1958, an open house was held to acquaint business and community leaders with the new Waters Building. Since then, the Waters Building has undergone extensive conversion. Today, the building has 98 percent occupancy and—with the exception of the Wolverine Showrooms from the old Furniture Market Era—has been entirely converted to offices.

In November 1968, the property was acquired by David Cassard, great grandson of Daniel Waters. In 1979, his son, David M. Cassard, joined the Waters Building Corporation and today is the building manager and vice president of the corporation. Also, in 1979, the Waters Building Corporation acquired the Medical Arts Building as well as the nearby Doctors' and Nurses' Parking Garage. As with the Waters Building, the property has undergone extensive remodeling to bring it up to today's standards of comfort and utility, yet it retains the warmth and tradition of the original era.

A spirit of community involvement has also been passed through the generations. David Cassard Sr. served as co-chairman of the Downtown Improvement District Committee which acted as liaison between the public and private sectors of the downtown in the planning and construction of Monroe Center. A founder and president of the Building Owners and Managers Association of Grand Rapids, he now serves actively on the boards of Downtown, Inc, the Convention Bureau and the Downtown Development Authority.

ONE OF THE FURNITURE EXPOSITION BUILDINGS

The earliest known illustration of the Waters Building shows a building of five stories (above). A sixth floor was added later. During the national-furniture-market era (below), furniture was displayed on the first three floors of the Waters Building.

From hometown business to worldwide industry

One of the fastest growing of America's office systems furniture manufacturers, the Westinghouse Architectural Systems Division, had its beginning in a chance remark exchanged between two Grand Rapids businessmen.

In the mid-1950s, a customer of the division's predecessor, Architectural Systems, Incorporated, observed that his contemplated office remodeling project could be accomplished more quickly and inexpensively if the walls were movable partitions instead of fixed barriers. The idea started the manufacturer thinking about a virtually untapped market.

In 1957, the small concern began to manufacture floor-to-ceiling office partitions that would be easy to install and inexpensive to move when corporate growth made changes necessary. The little company started with a handful of employees

Today's Westinghouse Open Office System saves space and rearrangement expense and increases office worker productivity (above). The Westinghouse Modular Factory System (below), applies the principles learned in office systems to manufacturing and materials handling.

and a work space not much larger than a garage. But the product was well received, and the company prospered. Just four years after its founding, the successful firm caught the attention of Westinghouse Electric Corporation.

Westinghouse saw in Architectural Systems' product an ideal application of the corporation's Micarta plastic laminate which provides greater durability than wood, with easier maintenance. During the next few years—after becoming a part of Westinghouse—the Architectural Systems' line expanded to include access flooring and laboratory clean rooms, as well as floor-to-ceiling panels, and the new Westinghouse division enjoyed a modest but steady growth.

In 1970, the division took aim at a newly emerging market and developed the Westinghouse Open Office System. In developing the system, such technical capabilities as acoustics, lighting and human factors engineering readily available through Westinghouse Research Laboratories, were applied to the new product line. The new concept envisioned furniture and its function, space, communications and lighting as a total operating system.

Today, the Westinghouse Open Office System is a coordinated group of panels, work surfaces, shelves, storage components, lighting fixtures and seating. And because the components can be arranged in a variety of ways, each workstation can be located and designed for maximum office worker productivity. In addition, the system

substantially reduces the amount of space an office worker requires and can dramatically save on the cost of office rearrangement, compared to conventional offices.

The systems furniture industry has experienced phenomenal growth in recent years, and the Architectural Systems Division has experienced growth rates that were unparalleled in the parent corporation. In recent years, employment at the division's 36th Street SE plant grew nearly sixfold, requiring a half dozen major facilities expansions.

Most recently, the Westinghouse unit introduced its innovative Modular Factory System that applies the principles learned from the open office business to the manufacturing and material handling areas.

In addition to the Grand Rapids plant, Westinghouse also operates systems furniture manufacturing facilities in Puerto Rico and in the Republic of Ireland and has established a broad network of showrooms, sales offices and dealerships in major cities throughout North America, the United Kingdom, Europe, the Middle East and the Far East.

Despite its national and international outreach, the Architectural Systems Division remains close to its Grand Rapids origins. Westinghouse is proud of the part it has played in the rebirth of Grand Rapids as a major center of the furniture industry, and the division looks forward to continuing in close association with its hometown as both a good corporate citizen and a good neighbor.

235

Fine furniture for over a century

In 1858, George Widdicomb, father of John Widdicomb, came from Devonshire, England, to settle in Grand Rapids. He gathered together twelve craftsmen and set up a small cabinet shop which prospered from the start. His English training was different from the frontier training of the average small town cabinetmaker and his well-made furniture found a ready market. The outbreak of the Civil War put a sudden end to his new enterprise when the entire work force, including his sons, joined the Union Army.

Following the war, George Widdicomb was joined by his four sons, John, Harry, William and George Jr., and the business started up again. The trade, entirely local to start with, was quickly expanded. The Widdicomb name soon became known in Chicago, then as far east as Philadelphia, New York and Boston. In 1897, one of the boys, John Widdicomb, felt the need of a plant of his own and started in a small way making interior woodwork and fireplace mantels on a site across the street from that of his father. (This building is now part of the present plant.)

Ralph Widdicombe, a nephew of John, who retained the old English spelling of his name, had earlier become interested in the designing of furniture, and when his uncle branched out for himself, Ralph joined him. For 53 years, until his retirement in 1951, all John Widdicomb Co. furniture was designed by Ralph Widdicombe, known as the dean of furniture designers. Although Ralph Widdicombe is remembered best for his classical designs, it was his modern turn-of-the-century bedroom suite that was awarded first prize at the Paris Exposition in 1900.

In 1924, working from models he had procured in Europe, Ralph Widdicombe introduced Louis XV Provincial designs, the first of their kind to be made in the United States. He started a wave of popularity for French Provincial which still continues. A bombe bureau, the first such design, is still a much sought after pattern in the John Widdicomb collection today.

In 1950, John Widdicomb Co. acquired the famous Wm. A. Berkey Furniture Co., another old established maker of fine quality English furniture, founded in 1879 by one of the brothers who had previously established Berkey & Gay Furniture Co.

The Widdicomb name, shared by two manufacturers since John left his father in 1897, was brought together again in November 1970 when John Widdicomb Co. purchased the name and goodwill of the Widdicomb Furniture Company, the latter having ceased production several years previously.

The company's craftsmen and artisans still come from many parts of the world and still continue the traditions of rare

Grand Rapids EXHIBIT

PARIS EXPOSITION 1900

A Splendid Conception in Mahogany ⌀ Colonial

JOHN WIDDICOMB
⌀ ⌀ **COMPANY** ⌀ ⌀

The turn-of-the-century mahogany furniture shown here, (above) was handcrafted in Grand Rapids at the John Widdicomb Company and displayed at the Paris Exposition in 1900. A John Widdicomb artisan, (right) continues the tradition of craftsmanship and attention to fine detail.

craftsmanship and of teaching their skills to new generations.

John Widdicomb Co. is also a leader in manufacturing oriental reproductions of the ancient Chinese art of incised carving, a method of etching fine detail in many coats of lacquer.

John Widdicomb furniture is available to interior designers through franchised showroom distributors in many major cities in the United States and is sold by fine furniture stores throughout the country and Canada.

236

Growing with our best foot forward: past present and future

The Wolverine story can be traced back to the end of the Napoleonic Wars when Valentine Krause returned from the fighting to become a tanner in his hometown in Prussia. In 1844, at the age of 24, Valentine's son Henry had served his apprenticeship with his father and left his hometown to come to America. He located in Ann Arbor, Michigan where he and his brother-in-law established a tannery. Skillful in their craft, the two tanners won first prize at the Michigan state fair in 1850. In 1866, they added shoemaking to their business.

Henry's second son, G.A. Krause, learned the leather and shoe business from his father, but he also wished to strike out on his own. In 1883, G.A. and his uncle formed a partnership and opened the Hirth-Krause Company in Grand Rapids which bought and sold hides and leather and wholesaled shoes and findings. Their beginning capital was only $2,900. (After nearly a century of growth that partnership in Grand Rapids has become one of the leading manufacturers of branded footwear in the country. In 1983, Wolverine World Wide, Inc., as the business is known today, celebrates its 100th anniversary of continuous business operations as well as the 25th anniversary of its most famous brand, Hush Puppies® shoes).

After almost twenty years of business success in Grand Rapids, G.A. Krause is said to have taken a horse and buggy ride that changed the history of Rockford, a prosperous village located on the Rougue River about ten miles north of Grand Rapids. The year was 1901, and the buggy ride provided G.A. with his first glimpse of the town which later would become the home of Wolverine World Wide, Inc. (a name the company adopted in 1966 to better reflect its international stature).

With Rockford providing a stable community framework, the company, later known as the Michigan Shoemakers, flourished as makers of Wolverine® footwear and tanners of Shell Cordovan Horsehide leather. In 1921, the company changed its name to Wolverine Shoe and Tanning Company and, in 1925, began national advertising. The company continued its record of growth in tanning and shoemaking as well as in glove manufacturing which was added in 1920.

As the automobile and tractor became fixtures in the American city and on the farm, the horse population declined and Wolverine tanners, in search of new raw material began to tan unsmoked pigskins. Years of research followed, and in 1950 the company developed a new pigskinning machine for use on the packinghouse floor. Even today, Wolverine's pigskinning technology assures a steady supply of raw hides to what has become one of the largest pigskin tanneries in the world.

In 1958, Wolverine first marketed a casual line of pigskin footwear with a unusual brand name—Hush Puppies.® Until then, the phrase, "hush puppies," referred only to little corn fritters served with fish in the South—the name coming from their occassional use as food to quiet hungry puppies. Wolverine adopted the phrase and began to advertise Hush Puppies® as comfortable shoes which were said to "quiet your barking dogs." A study in 1978 revealed that the Hush Puppies® brand had achieved a 97% aided-brand awareness among American adults. Today, more than 215 million pairs of Hush Puppies® shoes have been sold in the United States and in more than 50 countries through Wolverine's international licensees.

With more than 7,000 employees and plants in twelve states and two countries abroad, Wolverine has become a broadly based footwear manufacturer and marketer and has an extensive Hush Puppies® brand licensing program for products other than footwear. Wolverine's brand names include among others, Wolverine® boots and shoes, Hush Puppies® gloves, Brooks® athletic footwear, Wimzees® casuals, Tru-Stitch® Slippers, Breathin' Brushed Pigskin® and Kroupana® pigskin upholstery leather.

Wolverine World Wide, Inc., a name synonymous with progress, is committed to continued growth and to keeping its best foot forward. Proud to have its roots in the Greater West Michigan business community, Wolverine is equally proud to share in Grand Rapids' sense of history and resurging spirit.

The famous Hush Puppies dog was chosen to reinforce the brand's image and today represents quality footwear for men, women and children around the world (above). In the early 1900s, floats like this one promoted the tanning and shoemaking of the company. The painted leather banner on the horse today hangs in the Wolverine Shoe Museum in Rockford (below).

Triakaidekophilism promoted two decades of successful broadcasting

On November 1, 1962, at 6:30 p.m., WZZM-TV-13 became a reality, fourteen years after television came to West Michigan. "Get TRIAKAIDEKOPHILISM" was the invitation in the young station's first promotional campaign, referring to a great fondness for the number thirteen. That fondness was already part of the make-up for the staff of approximately 65 people, most of whom substituted devotion and drive in place of television experience. This was, after all, their new baby and they worked long days and nights to deliver it, with little or no overtime pay. And there were hurdles. Twenty minutes after signing on the air, WZZM-TV went off again as the first of two transmitter tubes failed during its debut, causing an interruption of nearly ten minutes.

The original home of WZZM-TV was in the old Pantlind (now Amway Grand Plaza Hotel). There, in a banquet room turned studio, camera operators dodged around pillars to broadcast their live programs: "This Morning" with Bud Lindeman, "Shirley's Show" and one daily fifteen-minute newscast at 11 p.m. consisting of five minutes each of news, weather and sports.

The challenge facing TV-13 was to break customary viewing habits and become competitive with established local stations which enjoyed a long headstart and wide lead. The key was to offer an alternative, to give viewers something to watch that they couldn't get elsewhere. One approach was to follow the lead of ABC, which turned to sports in an effort to attract viewers. While the network was developing "Wide World of Sports," "Monday Night Football," championship boxing and coverage of

winter and summer olympics, TV-13 was broadcasting live coverage of the Michigan High School basketball finals and of the University of Michigan basketball team led by a young Cazzie Russell. It was an ambitious undertaking for the young station but nothing compared to the effort given TV-13's first, and most successful priority, "Eyewitness News."

The philosophy of managment saw a dynamic news operation as the key factor in spawning a successful television station. Financial resources were poured into the department to purchase the necessary equipment. What followed was a succession of firsts for the West Michigan market. In 1971, "Eyewitness News" introduced the first weather radar. It was a sophisticated black and white aircraft radar system which visually depicted for viewers any approaching rain showers or severe weather. Three years later, the system was replaced by the first computerized color radar, and "Eyewitness News" provided viewers with the area's first broadcast-trained staff of three professional meteorologists.

At the same time, "Eyewitness News" was being equipped with state-of-the-art electronic cameras and recorders to replace film equipment. The new technologies supplemented a top-notch team of professional broadcast journalists who had already made their mark in 1971 by winning a National Emmy for a documentary entitled, "Sickle Cell Anemia: Paradox of Neglect." TV-13 was the first and only Michigan Broadcaster to be so honored.

Soon "Eyewitness News" began to domi-

nate state journalism awards as well. It captured significant regional and national recognition. The News Department had established a reputation for probing, incisive and award-winning investigative reporting. In 1981, judges for the Associated Press Awards commented, "There is an obvious concern for the quality of life for the station's viewers. No one could help but be impressed with the ability of its personnel, and the depth of stories they turn out. WZZM-TV has a quality news operation that should be the envy of many stations in larger market." "Eyewitness News" had succeeded against heavy odds and become a leader in the market.

The locally owned West Michigan Telecasters, moved the station to spacious new multi-million dollar quarters on Three Mile Road in Walker. President Gerald R. Ford, then a congressman, presided over dedication ceremonies.

In 1978, the investors—who comprised West Michigan Telecasters—were rewarded for their patience and good business sense when TV-13 was purchased by Wometco Enterprises, Inc., of Miami, a diversified corporation serving communities across the United States.

Today, it is almost taken for granted that TV-13, a station which once gave away TV antennas to prod viewers into finding the fledgling broadcaster's signal, will annually be named "Station Of The Year" by the Michigan UPI, or lauded for overall "General Excellence" by the Michigan AP. WZZM-TV-13 has become a vital part of the West Michigan community. The new baby on the block has matured into a dynamic force.

Multimillion-dollar studios (right), now provide a comfortable environment and efficient, award-winning production facilities. A phone-booth sized newsroom and film processing in a hotel bathroom (left), accommodated the modest beginnings of WZZM-TV-13.

World-wide ministry began as a family partnership

During the Great Depression, Grand Rapids, like other cities, was plagued with unemployment, stress and hardship. Rather than buckle under the difficulties of those times, two brothers, Pat and Bernie Zondervan, used them as a catalyst for starting what was to become a world-wide ministry. The Zondervan Corporation was the result of their vision.

With ingenuity and hard work, the brothers pulled together the materials needed to spread God's word. In 1931, Pat made a trip East to purchase religious books that had been reduced in price due to the Depression. The merchandise was brought to Michigan, and the seeds of Zondervan Corporation were planted.

What began as a mail-order business for books quickly grew into a much larger operation. In 1932, the Zondervans moved their enterprise from a farmhouse in Grandville to their first store in Grand Rapids. Pat's sales and promotional abilities coupled with Bernie's knowledge of finances and production produced a partnership that was solid until Bernie's death in 1966.

One of the reasons for creating Zondervan's was to enter the publishing world. Now that the company was formed, the next task was to decide what to publish. Books by the Zondervan Publishing House were to rank as the finest and best in their particular field, with each book having hearty approval and endorsement by the company. The pledge was made to publish only the soundest of fundamental, evangelical literature.

The first book chosen to wear the Zondervan seal-of-approval was *Women of the Bible* by Dr. Abraham Kuiper. The book was later divided into two books, *Women of the New Testament* and *Women of the Old Testament.* These set the precedent for excellence and still remain popular members of the Zondervan family of books.

After distributing different editions of the King James version of the Bible, the Zondervans ventured into a new area of the Bible with the publication of the *Amplified New Testament* in 1958. The edition included alternate words to show the subtle meanings of original languages.

There were many editions of the Holy Writ that followed the *Amplified New Testament,* but none with the impact of the *New International Version of the Bible,* which made its first appearance in 1973. The widely used, accurate and understandable translation represents the work of more than 100 scholars and years of research using original Greek and Hebrew texts.

During World War II, the Zondervan brothers expanded an important part of their ministry by entering the religious music market. The subsequent purchase of

Singspiration Music and the recent acquisition of the Benson company placed Zondervan at the top of the religious music field where it has been a guiding force in the areas of spiritual and gospel music.

Over the years, The Zondervan Corporation developed a chain of Zondervan Family Bookstores, located almost exclusively in high-traffic malls and designed to meet the needs of families, teachers and pastors. Today, there are more than 70 Family Bookstores nationwide.

Zondervan retail interests also include *The Book of Life,* a set of books that is sold door-to-door. Purchased in 1972, the publication became a division of the company. The set was then revised and reissued as a completely new set illustrated with more than 6,000 photographs, charts, maps and

drawings.

In 1970, Peter Kladder, treasurer of the company since 1956, became president of the newly recognized corporation. At that time, a board of directors was established and is still headed by Pat Zondervan.

Since the leadership of Kladder, growth and changes have been substantial—changes that remain in keeping with the high standards first established by the founding Zondervan brothers.

It has been more than 50 years since Pat and Bernie first had the vision to create a company devoted to spreading the Word of God. Through music, books, Bibles, retail outlets and records, the Zondervan Corporation had made an impact not only on the city of Grand Rapids, but throughout the world.

Bernie (left) and Pat Zondervan (right) go over Zondervan publications. (below). One of the first Zondervan Family Bookstores (above), was a familiar sight in downtown Grand Rapids.

239

The Morton House Livery was located where the Keeler Building now stands. At the turn of the century, most of the hotels ran their own livery service, transporting guests to and from the railroad depot and riverboats.

Index

"Accent on: City Planning." *Accent Grand Rapids,* January/February 1978.

"Airport '74." *Grand Rapids Magazine,* November 1974.

Allen, Hugh, "Focus on: Fund Raising in West Michigan." *West Michigan Magazine,* September 1980.

Arlinsky, Ellen, "Citizens Designing Continuous Riverbank Park System for Future Generations." *Accent Grand Rapids,* June 1979.

Arlinsky, Ellen, "The Matter of Finances," *West Michigan Magazine,* October 1980.

Arlinsky, Ellen, and Marg Ed Conn, "Hospital Costs—A Curable Malady?" *West Michigan Magazine,* March 1981.

Ashman, Mary, *Pathways and Clearings: Pioneer Living in the Grand River Valley, 1825-1850.* Grand Rapids, Grand Rapids Public Museum, 1981.

"Banks and the Men Who Made Them." *Michigan Pioneer Collections,* Vol. VI (1884).

Baxter Albert, *History of the City of Grand Rapids, Michigan.* New York, Munsell, 1891. Reprint, Grand Rapids Historical Society, 1974.

Belknap, Charles E., *The Yesterdays of Grand Rapids.* Grand Rapids, Dean-Hicks Co., Reprint, Mayflower Congregational Church, 1958.

Blaich, Jan, "Born Again Buildings: New Uses for Old Places." *Accent Grand Rapids,* March 1980.

Bolt, Robert, "Reverend Leonard Slater in the Grand Valley," *Michigan History,* Vol. LI, No. 3 (1967).

Bradshaw, James Stanford, "Grand Rapids Furniture Beginnings." *Michigan History,* Vol. LIL, No. 4 (1968).

Brinks, Herbert, "The American Letters." *The Grand River Valley Review,* Vol. II, No. 2 (Spring-Summer 1981).

"Celebration on the Grand." *Grand Rapids Press,* September 13, 1981.

"Celebration on the Grand." *West Michigan Magazine,* October 1980.

Clarke, Robert, "The Great Accommodator: The Right Stuff for the Right Time." *West Michigan Magazine,* September 1981.

Cleland, Charles E., *A Brief History of Michigan Indians.* Lansing, Michigan: History Division, Michigan

Department of State, 1975.

"The Comstock Row." *Evening Leader,* April 9, 1980.

Conn, Marg Ed, "Accent On: The Grand Rapids Public Museum." *Accent Grand Rapids,* November, 1979.

Conn, Marg Ed, "The Care and Feeding of Grand Center," *West Michigan Magazine,* October 1980.

Conn, Marg Ed, "Concern for Animals Sparks New Zoo Program." *Accent Grand Rapids,* May/June 1980.

Conn, Marg Ed, "A Celebration of Ethnic Communities." *West Michigan Magazine,* August 1980.

Conn, Marg Ed, "Is Higher Education Making the Grade? Area Colleges Reply." *Accent Grand Rapids,* September 1979.

Etten, William J., *A Citizens' History of Grand Rapids.* Grand Rapids: A.P. Johnson Co., 1926.

Flanders, Richard, "Digging the Past." *Grand Rapids, Present and Future.* Grand Rapids: Urban Concern, 1981.

Furnas, J.C., *The Americans, A Social History of the United States, 1587-1914.* New York: G.P. Putnam's Sons, 1969.

Garraty, John A., *The American Nation: A History of the United States.* New York: Harper and Row, 1960.

"Gerald R. Ford: A Special Report." *Grand Rapids Press, Wonderland Magazine.* September 13, 1981.

Goodwin, Tim, "The Man Who Built the Civic." *Grand Rapids Magazine,* October 1975.

Grand Rapids Citywalk. Grand Rapids, Urban Concern, 1981.

Grand Rapids Daily Eagle, April through July, 1864.

Grand Rapids Press, September 13, 15-20, 1981.

"Grand Rapids: Furniture Capital of the World." *Accent Grand Rapids,* March 1979.

"History: Memories of How Festival Grew." *Accent Grand Rapids,* May 1979.

Holden, Robert, "Lyman Parks, 'The Realist': How a Black Man Became Mayor of Grand Rapids Without Anyone Noticing." *Grand Rapids Press, Wonderland Magazine,* October 10, 1971.

Jennings, Carrie B., *The Grand Rapids Fire Department: History of Its Progress From Leathern Bucket to Steam Engine and to the Present

Time.* (1899). Reprint, Black Letter Press, 1971.

Johnson, Ida, *The Michigan Fur Trade.* Grand Rapids, Black Letter Press, 1971.

Kent Community Action Program 1979 Annual Report. Grand Rapids, Kent Community Action Program.

"Kent County Building Honors Phillips." *Outreach,* Michigan Department of Social Services, Vol. IV, No. 11 (April 1979).

Kurzhals, Richard, "Initial Advantage and Technological Change in Industrial Location: The Furniture Industry of Grand Rapids." Doctoral dissertation, Michigan State University, 1973.

Kurzhals, Richard, "What Price Progress?" *Grand Rapids Past, Present and Future.* Grand Rapids, Urban Concern, 1981.

Lewis, Mary Lu, "Rowing, Not Drifting: The Grand Rapids Study Club." *The Grand River Valley Review,* Vol. II, No. 1 (Fall-Winter 1980).

Lydens, A.A., ed., *The Story of Grand Rapids.* Grand Rapids, Kregel Publications, 1966.

Mapes, Lynn G., "A Century of Growth through Annexation." *Grand Rapids Magazine,* 1975.

Mapes, Lynn G., "The Gay Nineties." *Grand Rapids Magazine,* September 1976.

Mapes, Lynn G., "Grand Rapids Encounters the Depression." *Grand Rapids Magazine,* November 1976.

Mapes, Lynn G., "Grand Rapids in World War I." *Grand Rapids Magazine,* October 1976.

Mapes, Lynn G., "The Great Furniture Strike of 1911." *Grand Rapids Magazine,* September 1975.

Mapes, Lynn G., "Saloons and Prohibition." *Grand Rapids Magazine,* June 1975.

Mapes, Lynn G. and Anthony Travis, "Clubs, Concerts, Social Issues and Suffrage." *The Grand River Valley Review,* Vol. II, No. 1 (Fall-Winter 1980).

Mapes, Lynn G. and Anthony Travis, *Pictorial History of Grand Rapids.* Grand Rapids, Kregel Publications, 1976.

Mapes, Lynn G. and Anthony Travis, "Pounding a Typewriter, Punching a Clock." *The Grand River Valley Review,* Vol. II, No. 2 (Spring-Summer 1981).

Menninga, Clarence, "What Rocks and the Rapids Tell Us." *Grand Rapids Press, Wonderland Magazine,* May 13, 1979.

Morison, Samuel Eliot and Henry Steele Commager, *The Growth of the American Republic.* New York, Oxford University Press, 1958, Vols. I and II.

Olson, Gordon L., *The Calkins Law Office: Its History and Restoration.* Grand Rapids, Grand Rapids Public Museum, 1976.

"Open the Door to Your Downtown." *Grand Rapids Press,* September 11, 1980.

"People of the Grand." Grand Rapids Public Museum exhibit.

Ransom, Frank Edward, *The City Built on Wood: A History of the Furniture Industry in Grand Rapids, Michigan, 1850-1950.* Ann Arbor, Edwards Brothers, Inc., 1955.

Sommers, Lawrence M., ed., *Atlas of Michigan.* Lansing, Michigan State University Press, 1977.

Stewart, Lewis G., "A Review of Michigan as a Province, Territory and State." *Publications of the Historical Society of Grand Rapids, 1906.*

Travis, Anthony R., "Mayor George Ellis: Grand Rapids Political Boss and Progressive Reformer." *Michigan History,* Vol. 58, No. 2 (Summer 1974).

Tuttle, Frank W. and Joseph M. Perry, *An Economic History of the United States.* Cincinnati, Southwestern Publishing Co., 1970.

Whinery, Katherine Pantlind, "From Soup to Sadlers." *The Grand River Valley Reveiw,* Vol. III, No. 1 (Fall-Winter 1981).

Van Vulpen, James, "A Whole New Ballgame: Baseball Under the Lights at Ramona Park." *The Grand River Valley Review,* Vol. II, No. 1 (Fall-Winter 1980).

Wall, Vander; Heyda, Douglas and Dr. Marie, O.P. "In Honor of the Soldiers from Kent County, 1861-1865." *The Grand River Valley Review,* Vol. I, No. 1 (Fall 1979).

White, Arthur S., *Old Grand Rapids, Pen Pictures.* Grand Rapids: White Printing Co., 1925.

Williams, Betty, "The Truth About the Furniture Industry." *Grand Rapids Magazine,* February, 1978.

Authors' Acknowledgements

The authors would like to thank the following individuals and organizations for their time, help and contributions to *Grand Rapids: Renaissance on the Grand:*

Dr. David Armour, Mackinac Island State Park Commission
Arts Council of Greater Grand Rapids
Leon Borucki, photo department, *Grand Rapids Press*
Helen Claytor
Stu Cok, President, Grand Rapids Area Chamber of Commerce
Maury DeJonge, Kent County Clerk

Nancy Douglas, Information Specialist, Grand Rapids Public Museum
Mary Edmond, Supervisor of Social Studies and Multicultural Education, Grand Rapids Public Schools
W.D. Frankforter, Director, Grand Rapids Public Museum
Heritage Hill Association
Robert Israels
Michael Lloyd, Editor, *Grand Rapids Press*
James Markle
Buck Matthews
Marilyn Merdzinski, Registrar, Grand Rapids Public Museum

Michigan Room Staff, Grand Rapids Public Library
Gordon Olson, Grand Rapids City Historian
The Reverend Lyman Parks
Jim Searn, Grand Rapids Public Library
Catherine Stryker, Curator of Exhibits, Grand Rapids Public Museum
Monique Timmer, Grand Rapids Public Library
James R. VanVulpen, Consultant Historian
Diane Wheeler, Librarian, *Grand Rapids Press*
Ray Whelan, Robinson Studio

Publishers' Acknowledgements

The editors and publishers of *Grand Rapids: Renaissance on the Grand* are indebted to a number of individuals and organizations who gave invaluable assistance and encouragement in making this volume a reality for the people of the Grand Rapids community.

Our special thanks, of course, to Gerald Elliott and his associates Ellen Arlinsky, Marg Ed Conn Kwapil and Barbara McGuirl whose talent and cooperation helped create the book.

Thanks also to former President Gerald R. Ford. His encouragement and commitment to this hometown tribute was especially appreciated.

In addition, we thank the fine professional staff and volunteer leadership of the Grand Rapids Area Chamber of Commerce for their continuing guidance, including Robert C. Bodine, chairman; George U. Lyons, immediate past chairman; and Stuart Cok, president, who lent strong support and sagely advice. Beverly L. Boehnlein, Ann LaReau and Debra Grewats on the Chamber staff were also extremely helpful. We are indebted to you.

A salute to the family of Joyce Moffett for their sensitivity and understanding when mom couldn't be there. Transplants Craig and Vicki Kinseth, who are unabashedly proud of Grand Rapids and Michigan, deserve special note.

Others who contributed to the success of *Grand Rapids: Renaissance on the Grand* include Lynn Alexander, Tim Colwell, Tony Flatt, Ginny Katz, Karen Keim, BJ Mallinger, Nina LeMaire, Ann McGill, Laura Murphree, Nancy Myers, Pat Plunkett, Mark Radcliffe, Peggi Ridgway, Rick Robinson, Mickey Thompson and Joel Turner.

Photo Credits

Sources of photographs, maps and art appearing in this book are noted here in alphabetical order and by page number (position on the page is noted). Those photographs appearing in the chapter "Partners in Grand Rapids' Progress" were provided by the represented firms.

Amway Corporation: 179 all, 180.
Archives of Labor and History, Wayne University: 58 left.
Armour, David: 18 (painting by Homer Lynn).
Arts Council of Greater Grand Rapids: 171 center left, right and middle.
Bissell, Inc.: 66 top.
City of Grand Rapids: 170 top left.
Detroit Public Library, Burton Historical Collection: 17 center, 23, 58/59 spread, 144 center right.
Edmund, Mary: 113 top.
Gerritsen, James: 162 top right, 162/163 spread, 163 top left.
Gerald R. Ford Presidential Library: 141 top, 167 all.
Grand Rapids Press, the: 143, 146, 151 bottom, 158, 163 inset, 170 top right and center, 171 lower left, 177, 178 lower right, 181 top right and center left.
Grand Rapids Public Library: 6/7, 8 bottom, 15 top, 17 top, 19, 20 top left, 21, 22, 24 center, 25 all, 26, 27 all, 29 all, 32, 33 all, 34 center, 35 all, 36 all, 38/39, 41, 42/43 all, 44/45, 47, 48/49 all, 50/51, 52, 53 all, 54/55, 56 top, 57, 64 all, 65 bottom, 66 center left, 66/67 spread, 68, 69 all, 70 all, 72 all, 74/75 spread, 76/77, 78 bottom, 79-81, 82/83 all, 84, 85 all, 87, 88/89 all, 90 top and lower left, 92, 93, 94 top, 95 right, 96/97, 98 top right, 99 top left, 100, 101, 102/103 all, 104/105, 107 top, 108 bottom, 109 bottom, 111 all, 117 all, 118, 120/121, 122/123, 124/125 all, 126/127 all, 135 top, 137 top, 140 top, 150 top left, 151 top left, 247, 248.
Grand Rapids Public Library/Judd Collection: 90/91 spread.
Grand Rapids Public Museum: 2/3, 10, 16 top, 24 top, 30/31, 34, 46, 56, 61, 62/63, 65 top, 67 top, 71 all, 73, 74 lower left, 78 top, 86, 94/95 spread, 98/99 spread, 107 bottom, 108 top, 109 top, 114/115 all, 151 top right, 154 top right, 240.
Grand Rapids Public Museum/Richard Szczepanski: 14.

Johnson, Rusty: 12 top, 13 top, 20 top right.
Markle, James: 171 top left.
Michigan Bell Telephone Company: 11, 12/13, 15 center, 16 center, 37 center.
Michigan Historical Collections (XXX, 326): 40 top.
Parks, Lyman S.: 174.
Radcliffe, Phillip: 4/5, 8 top, 9 all, 144 top right, 145 all, 146 top, 148 lower right, 149 all, 150 top right, 152 all, 153 all, 155 top, 156 all, 157, 159 all, 160, 161, 164 bottom, 165 all, 166, 168 all, 169 all, 171 lower right, 172 all, 173 all, 174 top left, 175, 176.
Rasberry, Ted: 119, 147 center.
Robinson Studio: 128 top, 129 all, 132/133 all, 137 below, 139 all, 140 below, 141 below, 142 all, 147 top right, 148 center left.
Russo, G.B. (family): 128.
Skinner, Floyd (Mrs.): 112 right.
Smith, Pierson: 113 bottom, 147 top left.
Spielmacher, Earl: 134/135 spread.
Tate, Mary Roberts: 112 top.
Urban Concern, Inc.: 155 lower left.
Whinery, Katherine Pantlind (Mrs.): 86 top.
Watson, Bob: 178 top.
WOTV News: 154 lower right.

247

Municipal campground along the riverbank at Comstock Park in 1932.

Michigan Hill, looking east along Michigan Street, during the 1930s.

Concept and design by
Continental Heritage Press, Inc., Tulsa.
Printed and bound by Walsworth Publishing Company.
Type is Cheltenham
by The Type House, Inc. and Western Typesetting.
Text Sheets are Warren Flo • Endleaves are Eagle A.
Cover is Holliston Kingston Linen.